A Hundred Y

Writing

CREW

CREW series of Critical and Scholarly Studies
General Editor: Professor M. Wynn Thomas (*CREW*, University of Wales, Swansea)

This *CREW* series is dedicated to Emyr Humphreys, a major figure in the literary culture of modern Wales, a founding patron of the *Centre for Research into the English Literature and Language of Wales*, and, along with Gillian Clarke and Seamus Heaney, one of *CREW's* Honorary Associates. Grateful thanks are extended to Richard Dynevor for making this series possible.

List of forthcoming titles
Kirsti Bohata, *Postcolonialism Revisited* (0-7083-1892-4)
Barbara Prys-Williams, *Twentieth-century Autobiography* (0-7083-1891-6)

A Hundred Years of Fiction

Writing Wales in English

STEPHEN KNIGHT

UNIVERSITY OF WALES PRESS
CARDIFF
2004

British Library Cataloguing-in-Publication Data
A catalogue record for this book is available from the British Library.

ISBN   0–7083–1846–0 paperback
        0–7083–1847–9 hardback

THE *A*SSOCIATION FOR
*W*ELSH *W*RITING IN *E*NGLISH
*C*YMDEITHAS *L*LÊN *S*AESNEG *C*YMRU
Recommended text

Published with the financial assistance of the Welsh Books Council

Typeset by Bryan Turnbull
Printed in Great Britain by Cromwell Press Limited, Trowbridge, Wiltshire

Er cof am fy nhad

In memory of my father

CONTENTS

General Editor's Preface

The aim of this series is to produce a body of scholarly and critical work that reflects the richness and variety of the English-language literature of modern Wales. Drawing upon the expertise both of established specialists and of younger scholars, it will seek to take advantage of the concepts, models and discourses current in the best contemporary studies to promote a better understanding of the literature's significance, viewed not only as an expression of Welsh culture but also as an instance of modern literatures in English world-wide. In addition, it will seek to make available the scholarly materials (such as bibliographies) necessary for this kind of advanced, informed study.

M. Wynn Thomas,
Director, CREW (*Centre for Research into the English Language and Literature of Wales*)
University of Wales, Swansea

INTRODUCTION

In 1900, Welsh fiction in English was basically a way for English readers to tour Wales without leaving the armchair. There were collections of stories about travel, topography and the quaint, even mysterious, habits of the natives; there were novels where visiting characters and readers alike could be excited by beauty and strangeness, but never surrender their English values; there were historical novels to laud, in a safe past, the military spirit of this country which was now subservient to England; there was even the beginning of a fiction of industry, though nothing yet like the radical challenge to appear thirty years ahead. Most of this fiction, produced in London, often in handsome formats, partly by Welsh writers, in some way validated the colonial presence of the English and their language in Wales by shaping the views given of Wales and the Welsh people in terms of English attitudes and varying forms of condescending curiosity. There were some challenges to the general acceptance of colonization by these authors: Allen Raine and Amy Dillwyn approached a critical and liberal scrutiny of the Welsh situation, the Williams sisters, known on their title-pages as 'The Dau Wynne', used English to campaign for Welsh independence and Joseph Keating, enmeshed as he was in colonial romance, was at least working towards a credible account of life in a mining valley. But they all still published in London and operated at best as a mild corrective to the dominant colonial treatment of Wales and its people.

A hundred years later, the year 2000 saw a rich number of novels by Welsh authors writing in English, and even more important than their number and their success was the fact that most were published in Wales. The influence of London editors on Welsh fiction in English will be a recurrent topic in this book – it directed Dylan Thomas away from potent modernist fiction, delayed the career of Gwyn Thomas, contributed to the tragic death of Dorothy Edwards, denied readers a substantial number of novels by rejection and influenced in negative ways a whole series of major writers, from Jack Jones to Emyr Humphreys. Welsh editors can still argue with Welsh authors, but the terms and concepts are not going to be implicitly colonial, as is evident in the London connection over the years.

The themes and tones of the 2000 authors are very far from colonial complicity. Emyr Humphreys and Chris Meredith are well-established voices of a culture which, in the last section of this book, I will describe as espousing for the whole of Wales both integration and independence. Younger writers expose the aftermath of industrial colonialism as they write of a workforce developed and abandoned as in any Third World country. Though some of these authors are now publishing in London again – the loss of interest in Welsh writing after the 1960s has changed with the new devolution in Britain – there is no sign that Trezza Azzopardi or John Williams are working in terms of colonial stereotypes.

This new energy and self-identification come as the most recent changes in a long series of developments in Welsh writing in English over the twentieth century, which in this book I have described in three major movements. The first is the encounters with Wales from an inherently external viewpoint which I call 'first-contact romance'; the second is the internally focused self-description by authors from the English-language culture that was settled by colonial capitalism in south-east Wales; and thirdly, and more disparately, the wealth of responses after the Second World War, which have in various ways – aesthetic, nostalgic, feminist and consciously political – resisted the separations and disempowerments that colonialism brought to Wales, responses which all tend towards a view of Wales and its people that seeks integration and independence.

It will be clear that the approach I am using here is not only to read and consider a very wide range of material – effectively all the fiction of note written about modern Wales in the twentieth century – but also to assess that material and its meanings from a viewpoint known as post-colonialism. This is a widely spread and broadly accepted way of reading the literature that is involved in the process of colonization and empire – whether from the doubtful viewpoint of the colonizer, like Shakespeare's *The Tempest,* or from the critical viewpoint of the colonized, like Ngugi's *Petals of Blood.* There are many different kinds of post-colonialism, ranging from the political resistance embedded in the founders of the approach like the African liberationist Frantz Fanon and the Indian 'subaltern studies' writers to the emphasis on gender, identity and psychoanalysis in writers like Gayatri Spivak and Homi K. Bhabha. While these approaches certainly have their relevance to the Welsh situation, and an understanding of the past and the present in Wales would be – I hope will be – greatly enlightened through those powerful kinds of analysis, that is not the purpose here. This study is essentially post-colonial literary criticism with a social emphasis. It sets out to read Welsh fiction in English to understand how the literature of a colony, in the language of the colonizer, has been affected by its situation, how the authors respond, consciously and unconsciously, to the constraints of their situation, by creating acceptable symbolic forms of dissent like Rhys Davies or Gwyn Thomas or becoming, like Emyr Humphreys and Raymond Williams, increasingly radical in their analysis of the situation in their country, or by dealing with inherent social and personal forces behind colonialism, as do many of the women writers from Allen Raine to Siân James. Post-colonial analysis notes the impact of the pre-colonial world, as authors working under colonialism often deploy elements of their native culture both to entertain and also, if subtly, to undermine the colonizing power. There are more, and more varied, instances of this use of nativism in Welsh writing in English than in most colonized cultures; they range from occasional non-English phrases to the use of traditional Celtic narratives, or from the symbolic and historical meaning of the topography of Wales to fiction which deals directly with Welsh-only issues but uses the language of the colonizer to disseminate those debates more widely, as in the case of Emyr Humphreys.

Complexities arise in using a post-colonial approach to Welsh fiction in English: some of the most politically resistant writing, such as that by Lewis Jones, is in fact itself in a mode imported to Wales. Like Frantz Fanon, the African liberationist, Jones deployed the inherent contradictions of colonial capitalism against itself, and his interest was much more political than national: the debate about the relative status of nationalism and radicalism continues to the present in Wales and similar countries. Equally complex is the relation between national colonization and the parallel – inherently interlinked – subjugation of women in the home and in society; this has become a major issue as the growing strength of Welsh women's writing, and the scholarly study of it, has developed. Women writers have contributed substantially to the new confidence of writing in Wales and have indicated that integration of gender, as well as of class and region, is a necessary basis for a full independence, personal, social and national.

There will surely be those who resist the idea of speaking post-colonially about Wales and its literature. Some people are too comfortable with colonization to even identify it, or are more hostile to what they see as the threat of the natives to separate themselves from the English viewpoint. These are of course colonial positions, and several writers have used them – notably, though not simply, Caradoc Evans and, even more successfully, Richard Llewellyn. Then there are people in the Lewis Jones left-wing position who feel that all oppression is financially based and that to speak about colonization and its cultural politics is to obscure the real forces at work and thus delay the revolution. It is certainly true that both lived experience and a good deal of fiction in Wales, especially the settlement fiction of industrial Wales, must deal with the way in which capitalism interweaves with and indeed can often direct colonialism, but it seems equally true that the experiences Welsh people have had and have communicated through fiction are primarily those of colonization, whatever the main dynamic in any particular situation, and post-colonial analysis is the best way of understanding the complexities and the products of those experiences.

Other, less far-ranging, decisions taken in developing this book may also give rise to dissent. Though I have covered a substantial number of writers, to give them adequate treatment and still make the book manageable has meant that many writers are not covered, either in any detail or not at all. I have only dealt with authors who write, in whatever way, about themes, issues or conflicts in modern Wales. For the most part I have not dealt with historical fiction except where it seems relevant to contemporary positions as, to some degree, in the later nineteenth century and the post-industrial period. I also have not discussed fiction by Welsh authors which deals with other countries: again focus and space is the motive, and I would not want to imply that internationalism is not a major value in world writing. For these reasons I do not discuss John Cowper Powys, Richard Hughes, James Hanley, Edith Pargeter and Howard Spring, all of whom came from or chose to live in Wales but had very little to say about the modern period in the country. Similarly, the selection of materials from prolific authors like Rhys Davies, Hilda Vaughan and Emyr Humphreys focuses on the Wales-related material.

In a book which argues for both the value and the growing presence of a sense of integration between the English-language tradition and the native culture of the country, it would seem odd to have little sense of the Celtic culture of the country and the people, whether in ancient mythic stories or in more recent Nonconformism. A post-colonial reading of the native non-English culture of Wales in the last centuries is an obvious topic, and one that is being worked on at present by a number of scholars: I have had neither the expertise nor the space to deal with it. But in this book it has frequently been appropriate to refer to the non-English culture from which native materials are used in English – especially because a striking number of the English-language authors are themselves fluent in the other language of the country. I have not been able to bring myself to call this language *Welsh,* as the use of this term (a Germanic adjective meaning 'foreigner') seems to me a damaging mockery of the status of the native language, which I will call *Cymraeg,* the native language's name for itself, as seems appropriate in a country that is officially bilingual. I hope others will increasingly do the same. I will also use the perhaps clumsy phrase 'Welsh writing in English' for the material I will primarily be discussing, since the once-used term 'Anglo-Welsh' is found unacceptable by most authors, and indeed many others, on the grounds that it refuses Welsh status to Welsh people who, not speaking Cymraeg, nevertheless do not feel at all English. A much better term is *ffuglen Gymreig,* using after *ffuglen,* fiction, *Cymreig,* the term for 'Welsh-but-not-Welsh-speaking', but to use that might be – now at least – to take one integrative step too far.

Conscious as I am of trying to shape for the first time an account of Welsh fiction in English and the way in which its authors have described their country, their people and their experiences, I am just as conscious of how much work has been done, especially recently, that has enabled me to construct this guide to self-understanding and self-realization in this country. In instance after instance I have found that some scholar has done the basic work, analysed the career, read the letters, sorted out the themes, exposed the influences and so enabled me to see one writer's work in the light of another's and construct this book as an overview rather than a detailed engagement with data. The many footnotes must stand as specific acknowledgements to these authors, but some names must be noted as having had special importance in the development of an understanding of Welsh writing in English and in particular on the development of this book. As will be indicated in appropriate footnotes, major accounts of parts of the tradition have been offered by Gwyn Jones, Glyn Jones and Roland Mathias; Meic Stephens has been a constant source, both in his indispensable *New*

Companion to Welsh Literature and for his indefatigable editing (with R. Brinley Jones) of the 'Writers of Wales Series', which contains some real classics like Sam Adams on Geraint Goodwin, Tony Bianchi on Richard Vaughan and Sally Roberts Jones on Allen Raine. Tony Brown's inspired editing of *Welsh Writing in English* has made available a range of new research, including work by young and very promising researchers, and under the sadly late Robin Reeves *New Welsh Review* produced a remarkable number of essays that I have used. Across the field major contributions have been made by James A. Davies, John Harris, Ceridwen Lloyd-Morgan, Michael Parnell, John Pikoulis and Daniel Williams.

My thanks are due to all these scholars, on whose shoulders I have been able to stand to shape this book, but special thanks go to people who have been over recent years very generous to me in their provision of information and assistance: in the *ffuglen Gymreig* business, Jane Aaron, Katie Gramich and, *wrth gwrs*, M. Wynn Thomas; at Cardiff University Martin Coyle, Sioned Davies, Faye Hammill, Dawn Harrington, Radhika Mohanram and Angharad Price; at the University of Wales Press, Duncan Campbell, Susan Jenkins, Ceinwen Jones and Claire Powell. I should also thank the Arts and Humanities Research Board for the award of funded research leave to enable me to complete this book. I am sure that many – probably all – of these scholars and critics will, through their own expertise and commitment, find matters to debate and disagree with in this book, but I believe that they will not disagree with the principle behind the book, that the achievement of the Welsh writers in English is unduly unknown in their own country – let alone elsewhere – and that a proper way to start a discussion and disseminate knowledge about their work – its patterns, influences, qualities and values – is to look at the whole field of Welsh writing in English, to make available to readers, and perhaps especially to teachers, an account of just what has been achieved in writing Wales in English.

Literally this book has been written in the last few years, as returning to Cardiff has almost closed a circle that started when my parents, like half a million others, left Wales for work in England. But in a way the book was being developed all that time. As aspirational littérateurs in very petty bourgeois England, my brother, sister and I read from the local library the products of the post-war Welsh novel boom, from Michael Gareth Llewelyn to Menna Gallie, and saw in them a literary convergence with our parents' continuous discussion of the where-abouts, religious posture and moral standing of everyone they were related to or, it seemed, had ever heard of in the Rhymney valley – they lapsed into Cymraeg for the asterisked bits. For us the library literature elaborated an amputated experience, and, knowing our uncle Tom, nobody in Gwyn Thomas seemed in the least strange to us.

A further separation was as productive. After leaving Jesus College, Oxford, where the company was great, mostly Welsh, and the teaching at best patchy, I lectured at Sydney, in ironically New South Wales where the late Bernie Martin, wit and scholar par excellence, taught Old Irish: after I took the course he suggested I work up another on Middle Welsh, which, on the basis of my familial rudiments and some excellent editions and grammars, was not hard. This exiled relocation was extended by another sadly late friend, Jos Davies – philosopher, soldier and bon viveur – who in the spirit of his adult education work in Wales ran a *dosbarth Cymraeg* for a few of us, in his flat, for nothing. Discussions with him led me to read through, starting with the Jones trinity, Jack, Gwyn and Lewis, the industrial literature of the Welsh 1930s, and even teach some in a course on working-class literature at Melbourne University.

Those voices, literary and lived, were still with me when, my feet freed from the chains of administration, I was able to start orderly work on this book. But the strongest voice remains that of my father, who left school at the age of twelve when, after the Senghenydd pit disaster, he was the oldest male in his family, did with dignity a range of service jobs, cut into elegant squares the bread for chapel communion and took pleasure in his children's academic achievements – a mix of J. T. Miles and Harry Price. His experiences and values permeate the fiction. Indeed, this literature conveys many contacts. Fact is different from fiction, but fact only survives as statistics, traces, inscrutable fragments. It is the fiction of a culture, or a people, that preserves the memories as much as it constructs the models. It is the strong achievement of the Welsh that they have, in spite of everybody and everything, preserved into the present their native Cymraeg culture, but they have also, in the last hundred years, constructed another cultural tradition out of the potent, dynamic and often agonizing experiences of the English-language world that was created under the impact of English and capitalist colonization. From the colliery to the university is all a structure of a new world, and a diasporic life like my own is a literal spin-off, widely dealt with and deeply recognizable in the literature.

Chancy as the twentieth century was, and Wales was dealt one of the poorer hands, the people and the writers have survived it in perhaps surprisingly positive mood. Kate Roberts's great slender novel *Traed mewn Cyffion* ('Feet in Fetters') is, in English, even more gloomily entitled *Feet in Chains*. Emyr Humphreys long favoured for his series title the slightly less negative 'Bonds of Attachment', but he finally went for the definitely positive 'The Land of the Living', though he had a cautious gloss on it (see p. 154). In the same way Raymond Williams stressed the continuity of human community in Wales, entitling his unfinished trilogy the *People of the Black Mountains*. Basic as it is to the Cymraeg language culture of Wales, that sense of people, together, in place, is what the authors of Welsh fiction in English have also constructed, realizing a self-recognizable, and thus perpetuable, image of a particular world and way of life. Glyn Jones, in the conclusion to his learned and generous book about the literatures of Wales, both Cymraeg and English, comments that 'anyone can be Welsh if they want to, and are prepared to take the consequences'. Many make that choice, myself included. Not all the writers who chose to write Welsh fiction in English liked the consequences of being colonized – some preferred to masquerade in England-pleasing stereotypes, and others were directly resistant to colonial power – yet between them they mapped a rich and dynamic culture, one that can match the Cymraeg culture of the country, increasingly has developed elements of integration with it, and through its writers and readers, and through the ideas, influences and actions of both groups, is playing its own part in moving this closest, oldest, and in some ways still least understood colony of England towards its effective independence.

Section 1

First Contact and Romance

1.1 COLONIAL CONTEXTS

The low white farmhouse and the distant bleating of sheep; the dark pit-head wheel and a hooter screaming of disaster; families and communities interlinked in painful, colourful activity. These are focal images of Welsh writing in English. Yet there is much more than those central but often sentimentalized moments: over more than a hundred years, in novels and short stories, writers identifying with Wales have explored, criticized, celebrated and sometimes exploited the society and the culture that have been constructed in Wales by and for those who do not use the native language of the country. As this book will demonstrate, it is largely in fiction that these people have been able to know where their society and culture have come from, what conflicts it has known, and what values it has generated.

Fiction enables people to understand the nature of an earlier society – Chaucer, Shakespeare, Austen, Dickens epitomize major phases in the development of England – but this process is also contemporary. Writers create in their narratives and images an account of a period which generates self-understanding in the society they realize. The process will not be simple. Authors will have different evaluative and political positions in their analysis – Shakespeare's England is very different from Ben Jonson's – and their most powerful effects may be mythic: Virgil ideologized the new power of first-century Rome with a fantasy about Aeneas transplanting to Italy the traditions of Troy. But through those conflicts and myths a people are given a vocabulary and a structure through which to understand themselves. It is common when a new society emerges, whether nationally or class-based, that it will develop its own origin-legend; what Virgil did for Rome and Shakespeare did for Tudor England Dickens did for nineteenth-century bourgeois society and writers like Rushdie are doing for modern multicultural Britain.

A particularly complex and conflicted new society, in urgent need of self-description, emerges when one power takes control of another and subjugates it as a colony, imposing its law, traditions and in most cases its language. There will be in existence a native culture, often, as in the case of India, North America, Ireland and Wales, very ancient, but the imperial language will steadily gain ground and will be used both by the colonizers and the colonized in their varying and often competing accounts of the colony. Post-colonial analysis, which developed in countries that had emerged from colonial status like India, Pakistan, Africa, Australia and the Carribean countries, has identified both the types of writing that occur in the colonial context and also the responses that are made by authors, ranging from ready acceptance of empire through a complex set of mixed responses, often using some native materials and implying elements of resistance, to outright aggression towards the colonizing country, its methods and the effect it has had on the colony.

Wales, more as a grouping of tribes than a country in the modern nationalistic sense, was for about two thousand years home to the Cymraeg-speaking Celtic people, closely related to the Cornish, the Bretons and the Gauls. They were much more distantly related to the Irish Celts, who also settled in Scotland in the last of the Celtic moves across Europe. The Celts had themselves come to Britain as imperial invaders, but in recorded history have been the victims of a series of colonizing invasions, the major ones being the arrival of the Anglo-Saxons in the fifth century, which before long restricted the British Celts to Wales and Cornwall, and the steadily developing incursions of Norman and then English forces from about 1100 on. Castles, mercantile towns and ports, Anglo-French names like Williams and Lewis became widespread, but medieval Wales was never formally or substantially a colony. It was only from the sixteenth century that colonization became determined, when the new Tudor dynasty, itself claiming Welsh origins, legally made Wales a part, therefore a colony, of England under the 1536 and 1543 Acts of Union and subsequent legislation. Welsh soldiers, timber, livestock and some small-scale industry, mostly in metals, fed into the English economic system, and the Welsh gentry were encouraged to educate their sons in English. The first literary effect, as is common in early colonial encounters, was as Roland Mathias has recorded,[1] when Henry Vaughan and John Dyer became, in the seventeenth and eighteenth century respectively, significant as English poets, themselves elements of colonial appropriation.

Another literary feature of early colonialism is produced by writers from the colonizing power, who produce travel-books with descriptions of the natives, their customs, appearance and traditions. These first-contact texts, often illustrated, stress the mysterious, magical, even sinister elements of the colony and its people: they operate as a form of armchair travel but also validate the process of colonization through the courage of the observers and the intriguing wealth, both material and experiential, to be derived in this second-hand way. Common from all the English colonies, these first-contact texts range from quasi-scientific to crudely stereotypical – Moira Dearnley has explored those relating to Wales in the eighteenth century and shown how fully they validate the English imperial endeavour in Wales.[2] The first-contact texts tend to be limited in range – often called 'sketches' – and a fuller and more literary version of this imperial encounter with a new land is found in novels that elaborate at some length narratives about intrepid travellers who have exciting and sometimes dangerous encounters with the colony and its people and derive a stimulus that is a personalized, emotionalized version of the profit being drawn from the colony by the imperial power.

A sub-genre of the English novel as it developed locates English travellers – both men and women – in Wales, especially the fertile parts like the Vale of Glamorgan or the plains and foothills of Powys, both easily accessible from England. The story gives the visitor some encounter with an exotic native culture but finally enables the intrepid traveller, sensitivities heightened by romantic adventures, either to marry into an appropriately Anglicized context or, enriched with both the moral and often the financial profits of the visit, live a life fuller than the demeaning mercantile and urban activities that English Romanticism was already inherently criticizing. This is not writing about Wales so much as using Wales as context for English self-development. Dearnley has shown how these full-length novels about Wales develop in the eighteenth century as well as first-contact sketches, and Andrew Davies and Jane Aaron have continued the story into the nineteenth century, when Wales offered a mild variant to the exotic highlandery of Scott and his followers.[3] Anna Maria Bennett and

Ann Julia Hatton (writing as 'Ann of Swansea') are major producers, but there were many others writing in this mode. There is sometimes a genuine interest in improving Welsh society, either through Anglicizing the native landowners or sometimes by the development of Nonconformist faith and practices in Wales, and as Aaron shows there is a clear element of early feminist consciousness, as in the English novel at the time of Maria Edgeworth and Jane Austen.

The place and the people are treated in these novels in a consistently imperialist way and even the name of a country or its people can be part of colonial power, like the inappropriate 'Red Indians', the belittling 'niggers', the patronizingly Latin 'aborigine'. The name of the people of the regions beyond Offa's Dyke was not established simply: early descriptions tend to use the long-established native name Cymry, or its Latinate form Cambrians, literally meaning 'the compatriots'. Only in the full tide of nineteenth-century imperialist culture does the Anglo-Saxon name Welsh, meaning, in classic colonial mode, 'foreigners', come to dominate. The inherently imperial nature of the term Welsh, both in its meaning and its origin, is why this book will consistently use for the pre-colonial language and culture of the country the native term Cymraeg.

The early English-language fictions about Wales discussed by Dearnley, Aaron and Davies are basically imperial narratives with some first-contact features. It is clear that their major audience is in England and therefore they do not operate in any real way as texts that generate a self-consciousness among English-speaking Welsh people, who did not up to the early nineteenth century constitute a substantial audience for fiction or even factual writing. This soon changed, and so did attitudes to England and its power among the Cymraeg speakers. The development of Welsh writing in English is intimately involved with the massive changes that occurred in Wales in the nineteenth century, which would make the country both more like and also more subtly, and more crucially, different from England. These would be the bases for the different approaches of the authors who, from the later nineteenth century on, begin a conscious project, if uncertainly at first, of writing about a Wales that is now substantially and consciously colonized, and writing in the language of the colonizer.

Historians like John Davies, writing originally in Cymraeg, and Gwyn A. Williams, at once insistently Welsh and distinctively English-speaking,[4] have outlined how in the nineteenth century a major social and economic struggle broke the power of the Welsh aristocratic and semi-aristocratic landowners, since Tudor times inherently English in their orientation. The classic date is 1889 when the Liberal Party swept the Conservatives from political power, but these changes had been some time in the making and had religious as well as social force. The historians also show how Nonconformism, an originally English force which Kenneth O. Morgan comments 'had swept through most of rural Wales in the nineteenth century',[5] was reshaped in both Welsh and Cymraeg terms, seizing moral and intellectual power from the debilitated Church of England in Wales into the hands of a Cymraeg-speaking professional bourgeoisie with a large popular following. Policing the morals and the regulatory practices of the country with a millennial vigour, the chapels – of many kinds, and often deeply factional among themselves – wove an imposingly intricate web of popular devotion and institutional surveillance. A popular hymn-book, *Llawlyfr Moliant* (Handbook of Praise), first published in 1880, contains 942 hymns in Cymraeg: each one had to be sung at least once a year, often to magnificent tunes. Along with this religious hegemony was constructed a compelling social model known as the *gwerin* – or, after the definite article *y*, as the *werin* (initial mutation being one of the many native features which mystified the English incomer).

The *gwerin* ideal, still alive in Cymraeg Wales, was an image of a community which, while it recognized differences of status and income, rejected class difference: the minister and the wealthy farmer spoke the same language, sang the same hymns, acknowledged the same values and traditions as the poor labourer or craftsman. In the *gwerin* myth – often enough seen in at least partial reality – the humbler members of the *gwerin* might be as scholarly, as religiously fluent, as poetically skilled, as any more privileged member of the *bro*, the small rural region throughout which the *gwerin* knew itself as a community. A powerful and democratic substitute for the feudal model of the squirearchy and their tenants, a quasi-Athenian *polis* in Wales, the idea of the *gwerin* dynamized nineteenth-century Liberal Wales, helped to empower the brilliant Cymraeg literary *dadeni* or renaissance (there is no English word) of the early twentieth century, and is a ghostly presence in much English-language writing from Wales, whether rural or industrial, until recent times.

But even as Liberal Nonconformism constructed a powerful new Cymraeg polity and ideology, the forces of English colonization were on the march. It is difficult to disentangle them in terms of cause and effect and a historical account seems the most useful. Wales had been from Roman times a source of minerals, but by the later eighteenth century a structural change from occasional profit-taking to programmatic capital-based exploitation was evident in the slate-mines of Gwynedd in the north-west and the industries of the south and the north-east. Copper in the Swansea area was being outpaced by the iron foundries that grew along the mountainous heads of the valleys in what is now Glamorgan and Gwent, where iron ore and first timber and then coal to smelt it were found together. At and around Merthyr Tydfil by 1800 insurgent capital, frequently transferring from the now discreditable and increasingly unprofitable slave-trade, funded the foundries that turned small villages into infernos of industry and here massive population shifts occurred as workers trudged in from the impoverished farms of west and mid Wales to earn undreamt-of cash in what were known as 'The Works'. Risky as the work was – death and injury were common in the primitive mines and dangerous foundries, and the new settlements were notoriously subject to disease – it was a highly acceptable alternative to the slow attrition of disease and malnutrition on thin upland farms. The development was not socially or politically peaceful. The largest town in Wales, Merthyr, was also a centre for the earliest major industrial battles: in mid 1831 the red flag was flown for the first time in Britain as workers seized the town for five days and were eventually brought under control by armed soldiers – though not by the first sent against them. Dic Penderyn (formally named Richard Lewis) was a name to resound through Welsh labour history after he was hanged for his alleged part in the events. In 1839 the men of the industrial districts marched on Newport in the most determinedly violent of all the physical-force Chartist actions, and again a military and legally punitive solution was the only response of English colonial capitalism. Rural Wales was little more peaceful. In the south-west the remarkable Rebecca Riots continued from 1839 to 1843: black-faced men dressed as women destroyed toll-gates and even seized briefly the regional centre Carmarthen in 1839, setting free prisoners from the jail. The name and the official ideology of their struggle against toll-imposing landlords came from the biblical Rebecca of Genesis because she is promised power over gates: the influence of the chapels ran deep. The tithe wars of northern Wales in the 1880s continued the same spirit of local resistance.

Violent resistance to the manifestations of financially motivated colonization in the earlier nineteenth century were taken as a reason for extending colonial power more deeply into Wales, even into the language and so the thinking of Welsh people. The hastily arranged 1844 report on the Rebecca Riots, as well as recognizing real ground for local complaint, also judged, in John Davies's words, 'that it was the existence of the Welsh language . . . that hindered the Law and the Established Church from civilising the Welsh'.[6] The means of that civilization were made clear in the notorious 'Blue Books' report on Education in Wales of 1847, discussed in detail by Gwyneth Tyson Roberts.[7] This addressed itself, as empire did in so many locations, to the morals and education of the natives – or more exactly, their *re-education* to be good colonial citizens. Written by three Anglican lawyers with little experience of education and no knowledge of Cymraeg, the report attacked both the learning and the morality of the Welsh – specifically the immorality of Welsh women: this epitomized the ungovernability of the Welsh and a solution was proposed through the imposition of education in English. It is a classic first-contact move: both ignorant of Western ways and strangely stimulating, the natives must be constrained. The report's impact gave it the Cymraeg name of *Brad y Llyfrau Gleision* (The Treachery of the Blue Books): in part this refers to the Welsh witnesses who by over-cooperating permitted a malicious distortion of the situation, but the name is also deliberately nativist, recalling the mythical fifth-century imposition of Saxon rule in Celtic Britain through the perfidious assault of 'The Treachery of the Long Knives'. The impact of the report was quickly understood; it signalled a London-based determination to repress the dangerous otherness of the Welsh, especially their separate language. Governmental enactment of this determination was relatively slow – London had other and more lucrative colonies to bear in mind in Africa, Canada, India and Australia, and the major governmental measure to Anglicize the troublesome country was not imposed until 1870 when the Education Act insisted that all children in Britain, including Wales, should be educated in English until they were thirteen. But before that, the Church of England in Wales, fighting back against the Cymraeg organization of the Nonconformist Liberal hierarchy, had with considerable efficiency organized its own schools – Davies reports that by 1870 there were more than a thousand Church primary schools throughout the country.[8] It was on this widespread basis, with English state and Anglican Church combined, that in 1889 the Welsh Intermediate Education Act extended with little difficulty the period of colonial re-education for the most able students and so created the secondary schools that were to direct people like Caradoc Evans and Glyn Jones, with opposite effects, away from their mother-tongue.

Nevertheless, at the time the impact of English was not always seen as negative. D. Gareth Evans comments on the widespread 'commercial, utilitarian and deferential attitudes to the English' and that even the Eisteddfodau tended 'to slide gradually into English monolingualism'.[9] English newspapers became common, especially in south Wales, by the mid nineteenth century and as in all colonies there were both those ready to exploit the commercial advantages of Anglicization and also those who saw progress and reform being possible through the ideas and developments brought by contact with imperial culture. As well as ideas, other structural changes were at work, closely allied to industry and its imperial imperatives and spreading Anglicization. John Davies notes the growth of railways, initially in the industrial areas – the head of the valleys area again led Britain, and the iron media that could rapidly communicate mercantile colonization ran soon to the cloth centres of mid Wales and the seaside resorts of the south and north coasts, bringing with them English newspapers, the English language of railway operation and the floods of mechanics, engineers, merchants, bankers, insurance-men and tradesmen who, like explorers presenting alarm-clocks to Australian natives along with European viruses, were to alter ineradicably an ancient, coherent, if also limited and pressured, way of life and language.

Fiction was slow to represent these changes, in both languages. It was not a genre natural in Cymraeg. One of the glories of the past was the *Mabinogi*, showing that, like the Irish *Táin Bó Cualngne* (The Cattle-Raid of Cooley), Celtic antiquity had mastered imaginative prose when the Anglo-Saxons could manage nothing more than clumsy charters and chronicles. But those texts were themselves the products of an earlier colonial encounter, as scholars used the new skills of imperial Christianity to preserve their own Celtic oral traditions – an early example of what post-colonial analysis would call hybridized resistance. In more recent times, however, prose for the Cymraeg-speaking Welsh was a matter for sermons, learned debate and occasionally memoirs. The alleged 'first Welsh novel in English', T. J. Llewelyn Prichard's *Twm Shon Catti* of 1828,[10] is a loose Fieldingesque saga about a sixteenth-century anti-English, anti-authority trickster. Like the mythographic work of other contemporary London Welsh, in form, title and theme it expresses a version of native resistance to the appropriation of Wales as a mere site of English romantic adventure. But few were to take such a position and the earlier patterns of fiction, focusing on an external visitor's contacts and self-interest, persisted, if apparently with reduced force. The mid

nineteenth-century loss of interest in Romanticism as a dynamo for the
novel and the increasing focus of the English novel on urban and
mercantile forces seems to have made the turn-of-the-century patterns
described by Andrew Davies less attractive to publishers, though first-
contact narratives began to flourish: James Motley's *Tales of the Cymry*
(1848)[11] provided sketches of the quaint locals and the title of Revd
George Tugwell's *On The Mountain, Being the Welsh Experience of
Abraham Black and James White etc., Esquires, Moralists, Photographers,
Fishermen, Botanists* (1862)[12] sufficiently expresses the approaches and
interests of rural colonial visitors. The social context was still seen as a
land of squires and peasants, as depicted in Benjamin Williams's *Arthur
Vaughan* (1856),[13] a three-volume novel focused on field sports,
maintaining the sense of Wales as a place where the armchair colonizer
could draw both wonder and self-confidence from a literary contact with
these strangely foreign and even more strangely contiguous people.

   Publishing about Wales in English by Welsh writers gathered pace in
what Roland Mathias describes as 'an unprecedented number of prose
works' from 1880 onwards.[14] This is when 'first-contact' writing about
Wales becomes an identifiably common phenomenon of publishing.
Clearly the railways were now inviting more visitors, and this is in any
case a period when book production booms in London as reading
becomes a mass skill and improved production techniques, advertising
and distribution increasingly make publishing an industry not a craft.
The growth of the first-contact literary material exactly matches also
the surge in the Welsh coal industry to major importance. It seems
likely that the fact that, by this time, Wales is an operating and
important part of English imperial industry gives the country a new
place in the British national consciousness. There is a contradictory gap
between the actual capitalist exploitation and importance of imperial
Wales in both profits and politics (the imperial navy relied on Welsh
steam coal for its range and efficiency) and the distinctly old-world
rural representation of the country in the first-contact literature; this
strongly resembles the early Australian and Canadian literary material
which celebrates the grandeurs of the land and overlooks the harsh
productive exploitations which make the places of basic imperial
interest. The new phenomenon of a late nineteenth-century colonial
Welsh literature appears to give added force to Gwyn A. Williams's
argument that Wales as a different, strange and interesting country in
need of cultural appropriation was itself 'at the heart of the imperial
economy'.[15] Whatever the full reasons – and the first-contact literature

about Wales has not yet been studied in any detail – this is when it is
first possible to see a substantial and coherent body of material written
in English about Wales.

1.2 FIRST-CONTACT TALES AND ROMANCES

From the late nineteenth century there is for the first time a steady flow
of material produced by Welsh writers which in some ways makes the
country, its people, their customs and traditions available for the
English reader. The titles themselves can be very revealing: H. Elwyn
Thomas's *Where Eden's Tongue is Spoken Still* (1904),[16] a set of
sketches of the simple purity of Welsh rural life, combines a fantasy of
noble savagery with a claim for biblical antiquity. It is a classic example
of the idea Matthew Arnold had made widely known through his
lectures on Celtic literature, published in 1867,[17] that the Celts were
somehow older, nobler, more spiritual than the Anglo-Saxons. Yet at
the same time they are more primitive, and their spiritual qualities
should contribute to a better Britain when combined with the modern
democratic know-how of the bustling, if also philistine Anglo-Saxons.
Ned Thomas first identified this idea of 'contributionism',[18] that the
Welsh can contribute something to the 'British' (i.e. English) nation – a
nation definitely ruled from London and speaking only English, and in
fact returning nothing to Wales but vague admiration and classically
imperial appropriation. As Daniel Williams has explored,[19] the message
is endemic to colonial literature from Ireland and Wales, and the
mixture of national identity and colonial deference can be variously
represented: Alfred Thomas's *In the Land of Harp and Feather* (1896)[20]
refers in its title both to the ancient and distinctive musical traditions of
Wales and also to the feathers in the badge of the prince of Wales, that
figure and instrument through whom Edward I in 1282 appropriated
the authority of Llywelyn, the last native prince of Gwynedd and
Wales. In these books and their titles, cultural admiration of Wales
does not reduce the insistent English authority: the two features are
combined in an elegant display of cultural colonialism. The texts are
usually produced by Welsh writers and published mostly in London,
sometimes in Wales or in both places at once, implying both an English
self-gratifying audience and a Welsh one moving away from native
ideas along with the native language.

Unknown as these first-contact texts are to literary history, any good library in Wales will have rows of them, easily visible from their often elegant bindings, frequently with Celtic motifs on the covers, and, most revealingly, recurrently dedicated to some agent of the Crown, either literal like a lord lieutenant of the county or displaced like an Oxford scholar or land-holding aristocrat. There are sometimes whispers of the political tensions that this literature seeks to elide: R. Rice Davies in *The Cambrian Sketch-Book* (1875)[21] not only dedicates his book to 'The Cambrian Race' rather than some imperial agent but also in his preface says: '. . . if this work deepens the Welshman's love of country, and induces the English reader to regard us in a more favourable light than that adopted by a class of Saxon critics, I will not have laboured in vain' (ix). Tentative as the tone may be, it does at least remember the Blue Books and their aftermath, and there were some English writers who seemed closer to a nativist sympathy than the effortless superiority of appropriation. James Kenwood said that his *For Cambria* (1868) was not only 'designed for the general reader and the traveller' but also was for 'the Cymraeg cause',[22] and the book was dedicated to the Breton scholar Villemarqué as 'a generous vindicator of Celtic nationality'. Connoisseurs of colonial irony will appreciate that Kenwood lived in Smethwick, later to be the site of the notorious racist 'rivers of blood' speech by Enoch Powell – of Welsh origin and a servitor of Toryism.

Such occasional gestures towards the separate and valued existence of Wales and its traditions only emphasize the powerful and consistently pro-colonial thrust of this first-contact material such as R. C. Halifax's *Among the Welsh Hills: A Novel* (1878)[23] and Marie Trevelyan's topographical sketches *From Snowdon to the Seas: Stirring Stories of North and South Wales* (1895).[24] The tradition flowed on into the twentieth century in books like Alfred W. Rees's *Ianto the Fisherman and Other Stories of Country Life* (1904)[25] and was enshrined in the Welsh Celtic twilight novels of Arthur Machen (1863–1947), an actor turned journalist who specialized in apprehensions of the mystical among the rural beauties of his native Gwent. In *The Hill of Dreams*,[26] published in 1907 but written in 1896–7,[27] sensitive would-be author Lucien Taylor (a non-Welsh surname like Machen's, which, born Arthur Jones, he took from his Scottish mother) dreams of 'Celtic magic still brooding in the Welsh hills' (8), but such living in a fantasy past only leads to his wretched lonely death. In *The Secret Glory*, not published until 1922 but apparently written in 1907,[28] Machen reworks the tragic *The Hill of Dreams*, as the hero, Ambrose Meyrick, bearing

Machen's initials but now a Welsh surname, like Lucien 'revisited the faery hills and woods and valleys of the West' (86) after a drastically material English schooling. Through his appreciation of 'the wonderful and doubtful mythos of the Celtic church' (281) he has a Grail-associated transcendent end. Giving narrative form and fluent emotive style to his individualist version of the Celtic twilight, a theme more common in the poetry of the period, Machen has gained persistent international admiration among alienated romantics, but in his period he was merely the most successful of the London-based purveyors of first-contact material.

Ernest Rhys, another London publishing professional of Welsh origin, did the same through his feebly Celticist poetry, a very long way short of Yeats, and more so through his weekly column in the *Manchester Guardian*, starting in 1898, on 'Welsh and Other Celtic Topics'. But his novels were set mostly in England, except the pirate story *The Man at Odds* (1904)[29] which (much like R. D. Blackmore's earlier *The Maid of Sker*,[30] where he crossed from Lorna Doonesque Devon) explores the maritime border of the Bristol Channel just as the earlier touristic novels had ventured into Powys and the Vale of Glamorgan. Rhys's major contribution in this context was to republish Arnold's thoughts on Wales in *On the Study of Celtic Literature and Other Essays*[31] in the very widely circulated Everyman's Library, which Rhys edited. From early sketches stressing topographic beauty, quaint customs and insistently recurring elements of superstition to the more sharply focused novels of Machen and the travel-books produced by Edward Thomas (his well-known 'Georgian' poetry has little to do with Wales), this first-contact material fleshes out for audiences in both London and Wales the implications of Arnold's idea of the value of things Welsh as a useful civilizing additive to the dynamic structure of neo Saxon mercantile society

It is important to recognize that as with first-contact literature around the colonized world – in the American 'Leatherstocking' novels, the Australian squatter sagas, the Canadian land-taking narratives – when this material develops beyond mere sketches into the full narrative of a novel, the literary mode is romance. This means more than a tale about boy-meets-girl and the aftermath. Romance is also romantic in the early nineteenth-century sense, in that it privileges the feelings of individual characters in a stirring setting, a pattern that meshes easily with the individualist heroics of early capitalism. But romance also has a direct contact with the land-taking habits of imperialism in both its medieval origin and in its romantic period redevelopment. The knights of Arthur's Round Table ventured forth to fight ogres and villain knights and to win beautiful maidens – but also to take a land both for themselves and for the greater aggrandization of Arthur's realm. In the first great romance, Chrétien de Troyes's late twelfth-century *Yvain*, a landless nobleman kills the husband and then marries the wife and rules her land: she is Laudine, who is both the inheritor and the symbolic sovereignty of Lothian in southern Scotland.[32] The poetry and prose of the Romantic period, from Wordsworth through to Byron, are also heavily involved with an imaginative domination of new territory, though the thrust of the possession is personal rather than political. Those two possibilities of romantic appropriation are combined in the early 'land-taking' fictions of the American, Canadian and Australian settlements. They routinely condense the romance of a man and a woman, and the enriching of their own romantic sensibilities, with the relocation of land into safe colonizing hands. Scott's *Waverley* is both a classic case and a major disseminator of the idea through the nineteenth century, and his work is often a model for those seeking to represent Wales and the Welsh.

Romance in this wider sense is the inherent mode of the first-contact material in Wales, whether in attenuated form in sketches and short stories, or in amplified form as novels. A particularly popular version of it was historical: by recounting their history in novels Welsh writers both made available the Celtic antiquity so admired by Arnold and also, as Dai Smith notes, constructed for themselves an English-language Welsh antiquity through 'a late nineteenth-century middle class need to identify itself and its nineteenth century origin with the quintessence of Welsh history as they defined it'.[33] Many of these historical novels were medieval, relating to the most visible remains of the past, the great castles – themselves Anglo-Norman colonial fortresses. E. Everett Green's *Cambria's Chieftain* (1903)[34] is medieval, about Owain Glyndŵr, while *The Jewel of Ynys Galon* (1895) by the well-known 'Owen Rhoscomyl'[35] (actually Owen Vaughan) is a lively eighteenth-century pirate saga with dramatic and sometimes erotic, even homoerotic, illustrations; a more recent and more sentimental story about the Tristan and Isolde of Glamorgan was the extremely popular *The Maid of Cefn Ydfa* (1881) by Isaac Craigfryn Hughes, revealingly published by the Anglophile and business-orientated *Western Mail*.[35] The history could be at times involved in the Noncon-formist triumph – Revd H. Elwyn Thomas (he of *Where Eden's Tongue*

is Spoken Still) also produced *The Forerunners* (1910), a story of
seventeenth-century Nonconformism published by and ideologizing the
origin of the 'Evangelical Free Church Councils in Wales'.[37] Or it could
from a more conservative viewpoint drastically rewrite more recent
Welsh history: R. Dancey Green Price's *Rebecca, or A Life's Mistake:
A Story of Country Life* (1882)[38] not only targets both the moralizing
and the tourist audience in its title but also diminishes the impact of the
Rebecca Riots in history by making its Rebeccaite no more than a
poacher – Price's dedication is to the Revd Richard Lister Venables
who 'did much to check the evils of Rebeccaism'. The English hero on a
fishing trip, falls in love with a Welsh girl, a native of what the author,
in a finely imperial phrase calls 'Tivyland', but she is merely the
beautifully noble savage with no inheritance worth appropriating and –
a telling revelation of the imperialist context – they go off to colonial
service in New Zealand.

Rich in multiple ideologies as these historical novels are, serving both
a newly Anglicized Welsh consciousness and also an English audience,
they too are the essence of first-contact fiction. However, the most
widely read of the nineteenth-century Welsh romancers were those who
dealt in romance of the traditional kind, but added a colonial element
to the difference of gender. Anne Beale (1816–1900) started with a
literal first-contact story about an English woman, like herself, settling
in Wales. It first appeared with the simply descriptive title, *The Vale of
the Towey* (1844) but then was renamed in more consciously colonial
mode as *Traits and Stories of the Welsh Peasantry* (1849). Beale then
produced a sequence of romances, typically combining a largely
ornamental but romantic Welsh setting, a young Welsh woman, a
decaying Welsh gentry, some respectable yeomen farmers, both Welsh
and English, and a handsome, dynamic English military officer who
restores order and marries the girl. He will personify English virtues, as
in Colonel Sir George Walpole in *The Pennant Family* (1876) or
Colonel Faithfull, an old India hand who is loved by the heroine of
Rose Mervyn of Whitelock (1879). Beale, as Moira Dearnley has
noted,[39] is quite sympathetic to Wales and fairly egalitarian; Jane
Aaron has discussed Beale in an essay in a similar way and in her book
comments that her heroines are 'less snobbish than some of the heroines
of the Welsh language novelists' of the period.[40] Nevertheless, Beale is
seeing Wales in an Arnoldian way: Aaron continues that Beale sees 'a
need to civilize and Anglicize the principality, but in a loving and
neighbourly context rather than a hostile one' (169).

A sharper version of Beale's colonial tone was present in some of the fiction by Rhoda Broughton (1840–1920). Born near Denbigh, growing up in England and then living with her married sister near Ruthin, where she started writing, she became well known as a wit and satirist in Oxford where she finally settled. Like many other colonial intellectuals – she was always more than a mere romancer – Broughton both exploits and rejects her Welsh connection, using the local romance potential in a few of her plots but also using a frequently hostile first-contact tone. In *Not Wisely But Too Well* (1867) she starts the story in 'a small, dull North Wales watering-place',[41] in *Red as a Rose is She* (1870) some of her characters 'happen to have stuck up their tent-poles in Taffy-land'[42] and the narrator soon confides that the Welsh language 'has always a querulous, quarrelsome, interrogative sound' (13). Aaron sees 'extreme racism' in Broughton's work (168) and the main reason this feature is underdeveloped is the limited use of Welsh settings: Broughton does not make the whole plot depend on an encounter between both genders and national identities, as Beale usually does, and her main work was as an England-orientated 'Queen of the Circulating Libraries', as Tamie Watters has outlined.[43]

1.3 FROM ROMANCE TOWARDS ETHNOGRAPHY: AMY DILLWYN AND ALLEN RAINE

But not all late nineteenth-century fiction is as firmly imperial in its attitudes as the medieval histories, the first-contact sketches or the romances. The conservative *Rebecca* of 1882 may well be a politically motivated response to the firmly liberal novel Amy Dillwyn (1845–1935) published in 1880, *The Rebecca Rioter*.[44] Dillwyn, a forceful and free-thinking woman who ran charities, a business and stood up for working women on strike in Swansea, tells the story of the Rebecca Riots in her own Pontarddulais area with a distinctly sympathetic use of a young rioter as the narrative focus. To match the radical nature of the topic, there is a conscious departure from romance – the genre is more like the police-detective stories that were becoming popular in the period. Evan Williams, a labourer's son, is aided and educated by Gwenllian Tudor (Dillwyn is obviously aware of the elevated nobility of this name in Cymraeg tradition), but although they are clearly attracted to each other, there is no possibility of even recognizing this feeling, let alone moving towards a resolution, and he dies in Australia, a transported convict. Vigorous in its realism and strongly liberal in its sympathies, the novel makes it clear that all the characters, whatever their class, speak in Cymraeg, and it presents them as nothing like the quaint superstitious natives of the first-contact texts. As Gramich notes, Dillwyn's own father, a powerful landowner, was involved in the Rebecca conflict, and she is 'questioning the beliefs and attitudes of her own class' (xxi).

If *The Rebecca Rioter* looks towards a radical understanding of reform in its representation of events in Wales, an opposite form of contemporary critique, equally far from imperial first-contact stories is to be found in *A Maid of Cymru* (1901) by 'The Dau Wynne', Mallt and Gwenffreda Williams.[45] Their first book, *One of the Royal Celts* (1889)[46] is a fairly straightforward modern imperial romance: the 'Royal Celts' is a British regiment and the hero dies as a heroic 'contributionist', fighting in the Sudan. *A Maid of Cymru* interprets its subtitle 'A Patriotic Romance' quite differently: Marion Löffler suggests that Mallt Williams wrote this herself.[47] The patriotism is now exclusively Welsh, and this is a powerfully ideological, anti-imperial anti-romance. The romantically named Tangwystyl Hywel, of the Breconshire gentry, meets a handsome Englishman Garry Troyts on a cruise, and then – as you do in romance – they coincidentally meet again. But she rejects him and commits herself to the cause of Cymraeg culture and identity: a real patriotism for Wales permits no room for contributionism. An exotic production that parallels the Gaelic League activities in Ireland and enlists a contemporary 'New Woman' awareness in the service of a conscious nativism, *A Maid of Cymru*, like other novels to be discussed later, uses the English language against itself, in order to press the case for the value of true native patriotism. As well as its exotic names and heightened sensitivities, there is a real sense of anti-colonial resistance as Tangwystyl finally presides over a pan-Celtic eisteddfod held in the Park Hotel, Cardiff, though as Aaron comments the novel is also socially conservative: 'It portrays anachronistically the gentry class as a social force which wins an easy triumph over the historical radicalism of the period.'[48]

Amy Dillwyn and the Williams sisters showed that intellectual Welsh women could resist the pressure to write colonial romances in English for the English. Another woman was the most successful of all Welsh novelists of the time and positions herself between the radicals like Dillwyn and the Williams sisters and the naive, England-serving

mainstream of the first-contact texts. 'Allen Raine', born Anne Adaliza
Evans, becoming Mrs Beynon Puddicombe, and then adopting her
masculine pseudonym after seeing it in a dream,[49] is certainly a writer of
romance, and was, it appears, read in England as a first-contact writer
making Wales available for a 'contributionist' use. Nevertheless, in her
commitment to writing about Wales, in her sometimes quite complex
treatment of her themes and in her power to realize and critique the
forces at work in the romances, she deserves consideration as a post-
colonial, rather than simply colonial writer, and certainly deserves, as
Sally Roberts Jones has argued, the title of the first major English-
language fiction writer in Wales.[50]

Born in Castellnewydd Emlyn in Cardiganshire, the daughter of a
solicitor, 'Allen Raine' (1836–1908) led, as Anne Adaliza Evans, an
unremarkable comfortable life among the newly powerful Welsh bourgeois Nonconformists. This included some education in England and,
following the colonizing connection, she married a Welshman who
worked for a London bank and they spent ten years in the distant
south-west London suburb of Addiscombe. Suffering there (like Amy
Dillwyn and many other Victorian women, including Florence Night-
ingale) the common mysterious debilitating illness which some think
was the result of sexual tension, others to be undiagnosed ME, she
returned to Wales after her husband became mentally ill. They built a
house at Tre-saith on the Cardiganshire coast and it was in that region
that she set most of her fiction. Her first novel shared a prize at the 1894
National Eisteddfod (before 1951 they were bilingual) but though it
was soon translated into Cymraeg and published, it did not appear in
the original English until 1909, after her death. She called it *Ynysoer*,
the name of the offshore 'cold island' where much of the action occurs,
but it was published under the more romantically topographic title
Where Billows Roll.[51] Sometimes clumsy in structure and uncertain in
style as it is, many of the central Raine features are present. Set on the
sea-coast, like a surprising amount of the first-contact material (Wales
was often easier to visit by sea than road), valuing the environment as
natural and valuable, focusing on young, innocent and naturally gifted
children (here the twins Iolo and Iola), telling a Cinderella-like story
about them in the context of quite realistic ordinary people, including
landowners who are, in *gwerin* mode, not separate from the community, Raine makes it consistently clear that this is a Cymraeg-
speaking world. All these features will recur. While there are clearly
links with the first-contact material – Wales is beautiful and natural, the

people's quaint customs are touched on, superstition hovers at the edge
of the story – there are also features which make the story seem more
like a diluted version of *A Maid of Cymru*'s deliberate nativism than a
London-pleasing appropriation of Welshness. The twins seem a symbol
of Welsh native innocence and quality – the name Iolo itself may refer
to Iolo Morganwg, the early nineteenth-century ideologue of the
London Welsh's recovery of Cymraeg culture. The twins' place of
origin – a near-island difficult of access from 'civilization', suffering
conflict through incomers – sounds remarkably like an allegory of
Wales itself in the late nineteenth century.

The presence of allegory should not be surprising. In an influential
essay,[52] Fredric Jameson has argued that allegory, the use of symbolic
and suggestive patterns in a narrative, is a mode of meaning-creation
characteristic of what he calls 'third-world' writers, who tend because
of their native traditions not to use the English-language novel's way of
establishing themes through making central characters realize
personally, individualistically, what is true and of value about their
world. Allegory is a way of coding a meaning that may well be hostile to
the colonizing publisher and audience, but is also, in being based in
collective signification rather than individual rationality, in itself much
closer to the socially based thought-systems of people not yet
dominated by Western European individualist rationalism and its
instrument in the traditional novel. Allegories of many kinds will occur
throughout Welsh writing in English, and it is not surprising that the
first major writer appears to use the mode instinctively.

The conscious Welshness of *Ynysoer* is also suggested by its direction
– to the National Eisteddfod rather than a London publisher – and is
confirmed by the patterns evident in Raine's first English-published
novel *A Welsh Singer* published in 1897. This step needed some determination: the manuscript was rejected six times and Hutchinson only
took it on with an author's subsidy of £20.[53] So began a remarkable,
and remarkably forgotten, career. By 1911 she had, Aaron comments,
sold two million books in Britain and many more overseas.[54] The
influential magazine *The Bookman* was to name Raine as one of the
four bestsellers of the age[55] – the romantic writer Marie Corelli was
another and the popular, woman-oriented appearance of Raine's work
seems to have led to her being sidelined in Welsh literary history. Gwyn
Jones famously called her novels and *The Maid of Cefn Ydfa* a
'sandcastle dynasty' to be washed away by the brusque tide of Caradoc
Evans and his followers.[56] Sally Roberts Jones in her book on Raine

and Katie Gramich in her introduction to the reprint of *Queen of the Rushes*[57] have both argued that she is the first writer to speak up substantially in English for Welsh culture, and although she retained the romance formula in which both land and heroine are seen as desirable properties, both will remain in native hands. Similarly, though she uses many of the images of first-contact writing, her novels communicate an awareness of a separate, independent and self-sustaining range of values for Welsh life and, even more challengingly, though with varying intensity, an awareness of the impact of colonizing English culture in the period in which she wrote.

A Welsh Singer reads startlingly strongly when seen through the eyes of post-colonial criticism. The central figure is Mifanwy – the spelling seems an English simplification of the Cymraeg Myfanwy – who, like Raine's own sister Lettie, is a fine natural singer. But she is also a peasant shepherdess, barefoot, in rags and very dark in the face – the image of an American or Australian native girl. These figures often symbolize the fertility of the colonized country, their beauty and sexual availability providing an exciting image of the profitability of the new land. When the colonizers encounter strong and organized native forces, as in North America or New Zealand, it is quite common for this figure to be a native princess like Pocohontas who can in her actual person represent native political power. This is paralleled in Celtic tradition: a woman often represents the 'sovereignty' of the country, and there is clear evidence for the surviving force of 'sovereignty' women in medieval Arthurian romance.[58] Some of this force, as well as the sexual appropriation images innate to colonial literature, seems to be remembered in some of the English writers of Welsh fiction, Raine among them. Apart from this symbolization, Mifanwy celebrates the joys of nature, and her only other pleasure is to be with Ieuan Gwyllt (Wild Ieuan), another nobly savage child who has, to match her singing, a special talent in carving. They are both in the harsh care of 'the master', John Powys, one of the many landowners in Raine who is not separate from a *gwerin*-like community, here Aberseithin, a small sea-port set among farming country in south-west Wales.

The history – or fantasy – of the Welsh liberal bourgeoisie, Raine's own context, asserts itself as Ieuan's talent leads to his adoption as protégé by Sir Glynne Meredith, a local man whose sculpting gifts have brought him a knighthood, and Ieuan leaves home and Mifanwy for London. Separation of young couples, mismarriage and eventual, often strained, happy resolutions mark in Raine's fiction more strongly than in Austen, Gaskell or Eliot the passive miseries that patriarchy must have imposed on many women – quite probably Raine herself. But this is fictive, not factual pain, and Mifanwy herself moves off, first to 'the works', but not here into industrial realism. By accident she falls in with a circus in Merthyr, becomes a singer and performer, travels to London and there is taken up for voice-training and turns into the most celebrated singer of her time and a great beauty: the natural whiteness of her body returns when she is out of the wind and sun. The strained plotting (the circus as a locus of humane values seems to rely on Dickens's *Hard Times* and the London career is managed by the convenient relocation to the capital of her local preacher) does not prevent Raine from some lively realizations of the strains of cultural change. In the circus Mifanwy sings Welsh words to a waltz tune, and in London she calls herself 'La Belle Rhoose', based on a Welsh place-name, but is thought of as 'La Belle Russe' (The Beautiful Russian). The hybrid instability of identity in such a transitional context is vividly caught, and then later ironized as one of the Aberseithin locals celebrates the famous singer by calling her canary in quasi-Cymraeg 'labelrŵs'.

Ieuan, now an elegant London artist, falls in love with the glamorous singer, but in an extended play on authenticity – and an insistence within romance on native value – La Belle Russe will only accept him if he is freed by his rustic childhood sweetheart, Mifanwy. Back in their sea-girt Eden, as her original uncolonized self, she forces him to tell the truth about his own sociocultural transition and then (a moment to justify Gramich's argument for a feminist consciousness in Raine's work)[59] reveals that she has gone even further in the same hybridizing mode, and that she understands, and accepts him as her equal and husband.

The novel may realize the process of colonial transformations, but it is not in any real way an anti-colonial text. The only villain is Laissabeth, the Welsh gentry girl who also loves Ieuan and, having schemed against Mifanwy and nearly killed her in one of Raine's recurrent fire scenes, marries without love an enfeebled English aristocrat. Raine also often relies on Welsh stereotypes – the singing, the talented youth, the stern landowner, as well as a set of mysterious births and wills straight out of the Victorian novelist's box of tricks. *A Welsh Singer* is, nevertheless, a richly realized and vividly presented account of culture-clash as the two major characters learn to mime the behaviour of fashionable imperial London, and then, asserting the romance of rustic virtue rather than of land-taking, recognize the value symbolized by their natural origins. Raine would write more serious, more restrained and more socially descriptive novels, but she would never again catch so vividly or allegorically the strains of contact between a native and a colonizing culture.

She followed up with *Torn Sails* (1898),[60] set this time entirely on the coast, and for the first time working out what Jones describes as 'the classic Allen Raine quartet' of men and women who mismatch.[61] But this is not Ruritania: Gwladys, a beauty and singer, is persuaded to marry the man she does not love, Hugh Morgan, the local landowner, while her beloved Ivor sails for distant Caernarfon. Gwen, a village woman who loves Hugh, becomes deranged and finally burns down his house. Ivor, having returned, rescues Gwladys after a nautical suicide bid – another melodrama – and the pair finally unite. Raine's sense of real strain in relationships and her realistic presentation of the social context is in this novel swamped by the mechanics of a tear-jerking plot. First-contact-style Welsh characteristics are more evident than before: the people are said to be impressionable (15), superstitious (29–30), emotional (167), sometimes liable to insanity (196). Also more like a first-contact story is the instructional element: footnotes explain laverbread and *cawl*, Cymraeg words and phrases are translated more than before and stereotyped – the phrase *caton pawb* ((God) keep us all) is overused. Overall, *Torn Sails*, as Raine adjusts her sights for the English audience, is closer to a first-contact romance than *A Welsh Singer*.

But Raine did not give in to those simple patterns. Now a bestselling novelist, she seems to have gathered herself to combine her romance mode with an attempt to give an account of Wales in her own day in her three strongest novels, each of which can claim some element of contemporary Welsh social description and represent a move towards an independent ethnography of Welsh rural society. In 1900 in *Garthowen: A Story of a Welsh Homestead*[62] she uses a crime motif rather than hectic romance as the central structure, presumably influenced by the rising tide of one-volume mysteries that were beginning to flood the market in the wake of the Sherlock Holmes phenomenon, but the effect is, as Gramich comments, 'a much more serious exploration of social themes'.[63] The heroine is a seaborne foundling called Morva, and she lives a simple and natural life, 'yet so full of love and wealth and happiness' (119). She loves Gethin Owens, a sailor, but they are estranged when he is suspected of stealing money from his sister's fiancé and Morva becomes informally engaged to his brother Will, who speaks good English and is, via education, upwardly mobile. Will in turn is found attractive by Gwenda Vaughan, of gentry stock. But this novel does not focus on its four-handed amatory melodrama. It transpires that it was the young men's father who stole the money in order to fund Will at college, and in a dramatic sequence, quite new in Raine's work, he confesses to the chapel deacons, who refuse to offer any forgiveness. The couples eventually pair up correctly, and the father finds some sort of peace, but this is a serious story about moral blame, reaching into the world of Nonconformist social ambition and hypocrisy, a world usually associated with Caradoc Evans rather than Allen Raine, as will be discussed below. *Garthowen* sold less well than Raine's other work and she did not again demote the romance interest, but it does show that she was at least trying to give some sort of account of Wales as she knew it.

A less challenging treatment of contemporary Welsh life varies the romance pattern in *A Welsh Witch: A Romance of Rough Places* (1902).[64] Again we are on the coast, with Goronwy, a sailor turned farmer, a rival male in the gypsy-like Walto and this time two Cinderellas in Yshbel Lloyd, abandoned by her probable gentry father, and Catrin Rees, a wild child who haunts the sea-coast and is widely suspected of witchcraft. Yshbel is warned off Walto by his ambitious mother and – here the novel becomes innovative and distinctly ethnographic – he goes off to 'the works', but unlike in *A Welsh Singer* Merthyr is a place of intense industrial activity, not a literary-derived circus. Eventually Yshbel and Goronwy will also move to the industrial world and, probably drawing on Joseph Keating's 1900 novel *Son of Judith* (see pp. 26–7), there is a pit explosion and an escape. The relative realism of the treatment of the industrial world is, however, no more than a context for the complexities of romance: Raine is not here trying as she did in *Garthowen* to shift the genre. The industrial material is her own rural Welsh version of first contact with a new world, but it is not the main source of excitement. Indeed back home at the seaside, before and during the shift to the east, all kinds of melodrama have broken loose: Yshbel herself saves a ship in distress, Catrin in turn rescues Yshbel from the seas, and an entire field in dispute between the two families crashes into the sea. Having escaped being sent to an asylum, Catrin takes to the gypsy life, then is rescued from being a shepherdess in Snowdon by the discovery that her father's true discovered will has left her the farm. Finally, as if exhausted by their escapades, the pairs form up properly.

A Welsh Witch is distinctly elaborate – Jones seems generous to call it 'ambitious' (41) – and this may stem in part from Raine's growing confidence as a bestseller but also from a generic imbalance between the romance matrix and an urge to speak about her country. This had worked well through allegory in *A Welsh Singer* but here, as she tries to bring in more realistic ethnographic material, the overall effect is increasingly one of strain on the fragile body and delicate tone of romance. In her next book Raine avoided this problem by venturing into history with *Hearts of Wales: An Old Romance* (1904),[65] but her ethnographic seriousness continues: far from the wide-ranging fictional sweep of the usual Welsh historical novels, this is closely and for Raine locally focused on the past of the castle at Castellnewydd Emlyn, combining historical reminiscences with rhapsodies of natural beauty but also describing, if a little touristically, the native customs. The original title was *The Sin Eater*, referring to a feature of local funeral practice that comes up regularly in the first-contact stories. But if historicism relieved Raine of the strain between romance and ethnography, in her next and finest novel, *Queen of the Rushes* (1906),[66] she both tackled and to a large extent resolved that problem.

She indicates in her subtitle 'A Tale of the Welsh Revival' her bold wish to give an account of an absolutely contemporary event – the Religious Revival swept across Wales in 1904 and the book was published in 1906. Once more on the coast, on a farm divided by the sea, a boat capsizes and farm-workers are drowned: a young girl, seeing her mother die, is struck dumb. Dramatic rather than melodramatic, and ultimately allegorical in a more focused way than *A Welsh Singer*, this opening provides a silent child of nature marked by suffering in Gwenifer, a shepherdess with 'lustrous brown eyes' (34): the fact that she is known as 'Queen of the Rushes' suggests her role as a figure of natural sovereignty. Her parallel in the usual Raine foursome is Nance, daughter of a broken-down schoolmaster. It is Nance, blue-eyed and flawed in character, who will marry Gildas, the owner of the farm and local 'master', whom Gwenifer silently loves, while the wandering sailor 'Captain Jack' will both learn to love the dumb Gwenifer and through his thoughtless flirting become the object of Nance's obsession. These are a more strongly demarcated foursome than Raine has used before, and as Gramich notes (19) the fact that Nance is a class hybrid (her father a bourgeois reduced to peasant status) and Jack a national hybrid (speaking both Cymraeg and English and widely travelled) brings into the book on a realistic basis some of the tensions that were only allegorized in *A Welsh Singer*. The real strength of the novel, however, is that its ethnographic drive is here woven deeply into the romance plot, not, as in *Garthowen* or *A Welsh Witch*, working against it. As the Revival comes, the people of Tregildas grow increasingly religious, and Nance, always liable to overexcitement, becomes an obsessive chapel-attender. Her husband Gildas, however, is cool about the emotive excesses he identifies in the Revival and is outraged when Nance, as he sees it, publicly shames him by having him prayed for. He becomes almost ostracized by the community: *gwerin* solidarity between people and master is riven by new, incursive, religious affiliations. The social and domestic storm gathering around Gildas, itself matched by the sombre setting and dramatic weather, climaxes as Nance runs off to Jack's ship, is told by him he loves Gwenifer, and disappears. A body identified as that of Nance is found on the beach and Gildas is suspected of murder – a brief turn towards the mystery novel. At the inquest it is Gwenifer, suddenly able to speak again, who clears him by describing what happened on the beach that night, and eventually Nance, now weak and deranged, returns from the mountains where she fled, and dies so that Gwenifer can marry Gildas. The romance closure here includes moral judgements, dispatching the two less than admirable characters of the foursome, and strongly asserts the long-oppressed values of both the dumb but faithful woman and the stubborn but calm Gildas.

The closely woven and seriously developed nature of the novel (with a few lurches: where did the body on the beach come from? just what enabled Gwenifer to speak again?) enables it to be interpreted in some depth. Gramich makes a good case for seeing aspects of feminist symbolism in Gwenifer's experiences, and Raine was no doubt aware that in naming her hero Gildas and the town Tregildas, 'Gildasville', she was using the name of the Welsh author who in the early sixth century excoriated his countrymen for their folly and fickleness. Unquestionably romance still, and not without the first-contact features that recur in all Raine's work, *Queen of the Rushes* nevertheless enfolds a thoughtful account of the Revival, and insists on the native virtues, however unable they are to make themselves heard. This is where Raine best manages to press romance towards a serious mode of representation.

But only the return to allegory in Gwenifer's dumbness permits the critique of the hyper-vociferous Revival. What Raine does not do to any extent here, or in *Garthowen* and *A Welsh Witch*, was to describe the community she knew so well in terms that were socially or fictionally realistic, that is terms which were generically appropriate to an ethnography of the developing world of English Wales. It would be tempting to assume that this was because of her class position and a romantic view of narrative outcomes, but the fact that Joseph Keating, a collier, was also unable to escape the embrace of romance and in fact did less well than Raine in realizing the ambient social world of Wales, suggests the problem was deeper. These writers, under publishers' and readers' pressure to continue with romance, had not discovered or worked out a genre or a narrative position that would enable them to describe with real depth the tensions of a native culture under rapid change from the pressures of external political and economic forces. As with Hardy, romance, whether positive or tragic, was the medium they used and this posed special problems for a Welsh writer: finding a genre that is not itself borrowed from the colonizer and so is not inherently coercive is one of the hardest tasks for the colonized writer. In fact when Raine is compared with the drastically limited work of the first-contact sketch writers, the simplicity of the historical novelists and the self-indulgence of the Celtic twilight writers, it is remarkable how far she did move towards an account of the world she knew that was more than 'contributionist', that realized a real, if partial, separate identity and value for a Welsh social culture. It is true that there is always an element of the colonizer's values in Raine's work. Aaron stresses this, arguing that both she and Beale offer 'some sort of subtle propaganda, concealed, on the side of English middle-class influences',[67] but Raine comes closest of these Welsh women romancers to being an ethnographer of rural Wales in her period. When compared with writers like the later Berta Ruck who churned out London-focused romances, it seems clear that even Raine's decision to set all her work, after the London-visiting *A Welsh Singer,* in western Wales was in itself an act of dissent against the English metropolitan power she had experienced in her years in outer London and that in this, as in the relative seriousness of her work, Raine was at least testing, even inherently resisting, the constraints of English colonial publishing practices.

1.4 THE ROMANCE OF INDUSTRY: JOSEPH KEATING

Joseph Keating (1871–1934), born in Mountain Ash and working as a collier for six years from the age of twelve, is the first Welsh working-class figure to write fiction in English. Raymond Williams has seen that as being of great moment,[68] but the *gwerin* tradition would have found nothing strange in such a situation – though it would have expected high quality poetry or sermons to flow from an intellectual of humble origin. Commentators may in fact have separated *gwerin* and working-class models of culture too much in Wales. Although the situation in industrial south-east Wales was increasingly one of class society where a moneyed elite, supported by a bourgeois professional class, exploited in classic terms the labour value of a proletariat, the responses of the workers at times followed the traditional (or newly declared traditional) paths of the Welsh *gwerin* ideal rather than the confrontational politics characteristic of the revolutionary industrial situation as found in Germany, Russia, England and indeed parts of early nineteenth-century Wales.

But Joseph Keating, like so many in both fiction and reality in industrial Wales aspiring to move through his innate and acquired skills beyond painful labour into a more leisured and better rewarded form of work, used in his novels neither a *gwerin* ideal nor the yet hardly imagined politics of class confrontation. He wrote by 1906 many short stories descriptive of mining for the *Western Mail* under the inherently romantic series title 'Adventures in the Dark', and this non-realist tone is stronger in his novels. He wrote four set in his native Cynon valley and, strikingly different as they are, all follow an inherently first-contact romance pattern in that they present the industrial context with as much sense of quaint wonder as the earlier sketch writers had employed and they consistently anchor their plots in an amatory romance dealing with the wealthier classes. The squirearchy had lost authority and the professional bourgeoisie never held power in the mushroom towns of industrial south-east Wales, so the social fraction where Keating finds authority and focal interest, the central figures in his fiction, are the owners and managers of the coal-pits.

His first novel, *Son of Judith: A Tale of the Welsh Mining Valleys* (1900), written while he was working for the *Western Mail*,[69] realizes the decay of the gentry and the doubtful rise of the industrial bourgeoisie, both caused by the incursion of capital. Its title alone locates it away from the local working classes who called a pit a colliery – a mine could as easily produce ironstone – and did not use in a routine way the distanced and inherently patronizing term 'the valleys'. Judith Morris is a gentry lady, who, abandoned by a young surveyor, raises alone their son Howel: it is never clear why she named him that (the aura of Hywel Dda, ancient lord of Morgannwg and much of Wales may be an unpursued allegorical thread). She brings him up in hyper-melodramatic fashion to avenge her by murdering his treacherous father when he can, even if – perhaps especially if – he hangs for it: she both loves and hates the boy. The bloody-handed Judith of the Old Testament comes to mind, but it is also tempting to think that Keating, of Irish origin as his surname suggests, was familiar with the murderous passions of early Irish saga.

The father, known only by his surname, Meredith, has risen to possess several pits and Keating exploits his own knowledge of collieries in a remarkable sequence of a hundred and twenty pages in which varied gentry, including Meredith, the young surveyor Howel, and Morwen Owen, a young woman of good family who is training as a pit-manager, are caught underground in a fall, wander around the pit, and are eventually rescued through the heroics of the titular son of Judith. Keating draws on Zola's *Germinal*, a source for so much in industrial fiction, as well as his own knowledge, but it is highly revealing that the people he traps in the disaster are the sort of people who would in fact stay well clear of trouble underground: gentry romance still, however improbably, dominates the action.

Judith's son rises in favour, especially with his unknown father, and he is soon in a financial position to enact vengeance on behalf of his mother who, true to the stereotypes of first-contact romance has a 'pale witch-like face' (239). Eventually, as her son refuses to do her vengeful bidding, she herself pushes Meredith to his death in a mountainous ravine, and then, trying repentantly to save him, also falls to her death. Melodrama consumes the fury of their relationship, and Howel can live on in happiness with Morwen: the plot neatly removes the passionate combatants and leaves a peaceful future for the inheritors of the social compromise in charge in the valley. Keating, though a denizen of the starkly industrial Cynon valley, writes a story as romance-oriented as Raine's *A Welsh Witch*, though the death of the errant bourgeois and gentry figures implicitly expresses the exhausted nature of that genre. A striking failure to ethnographize the world he knew, a sad hostage to the power in the publishing market of the established romance of first contact, Keating's work is testament to the way his own experience and knowledge are dramatically colonized by the imperial form of the English sentimental novel. Like Raine's *A Welsh Singer*, his first novel is the most expressive realization of the difficulties facing him as an author struggling to write about the world he knew in the context of an overpowering literary tradition replete with imperial authority.

His second effort at writing industrial Wales in fiction is a more stable statement of limited capacity. In *Maurice* (1905),[70] he deals, as so many English-language Welsh male writers would, with a boy. This is not only male narcissm. The isolation and powerlessness the authors feel and the vulnerable innocence of their own position find an objective correlative in a character subject to forces beyond personal control; these forces derive from errant and absent parents, symbolizing the loss of social certainties and confident control in the world around the authors. A Raine-like foundling, with an Irish informal foster-father, Maurice grows up to experience (apparently for the first time) the classic Welsh industrial fiction routine of a boy's first day down a colliery. He is befriended by Olwen, the daughter of a coal-owner, whose name seems to direct us back to the beautiful earth-goddess sovereignty figure of the ancient prose story *Culhwch ac Olwen* (found in the *Mabinogi* collection), a connection made explicit in the book (110–13). Olwen represents first-contact style Welsh natural values and loves the hero Jethro, of farming stock. His brother, with the nationally resonant name David, leaves the impoverished farm for work in the colliery. Recognizing in this way what the narrative calls 'the civilisation that had advanced so barbarously' (169) and including Olwen's other admirer the Honourable Odo Rhys, son to Lord Cynon, owner of many acres and mines, Keating quickly develops a drama where Maurice on his unlucky first day underground is involved in a disaster where, ultimately, Jethro dies saving him and Olwen falls romantically dead on her lover's corpse. Keating uses *Romeo and Juliet* as a way to the end, aided by the even more improbable source of Mafia-type Italian dissidents who 'personified sordid modernity' (358), a version of Zola's destructive anarchist Souvarine in *Germinal*. Powerfully realistic in detail and language but always avoiding a worker-based political drama, Keating's novel recognizes the way in which the coal industry radically changed lives, creating what he called in his autobiography 'a hideous industrial experience',[71] but he resolves that tension through a lament for the passing of gentry lives and antique communities. In retrospect, his work makes Raine's effort to involve her romance plots in the actualities of contemporary Wales look like a heroic enterprise.

It is in one way not surprising, though in another very disappointing, to find that Keating's third Welsh-set story, *The Queen of Swords: The Story of a Woman and an Extraordinary Duel* (1906),[72] is a bizarre trans-plantation of Rafael Sabatini's newly successful masculine fantasies to the battered Cynon valley. To 'our Glamorganshire village' (1–2) comes

Owen Wynne, a gentry adventurer, lady's man and duellist, whose drastically unlikely career and peacocking success proclaim Keating's clear sense that no publishing profit lies in anything tinged with Welsh realism, however useful a knowledge of a particular topography might be to the hard-pressed producer of pot-boilers – the novel reads like a travesty of the earlier sporting-gentry visits to Wales.

Not surprisingly, Keating fell silent on Wales for some time. It may well be – with some irony – the success of Caradoc Evans's savage Welsh satires in the English market, starting in 1915, that renewed his interest in his homeland as a setting. It was in 1917 that he published *Flower of the Dark*,[73] a confident, well-structured novel that combines a plot of the contemporary mystery thriller kind with a range of statements about events and values in the Welsh industrial context, though it still focuses on the pit-owning and professional class fraction. Aeronwy Parry, golden-haired, pretty and twenty years old, is a romance heroine in the twelfth-century tradition, inheriting as she does, just before the war, the possessions of her father in 'a straggling Glamorganshire pit village' (12–13) and so being highly available for marital appropriation. One candidate is the ominously named Samson Cragwyn who owns an adjacent mine; another is Idwal Morgan, a miner turned manager and part-owner of Aeronwy's own mine. The overbearing Samson persuades this valley Delilah to leak information that leads him to find 'The Big Vein' of splendid coal and even to lend him the £20,000 needed to exploit it, but like a contemporary thriller villain he then sells the product to the German enemy, through suitable intermediaries. Though Samson makes Aeronwy promise to marry him, he really loves Megan, his besotted housekeeper (Allen Raine still seems to be playing a part in Keating's plotting), and sees Idwal as a rival. Popular literature knew what to do about such rivalries and on a stormy night Samson murders Idwal and, with a pit-owner's eye, pushes his body under a flood-induced mud-slide.

So far this seems a narrative without a hero, but this is to be the mild-mannered assistant manager (and son of yet another surveyor – they seem to function like lawyers, good and bad, in Dickens's fiction), a figure held over from *Son of Judith* and racially transmuted, with the startlingly English name Osla Silvertop. Having led Aeronwy out of another gentry-underground situation, he helps put her pit back into profit after a brief patriotic spell in the army and works out the murder (he is an unnoticed early amateur detective). Megan has died without revealing her knowledge of Samson's crime but, neatly rather than meaningfully, the plot makes Megan's plodding proletarian admirer Caleb, now a soldier, shoot Samson dead by accident. He is on guard because of industrial problems caused by Samson's use of scabs in a deliberately induced strike (a shadow of Tonypandy in 1910). So Osla and Aeronwy can unite, and English professional skills can appropriate the image of Welsh fertile profit.

A riot of professional fictional motifs, as well as an insistently gentry version of what could have been a potent ethnography of industry, *Flower of the Dark* exposes the painful limitations of first-contact romance as a way of describing, let alone analysing, the new world of imperial industrial Wales: the closest it comes to critique is when a Nonconformist preacher refers to the owners' 'blood-stained gold' (226). Keating seems subconsciously to give away his Anglicized position: Osla in Welsh tradition is Osla Gyllellfawr (Osla Big-Knife), Arthur's opponent in *Breuddwyd Rhonabwy*, the archetypal Saxon whose name reiterates that treason of the Saxon long knives that was coupled with the incursive strategies of the treasons of the Blue Books. Later writers, by focusing their narratives firmly in the minds and voices of the Megans and the Calebs, would recirculate the melodramatic events of the coalfield in a new, self-sufficient ethnography of English-language industrial Wales and see the Samsons and the Oslas as the enemies of the Welsh working class. But, in thrall both to English publishers and readers and also the imperial traditions of fiction, Keating, for all his inventiveness and his frustrated boldness in writing about the coalfield, could only reduce his novels to grotesque melodramas and his Welsh workers to pathos. In fact, and it seems against some at least of his instincts, he reconstructed the romance of appropriation in a new location and as a new means of exploitative power.

That this was due to the contemporary lack of a way of writing in anything other than an inherently colonized way about industrial Wales is supported by other novels. D. Miles Lewis's *Chapel: The Story of a Welsh Family* (1919)[74] is a Keatingesque saga of a coal-owning family, oddly named Chapel. Irene Saunderson's *A Welsh Heroine: A Romance of Colliery Life* (1911)[75] starts like a predecessor of the 1930s leftist realism, presenting the harsh world of the miners and their resistance to the power of the mine-owners in a language clearly, aggressively, in the voice of the oppressed – what post-colonial analysts call 'abrogation', a refusal to share, and be contained by, the verbal style of the colonizer: even the novel's subtitle espouses some colliery realism. Nevertheless, the subtitle admits the ultimate genre of the novel: the focus on a beautiful and talented girl, rough-hewn though her language and radical attitudes may be, opens the path to a romance resolution of the apparently unresolvable political conflict that is realized. As the colliers and the troops stand face to face – Tonypandy in 1910 again – the inspired Morfudd Llewelyn, her name a combination of a Dafydd ap Gwilym heroine with the last Cymraeg prince of Wales, acts in an image of colonial harmony. She strikes up a hymn, the previously embattled miners accept her lead and, all singing in quaint Welsh harm-lessness, they pass over the bridge, through the soldiers and tunefully disappear. Morfudd herself crosses a wider divide as she and the soldiers' officer, an English gentry caricature, Lieutenant the Hon. Leslie Montcalm, fall in love. In the end, after she has, in a pit-disaster, bravely found her dying father – yet another wicked surveyor – the ill-matched pair marry. There is little credibility in the officer's explanation that 'love makes all things even; it is the greatest possible socialist extant' (237). What begins as a robust account of the industrial colony from the natives' side fizzles out as a deeply improbable romance. Whether basically avoiding the colliers' viewpoint like Keating (or indeed Raine in *A Welsh Witch*), or initially firmly espous-ing it like Saunderson, these first industrial Welsh fictions cannot position themselves for a full, sympathetic and consistent ethnographic account of the new world of industry in Wales as later writers from south-east Wales were to do.

1.5 RURAL ANTI-ROMANCE: CARADOC EVANS

The tales of south Cardiganshire folk caught between poor farms and harsh chapels produced by Caradoc Evans (1878–1945) have not been seen as romance because of their 'ferocious' tone[76] and the regularly dismal outcome of events. Yet their separation from the first-contact sketches is not as great as those, like Gwyn Jones, who have proclaimed Evans the first of the Welsh writers in English, might suppose.[77] Knowledge of the first-contact material makes clear similarities appear. Evans's stories are generically tales, often just sketches, of a folk, and his own location and approach to his distant setting is in its dark and belittling way another version of a London-based professional writing about 'Tivyland'. The negative tone is also familiar, going back to the 'Taffy' chap-books that Dearnley described rather than the sentimental late nineteenth-century material. First-contact stories were not always about beauties and profitabilities – accounts of the 'Red Indians' and the 'Aborigines' often stressed their disgusting, dirty, treacherous nature. Many of the early illustrations of colonized peoples represented them as close to animals, ludicrous in their attempt to speak English, bound to the land, often demonstrating a coarse sexuality of a despicable and yet, for the genteel audience, distinctly intriguing kind. Even the twelfth-century French romances consistently represent the people who till the land as ogres and beasts, animals ripe for dumb exploitation. This negative presentation is anti-romance, depicting the savagery that justifies the colonization as much as the natives' occasional nobility makes taming them an activity that is culturally (and in reality financially) rewarding.

If Evans is in several ways the dark reflex of first-contact romance, his relation with Raine is similar. He was from the same area, but at the very poor end of a professional family: his mother struggled to bring him and his disabled brother up on a tiny farm near Castellnewydd Emlyn. A classic victim of the 1889 Education Act, he went, deep in the Cymraeg heartland, to an English-only school where, for all his obvious intelligence, he learnt to hate learning, and in order to earn a living passed on to that classical site of Welsh servile respectability, work as a draper's assistant, first in Carmarthen and – tracing mercantile colonialism back to its source – then Cardiff and then London. Before he could recreate in fiction these two hostile environments of home and work, he educated himself in night-classes, another classic Welsh lower-class manoeuvre, but this time displaced to north London, and in 1906 with his new skills he obtained work as a junior journalist in the London popular press – a move which matches, almost parodies, the farm to Oxford fantasy (and sometime reality) of the *gwerin* ideal.

As John Harris, indefatigable scholar of Evans's work and life, has shown,[78] Evans's journalistic work, notably when answering readers' letters as editor of *Ideas*, was flexible, even warm, and several people have commented on how courteous and charming he was in person. His early stories set in London have a similar humane, even sentimental, tone: in 'A Sovereign Remedy' a forger gives himself up to the police to save a poverty-stricken woman who passes one of his bad sovereigns.[79] But this London-constructed genial professional persona never appears in the stories he produced to take revenge on what he saw as the crippling environment from which he had emerged. Like Zola, Swift, Langland, other great satirists, he had a creative vitriol for his own rejected world; Evans identified a particular dehumanizing force from which he had escaped but which still obsessed him. He felt that the power of the Nonconformist church as the regulator of rural Welsh life had acted as a magnifier of peasant rapacity in the area he ironically – and referring to first-contact idealism – names Manteg (Lovely Place). The Nonconformist *gwerin* ideal met its inquisitor in Evans: he called it a 'debased religion',[80] and the famously virulent reaction his work received in the Welsh press, charted by John Harris and T. L. Williams,[81] was the outraged response of a triumphalist ideology that felt betrayed from within.

The attack was certainly ferocious and two of the early stories in *My People* (1915)[82] are among the most brilliant, subtle and damning satires ever published. In 'A Father in Sion', the first in the collection, Sadrach rejects his wife Achsah – the names are redolent with Old Testament self-importance – after she has born him eight children. He declares her mad, locks her in the harness-loft and exercises her in reins. Nonconformist piety does not stop Sadrach taking another woman nor, it seems, for all his denial in chapel, having impregnated Achsah before their marriage, nor yet, the story even implies, from having sex once more with Achsah before he 'marries' Sara Ann. This is not a moral world: fate, not an angry God, seems the force which strikes Sadrach's children one by one, though Rachel is shown to die in deepest misery and horror because of her father's land-obsessed unconcern. Sadrach does not personally suffer nor repent, and the final viewpoint is that of the escaped Achsah, realizing only two of her children are alive and greeting her supplanter now as truly 'a lunatic' (56).

This condensed, potently suggestive story, little over three thousand words, permits Sadrach to justify his brutality in hypocritical Christian terms. It is also written in a unique style. The narration is restrained, formal, a language Evans acknowledged was based on the sonorous confidence of the Bible. But the characters speak in an English that is heavily, abrogatingly, marked by Welshness. With phonetic variation they say 'Iss' for 'Yes'; in terms of vocabulary 'little', the Cymraeg *bach*, is used as an affectionate diminutive throughout, and God is called 'the Big Man'; native syntax underlies the dialogue in bringing an emphasized complement to the front of the sentence – 'Wise was Sadrach', and constantly placing the adjective after the noun – 'woman bad', 'farm good'. Many hostile critics felt Evans was literally translating from Cymraeg to mock native speech, but it is more complex than that. The speech is a poorly learnt English – few of the characters know for

example that English, unlike Cymraeg, reverses subject and verb after
an adverb ('Why say you?' not 'Why you say?'), or more usually uses
the compound 'Why do you say?'. And just as imperfect as their
cultural transition to English, like Evans's own botched schooling that
made night-classes in English necessary for him in London, is the
characters' crude, narrow understanding of religion – 'Bod mawr' for
God really means 'Great Being', but to them God is only a big man. In
the same ironic way the use of biblical language in the narration
outlines the distance between the depths of Christian traditional values
and this harsh, competitive, self-centred world, and the title, 'A Father
in Sion' drily, and also bitterly, underlines the satire. Evans, as a skilled
journalist and editor, was an expert at suggestive titles, and he
originally, but less ironically, called this story 'The Man who Walked
with God'.

The other great story, 'Be This Her Memorial', focuses not on male
self-obsession but the way in which chapel ideology empowers such a
world. Nanni, a poor widow, supported thinly by the parish and
expected to work brutally hard in return, hears that the minister is
leaving – the 'call' of a wealthier parish is God's law to the pompous
Respected Josiah Bryn-Bevan, who combines the statutory Old
Testament first name (hardly a Christian one) with the double-barrelled
surname that is the mark of would-be gentry in Wales as in England
('Respected' literally translates *Parchedig*, the usual title for a Nonconformist minister). Nanni wishes to honour him by saving up for an
illustrated bible. The 'widow's mite' reverberates through the story, but
this is a fetishized world and the profit goes to the business-like 'Seller
of Bibles'. As she saves, parishioners notice that Nanni is growing
weak, unable to repay the parish in work, and her hovel smells worse.
She pays the sovereign for the bible and gives it to Bryn-Bevan, but is
unable to attend chapel the day he coldly passes it to the Sunday
School. With equal casualness, he finally visits – to find her dead. The
roasted rat in her hands reveals terribly how she has managed to save
for the Bible: shocked, and miming his own distance from Christ, the
so-called 'Respected' 'fled from the house of sacrifice' (112). Only for
Nanni and, to some extent, Achsah, does Evans relent in his generally
cold objectivity and permit the narration to value a character. These are
both the most cutting of the satires and also the stories where the
reader's interpretation of implications is most fully invoked to create
the impact of their full meaning. Elsewhere Evans less directly implies
the greed, cruelty and abuse of the poor and of women – the main-

stream activities of the dominant males in the native population that his stories presented for a double audience: London admired their power and Wales was traumatized by it.

Some other stories approach these two in their fierce revelations: in 'Lamentations' Evan Rhiw, a drinker who fails to give enough money to the chapel is attacked by the minister and publicly shamed by the townspeople. On his failing farm his wife works herself literally to death and his daughter, victim of his incest, grows deranged and roams naked through the area. Evan, with a rope, takes her to the Carmarthen mad-house and, because he 'did not sin any more' (144) grew rich and respected. As Katie Gramich notes, Evans shows how women are often forced into 'a position of bestial subservience'.[83] A reverse pattern of hypocrisy emerges in 'The Talent Thou Gavest', which tells how Eben, a shepherd, feels God wishes him to become a preacher. He is trained at the chapel's cost, but then criticizes their behaviour in the light of Christianity. Ostracized and pressured, he literally – and allegorically – digs a grave for his true talent and returns to preach in a mealy-mouthed, uncritical way, aware that he is using only 'half a talent' (44). Other characters resist the power of a selfish theocracy, with a similar lack of success: in 'The Woman Who Sowed Iniquity' Betti, 'a princess in Sion' (94) who owns her own farm, refuses to remain unmarried as her brother, greedy for her wealth, demands. She marries and moves to Carmarthen, but when she leaves her brutal husband her brother first damages then seizes her farm: finally, so 'The Lord's will be done' (101) he sends the locals in as a mob to unroof her house Rebecca-style – and, he expects, and hopes, kill her in the process. In 'A Just Man in Sodom', Pedr, a visionary hedge-preacher, tells the people (including Sadrach of 'A Father in Sion') that God is angry with them for their sins. He is stoned, takes to the moor and, when he sacrifices one of Sadrach's calves to his vision of an angry God, is hit, bleeding, against the chapel altar: allegory again is potent.

A short, dense book of fifteen merciless satires, *My People* brought both stylistic power and deep communal criticism to its writing about Wales. Realizing the strength of the stories, the publisher Andrew Melrose called them on the dust-jacket 'realistic pictures of peasant life' and said Evans's motive was 'to portray that he may make ashamed'. Evans's defence against critics was that the stories were realistic: he said that many incidents, including the tragedy of Achsah, were based on his own knowledge.[84] That notion of reportage and revelation is itself a first-contact manoeuvre, and there is a concordant professional, even exploitative, nuance to the way in which Evans continued with another series set in the same area: *Capel Sion*, which came out in the following year.[85] Some of its contents were simply grotesques like 'Three Men from Horeb', a knockabout battle for a body between two chapels, and 'The Tree of Knowledge' where a miser kills his wife, mistreats his sister and hangs himself – but his brother fails to find his gold: Harris feels this story, both grotesque and direct, 'buckles under the weight of mannerism'.[86] Just as stark but emphatic are the linked stories 'Sins of the Father' and 'Judges' which outline a family squabbling after their father dies: a third one 'The Day of Judgement', published separately, is included in the reprinted edition, and these seem to be parts of an uncompleted novel. Some stories rework themes from the earlier volume: 'A Sacrifice unto Sion' replays the Nanni theme as a son drives his father off the farm and he finally dies in the company of a pig, which has partly eaten him, while 'Calvary' continues the holy-fool adventures of Pedr, and 'The Acts of Dan' is very close to 'The Talent Thou Gavest'. But several stories match the power of the previous volume. In 'The Widow's Mite' a greedy woman makes her dying husband beg for money and then strips and humiliates herself in what is now a demented form of avarice. The limits of resistance are explored in 'The Pillars of Sion' when Silah, 'a doltish virgin' (43), goes dumb after a sexual attack by Amos Penparc: as he has her cleansed in chapel she pulls down the roof on him – but he remains unhurt.

The stories in *Capel Sion* may well be, as Harris suggests, 'a darker, more claustrophobic collection' (xv), but in general they lack the intensity and flexible subtlety of those in *My People*. The minister is more often a target of direct attack, and only 'The Word' has the masterly indirection of Evans's best work: it is a menacing manipulative sermon attacking all dissenters including, as 'Dai Lanlas', Evans himself (he lived when very young at Lanlas and his first name was David). The sense that Evans had gone as far as he could is reinforced by the fact that his next collection, *My Neighbours*, dated 1919 but actually, challengingly, published for St David's Day 1920, is directed at the London Welsh.[87] The stories are much simpler, focusing just on greed, social climbing and some sexual misbehaviour – the latter in the most interesting two stories, 'According to the Pattern' and 'For Better' which, as T. L. Williams notes,[88] clearly pillory David Lloyd George, that epitome of the Nonconformist ascendancy which Evans always attacked, as a manipulator of men and a seducer of their wives.

Having worked out his venom towards the environment that he felt had so strongly misshaped his own life, Evans turned his attention to the equally disabling work through which he had escaped his native region. One of the stories in *My Neighbours*, 'Joseph's House', is about a peasant boy turned draper who has, in his greedy and obsessive way, real success in London, but when he returns home he is tricked by his relatives and dies in misery. In his best-focused novel, *Nothing to Pay* (1930),[89] Evans developed this idea but did not blame the negative outcome on the Cardiganshire community. Amos Morgan follows a path very much like Evans's own, from Carmarthen to Cardiff to London. Rich with details about the practices and malpractices of the drapery business, and spiced with more than a little sexual adventure – some unlikely like the actress who seduces Amos in Carmarthen, some grotesque like the sickly but wealthy co-worker he finally marries – the novel exposes the same patterns of greed, manipulation and obsession that existed around 'Manteg', but here the ideological dynamo is no more than making money and getting on in business, not a hypocritical Nonconformist validation of wealth and competition.

Much less mannered in style than the early stories, but like them combining mordant detail with real narrative energy in a basically episodic structure, the novel combines sensation (a store-owner's former mistress poisons his new and pregnant lover) with a sour overall tone. Amos is always unpleasant, having nothing more than his self-belief and malice-directed energy to recommend him. With a hero who is totally complicit in his own vileness, like the sanctimonious peasants of Cardiganshire, but also close to Evans's own career, the novel could be seen as some sort of displaced apology for the author's own harsh and alienated literary persona. Post-colonial analysts often find such a sense of complicity in the work of an author who has shifted from an original colonized culture to that of the colonizer, and some clear examples will appear in some later Welsh writers.

Evans reduced his virulence considerably in his later work. His novel *Wasps* (1933)[90] is farcical rather than satirical in its treatment of Welsh village life, including some London scenes, and in 1943 he published the quite good-natured rural novella *Morgan Bible*. He made a semi-apology for his earlier ferocity when he said, of what would be his posthumous collection *The Earth Gives All and Takes All* (his only clearly positive title, 1946), that the stories were for once 'without bitterness'.[91] They were produced when he was married to the popular writer 'Oliver Sandys' – the Countess Barcynska – and was living in a partly revered retirement in Aberystwyth. But though the violent opposition to his early stories had been worn down by time, feeling remained negative. Glyn Jones, who has a generous word to say for everybody, finally judges that Evans's stories were 'a scurrilous portrait' and – using a firmly anti-colonial viewpoint – that he 'betrays . . . a small nation fighting desperately for its life'.[92]

A number of commentators note that *My People* appeared at a time when mockery of the Celtic parts of Britain was a profitable publishing practice. *The Perfidious Welshman* by Arthur Tyssilio Johnson (writing as 'Draig Glas', 'Blue Dragon' – correctly 'Draig Las'), appeared in 1910 in the tradition of *The Unspeakable Scot* of 1902 by T. W. H. Crosland, a journalist Evans knew, who went on to publish *Taffy Was A Welshman* in 1912.[93] These may seem lightweight compared to Evans's satire, but his first effort on his major theme was called 'Taffy at Home', reprinted in *Fury Never Leaves Us*,[94] and his play, first written as a novel,[95] which caused the London Welsh to disrupt the production, among other things by singing 'Hen Wlad Fy Nhadau', was provocatively called *Taffy*. The title *My People*, while obviously an ironic disavowal, still permitted the collection to be read in England as a first-contact narrative, and its grotesque satire is in fact in real ways in contact with the ancient chap-book tradition that, as Dearnley shows, made ill-spoken stage buffoons of 'chapbook Taffy, poor, naive and cunning'.[96] Not just the 'courageous reporter' that Harris calls him,[97] the scourge of the deforming hypocrisies of Nonconformist Wales, Evans also acts, or was read as, a foreign correspondent for imperial London and his work is best seen as a related opposite to that of Allen Raine: like her there are formative pressures from London publishing, and like her he has something evaluative to say about his native region.

Some have seen connections between him and J. M. Synge as realistic critics of their native culture: Austin Clarke, an Irish writer himself and friend of Evans, was clear on the point,[98] but Evans's position seems more fully linked to that of the Scottish writer George Douglas Brown. His *The House with Green Shutters*, published in 1901, also by Melrose, is a grim account of rural life in Scotland, and was seen then and since as an attack on the 'Kailyard' school of rural fictions, a genre drenched in a *gwerin*-like sentimentality.[99] Raine has herself been seen as a Welsh 'kailyard' writer,[100] but in fact her village reality is too strong to deserve that term, her romanticism being reserved for the physical setting and the love story. But it is no doubt her work that Evans referred to when he spoke of not writing 'the pretty-pretty novels that are dear to my race'[101] and opposing them must have been in his mind when he told Melrose 'It is the ugly side of Welsh peasant life that I know most about.'[102]

There have been other explanations of the negative thrust of his work beyond seeing it as a truth-telling kind of modernist rigour. Barbara Prys-Williams has, with a Freudian method, dug into Evans's family background to find 'a fear of the sense of his own wickedness',[103] and that approach certainly helps to justify a 'complicity' reading of *Nothing to Pay*. The basically materialist approach of W. J. Rees has asked intriguingly why Evans's hostility to the *gwerin* ideal should differ so greatly from D. J. Williams's well-known exaltation of that idea in *Hen Dŷ Ffarm*,[104] when they are near-contemporaries and their districts are only twenty-five miles apart.[105] One factor Rees suggests is that Williams, born in 1885, would not have remembered personally the severe rural depression of the 1880s, whereas Evans was just old enough to do so. But his main point is that Williams's Llandeilo area was reached by rail in 1857 and this became a main supply route for livestock leaving rural Wales, while Castellnewydd Emlyn waited until 1895 for the railway: 'the result was a social catastrophe'[106] in Evans's region. By then cattle-droving, for so long the main source of income in the area, had been destroyed by the railways – and for the same set of reasons the southern area was much less affected by the depression and found prosperity soon returning.

Transport and business are major agents and impacts of colonialism, and while Nonconformity no doubt participated in and even magnified much of the distress of Caradoc Evans's *bro*, the full weight of his charges against the chapels may be best answered with a verdict of 'not proven', even perhaps 'not guilty' except as an accomplice. And there is, as well as D. J. Williams, another local writer to be compared to Evans. In her final illness Allen Raine's doctor was Evans's wealthy (but unfriendly) uncle Joshua Powell,[107] and their writing has related opposition. Just as Raine's romance orientation and publisher's expectations bring strained harmonies to her work, so Caradoc Evans's journalistic ability to condense and intensify makes his work exaggeratedly inharmonious. The situations and the responses of both writers are those of colonized authors: what has made them seem so different is the complexity of the forces released in the colonial encounter, and their surviving value is to have retained in full, complex and often puzzling form the impact of English cultural and socio-economic colonizing forces on what had previously been Cymraeg Wales.

1.6 THE ROMANCE OF POWYS: GERAINT GOODWIN, HILDA VAUGHAN AND MARGIAD EVANS

The writers considered so far have been located in the south, from Raine's far west to the coalfield of Keating. Always open to English incursion both by sea and along the road to Ireland, long before industry amplified that effect, the south was nevertheless not the easiest part of Wales for English people to visit and settle in. Offa's Dyke was built along the western border of Anglo-Saxon England because it was so simple for the Welsh to raid into England across the rolling hills and plains of what was then, and is now again, called Powys – and it was just as simple for the English to move in the opposite direction. Towns like Newtown, Shrewsbury, Hereford and Monmouth, set on the rivers that irrigate the borderlands with mountain water, had for long been settlements where Welsh and English livestock, language, love and conflict interwove. Powys, between mountainous and deeply traditional Wales and the expanding English world, is another major site of English-language writing that debates aspects of Welshness in the earlier twentieth century. It also uses first-contact romance as its basic mode, though, as before, in different ways depending on the position, self-concept and imagined audience of the authors.

Hilda Vaughan (1892–1985) was from a Radnorshire gentry family; she grew up in Builth Wells as a solicitor's daughter and, experiencing the new roles possible to women of her generation, worked as a nurse during the First World War. Like Raine she married a London professional, but this was no erratic Welshman whose illness returned his wife to Wales, but Charles Morgan, who was to be a prestigious dramatist and novelist. He firmly supported his wife's writing career, and his circle and interests are no doubt the reason why her later work moves away from a close concern with modern Wales. Her first novel, *The Battle to the Weak* (1925),[108] is set near Builth Wells and is in structure a Raine-like romance, an extended and eventually happy Romeo and Juliet story. Esther and Rhys are separated for years, largely because of an inter-family feud, and eventually reunite after the man's first marriage. Also like Raine, Vaughan includes a good deal of rural and domestic observation – the English readers could use the novel as a fictionalized tourist text. More overtly than Raine it recognizes the colonizing of Wales: the man's family is stereotypically native, the hot-tempered hill-farming Lloyds, while Esther's family are Bevans, equally Cymraeg in name, but closer to town, and her father has lost his

Cymraeg, though he is also drunken and violent. It is Esther, like one of Raine's flexibly sturdy women, who represents an enduring, Anglicized, yet still naturally sensitive Welshness.

Vaughan moves on from a simple opposition of native and hybrid-ized identities. Esther also represents a strong woman, not only chop-ping logs for the fire but also enduring loneliness and recognizing that virtue and family loyalty are in some ways painful: her friend Megan has two illegitimate children to warm her own isolation. Rhys too, when he returns from America, represents more than native vigour: angry about the 'petty enmities that are the ruin of Wales' (247), he is also a radical (the parson calls him a 'revolutionary', 275) and – here Vaughan refers to one of the dialectical effects of colonization – sets up an Institute for workers' education in modern politics. The plotting can be strained: Megan makes an unlikely manager for Rhys's Institute and it is never clear where Esther has been away for seven years, as we suddenly discover, but, like Raine, Vaughan works to make the novel more than a naive nativist romance. Esther may love the countryside and even, as Rhys reflects, be 'of the land' (285) but she is more than the country-symbolizing maiden of medieval Cymraeg literature and first-contact sketches; she has a distinctly Powys hybrid personality and a lightly indicated local accent to match. At the end she decides she is not a fit mate for the new dynamic Rhys, but a last-minute love-moment removes the threat of an unhappy ending. Presumably she is therefore the triumphant 'weak' of the title, though the fitful Rhys might also be a candidate: it could be that Vaughan also suggests that the intrinsically weak people of a divided and overshadowed Wales can, by affectionate and purposive combination, gain real strength. The novel finally accepts and values the hybridization of English and Welsh, an unsurprising view in terms of the history of the border country, but, as with other Powys romancers, such a position seems overlaid with an equally historical set of irresolvable hostilities – just as post-colonial analysts would expect of any hybridized situation.

Thoughtful, often compelling, and to some degree not resolving in its happy ending the tensions it vividly realizes, *The Battle to the Weak* is, like Raine's *A Welsh Singer* and Keating's *Son of Judith*, a first response to the colonized situation, a mixture of allegorical suggestion and semi-realistic obfuscation. However, where Raine went on to gain in social realism, to organize her plots thematically and even develop areas of effective social reporting of the Wales of her time, Vaughan, presumably because of the elevated literary life she was leading in

London, moved away from the complex interface of colonized Wales into accounts that became more simplistic, more like first-contact novels without even the aspirational value and allegorical possibility of romance to enliven them.

In *The Invader* (1928)[109] she uses a narrow space and restricted time-scheme to outline conflict between Daniel Evans, a horny-handed, thick-skinned native farmer, a kind of cross between one of Raine's harsh masters and a Caradoc Evans schemer, and his improbable opponent, Miss Webster, a lecturer from an English women's agricultural college who has inherited the farm from which he is evicted. Crisp as Vaughan's scenes are, and pacy as her action can be – this is technically more polished than the previous novel – it can hardly claim credibility after such a start. The English woman is pompous and impractical, the Welsh man is cunning and brutal, and the text seems to give him the last evaluative word after he and his Manteg-like cronies drive her off by various vicious ruses: her sheep die in the snow, those they have not already rustled, and the house of the only character who seems to be on both sides is destroyed in Rebecca style. Where in *The Struggle to the Weak* the Lloyd-versus-Bevan feud was soon elided for more up-to-date debates, and Esther represents a viable form of hybridized, even feminist, self-consciousness, *The Invader* seems to relish crass difference, like an early first-contact novel where a gentry figure lands in darkest Wales. Described rather blandly by Christopher W. Newman as 'a comedy of Welsh rural life',[110] the novel seems to abandon, even contradict, the serious effort Vaughan made in her first novel to understand the issues and forces at work in a region like Powys.

If *The Invader* is memorable for crude nativism, Vaughan's last version of cultural interface in Powys is as strangely old-fashioned, but in reverse. *The Soldier and the Gentlewoman* (1932),[111] which was her most successful book – perhaps because the title promised various excitements – is even stranger than its predecessor. The soldier of the title is Dickie Einon-Thomas, a war-damaged man who in 1919 inherits an estate after its sons die in the war. The only unmarried daughter is Gwenllian, whose masterful nature and stern good looks match her noble Cymraeg name. Determined to hold onto the estate in her own family line she inveigles Dickie into marrying her, and produces a son. In spite of his name and blood her husband is feeble, Anglicized, fond of drink and his army friends, and after the couple drift apart, and have many quarrels, she ensures the inheritance to her son by murdering his invalid father.

Hardly less direct, or clumsy, than the plot of *The Invader*, this changes the roles but not the critique: the native Welsh are still dominant and it is still the woman who is stiff and ultimately criticized by the novel. The change is that the woman triumphs, but without vigour or value. There is a final flicker of approval for Gwenllian's sister Frances (they named variously in this family), who understands what has happened and may be a much reduced version of Esther's hybridized value. Unappealingly negative in tone, and bleakly devaluing every position like a Welsh-set Evelyn Waugh novel, toying sometimes with sado-masochism as befits what Newman calls 'something of a psychological thriller'[112] (a genre which was a new taste in the early 1930s), *The Soldier and the Gentlewoman* seems a brittle reworking of the first-contact pattern that has as little contact with Welsh actuality as Vaughan herself now had.

She was always various, even dilettantish: G. F. Adam calls her a 'neo-romantic'[113] but this takes several forms. *Here are Lovers* (1926)[114] is an unironized full-blown historical romance set in 1866, where the squire's daughter loves the son of a Chartist imprisoned after the Newport rising. The possibility of cross-class feeling implied in Dillwyn's *The Rebecca Rioter* is dissolved in a quasi-mythological ending as they are consumed in a tragic end in the river. Other historical novels like *Harvest Home* (1936)[115] are equally melodramatic without this connection with politics, but Vaughan's mid-career tendency to move towards nostalgia and allegory is more potent in the novella, *A Thing of Nought*, first published in 1934 in a notably fine edition.[116] Here as in *The Battle to the Weak* a couple are separated; the woman lives on in their strangely isolated valley, a locational symbol, it seems, of the cut-off Wales Vaughan had left. Eventually she marries the coldly respectable local minister; her much changed lover returns; they remain separate, but she bears a child in his image. Vaughan's willingness to let her mystical interests flow (perhaps a version of the modernism of her London literary circle) is set fully free in a novel published first in America when she and her children were war refugees: there entitled *The Fair Woman* (1942), it appeared in Britain as *Iron and Gold* (1948).[117] A frankly nativist mythic recreation, it exhibits Vaughan's capacity as a writer of effective power and feminist insight (as Jane Aaron shows in her introduction to the reprint)[118] as well as her career trajectory from a substantial post-Raine position as a writer of at least one thoughtful Wales-inspecting romance to move back in genre and time to become a creator of first-contact style romances, most of them crudely caricatured but at their best, as in *A Thing of Nought* and *Iron and Gold,* combining elements of Celtic Twilight material with her continuing commitment to a broad-based feminist agenda.

A parallel position, in both Powys setting and steady self-distancing from describing the forms and issues of modern Wales, is found in the work of Geraint Goodwin (1903–41). Like Caradoc Evans and many others – including the powerful Cymraeg writer Caradog Prichard – he became a journalist in London after an English-language education in an Education Act intermediate school. Born on the edge of a border town (as Sam Adams notes,[119] it was important to him to identify it as quasi-rural Llanllwchaearn not Anglo-bourgeois Newtown), he combined journalism with creative writing. His family, a Welsh-English mixture, spoke no Cymraeg – the mother's tongue, as so often, was lost – but in a classic Welsh irony he was educated in the native tradition by his English master at school, obviously one of the many who faced a hybrid situation with some resourcefulness. While a journalist Goodwin gained a standing as a poet, but developed tuberculosis, that ravaging curse of rural Wales. In 1932 he married Rhoda Storey, a journalist who gave him strong support, and soon, with a daughter named Myfanwy, he turned to full-time writing.

Like a striking number of male authors who describe the puzzlingly colonized Wales about them, he started with something close to autobiography: that this is much rarer with women writers is a matter that invites further analysis. *Call Back Yesterday* (1935)[120] is both a nostalgic quest for an early, less self-alienated Wales and also a positioning of the writer determined to make something of the cultural cross-fire in which he found himself. His work was fostered and redirected by Edward Garnett, talent-spotter for several London literary publishers. Goodwin already knew in person Mary Webb, the very successful writer of English border melodramas such as *Precious Bane*: then called regional novels they assured anxious urban workers that there still existed a world of natural feeling and high excitement outside the cities, and you could read about it without the inconvenience of living in the country. Garnett favoured a peaceful, contributionist approach of this sort for Welsh writers and insisted Goodwin read Richard Jeffries, the Edwardian ideologue of gentlemanly ruralism. In spite of this pressure towards Powys pastoral, what Goodwin actually produced in his first novel was more dynamic, and more focused on the strains of a position like his own, emotively inhabiting both Wales and

England but, as Adams comments, offering a 'steady assertion of Celtic, and especially Welsh, identity through the book'.[121]

The first edition of *The Heyday in the Blood* (1936)[122] is a handsome, dark-jacketed novel emblazoned with the banner of metropolitan canonization as the 'Evening Standard Book of the Month'. It starts with a standard first-contact scene: beautiful Beti romps in the dew before returning to the ancient solid building that is a pub run by her father Twmi, an almost equally deep-rooted native, but seeming more limited than Adams's suggestion that he has 'ancestral wisdom'.[123] The characters invite the gaze, even embrace, of an appropriating Englishman, but Goodwin shapes his account of the hybrid experience of colonization from the Welsh side. This is fishing country and two Manchester businessmen arrive: Mr Birbaum – not, especially in the period, an anti-semitic presentation – tries to persuade Beti to work for his sister in Golders Green, but she is able with her father's support to refuse this diasporic servitude.

The time is the present, and the narrator says in the spirit of Jeffries and the English ruralists 'The old way of things was ending . . . Wales would be the last to go – but it was going' (92). Beti is the focus of change. Clearly enough she is a figure of female sovereignty, natural native Wales embodied in a young woman, and the issue, as with the ancient sovereignty figures, is who will marry her? Lacking the triumphalism of the nineteenth-century historical romances, the rural confidence of Raine or the caricaturing dissonance of Vaughan, Goodwin offers two men who represent modern Welshness. Evan has won prizes for his Cymraeg poetry: he is the local miller but that trade is now exhausted, and he too is less than virile, or even healthy, ending up with tuberculosis. Llew is a journalist in England but his father was an early nationalist and he loves hunting. They are two aspects of Welsh debility, and of Goodwin's self-identification, rather than a clear choice between native and hybridized, and though the novel seems to be heading towards a choice for Llew and a hopeful ending, it is Evan that Beti decides to choose, though neither he nor her father seem to see much success ahead. This uncertainty is confirmed by Goodwin's final turning to a quite different colonial theme: the last two chapters deal with plans for a new road from England that disrupts, even destroys, the village. Even the sturdy Twmi cannot resist, and the final lines suggest that Beti has herself given in completely, and has joined Llew in London, suddenly, 'on the express' (286): transport is for the Welsh both a set of problems and way of resolving them.

There are conflicts of tone throughout *The Heyday in the Blood*: the title itself, which might suggest an H. E. Bates type of rural vitalism, was in fact spoken in *Hamlet* by Gertrude about her own weakened powers; the point seems to be to realize and then show as limited the truly Welsh vigour and fertility of Twmi and his daughter. In much the same way the language of the book strains so hard to be authentic it becomes alien: 'Shutapp you pugair' says Twmi frequently, not 'Shut up you bugger'. Cymraeg phrases are included, and Goodwin commented how much care he took to get them right against English printers and proof-readers.[124] As in Caradoc Evans, the native culture is weakened both in the theme and in the treatment; the distance between the original Welsh men and the actual alienated position of the narration is striking, and Beti, however much admired, is ultimately a token of exchange not a source of value. The situation is much the same as in Hilda Vaughan's novels, and this presumably comes from the fact that the authors are based in the London publishing world, not seeing any scope for Welsh resistance, nor even offering the position of a perhaps reluctant contributionist to the Welsh reader. In his best-known short story, 'The White Farm', which gave its title to his 1937 collection,[125] Goodwin sets out the situation clearly. A car brings an English husband and a young Welsh wife to visit her home region. Eschewing golf with his friends for the day – the English too are at home here – he takes her up the mountain to meet, and speak Cymraeg to, her ancient uncle, but not her injured brother: as with Evan in *The Heyday in the Blood* the younger native males are enfeebled.

As vignettes realizing and to some degree deploring Welsh weakness, and implicitly validating his own departure for London, however much he emotionally values an older Welshness, these works gained Goodwin a high standing. Following the Mary Webb pattern, his two later novels deal decreasingly with Welsh issues and are set in border towns – *Come Michaelmas* (1939) is set in 'Moreton', his name for Newtown and *Watch for the Morning* (1938) uses that name in passing for its setting.[126] Both communities, and both novels, are more concerned with social and industrial change than their border status, and authentically enough. Something very like internal colonization was happening in the ancient rural areas of England, which included the border with Wales, as high capitalist farming and the service of a national, indeed international, market economy ousted older, simpler, practices of productivity and distribution. Goodwin now restricts Welshness to a woman character who is in touch with feeling, even passion, in a way more

Lawrentian than traditional Celtic. Neither Menna in *Watch for the Morning* nor Branwen in *Come Michaelmas* are decisive characters nor do they make marriage choices that offer anything but further debility to their Welshness; nothing else thematic develops the issue of colonization. This is in part because they are border-focused, not Wales-orientated, but also because they are thematically limited: both novels are more a matter of rustic episodes than developed theme-oriented plots. Like Caradoc Evans, Geraint Goodwin shows that a popular journalist's skills of condensed vigour are not an ideal basis on which to mount a full-length serious novel.

Goodwin's work moved steadily away from the inner Wales that his English teacher and his mother's memories had evoked for him as a source of value. Personally he resisted this: he came finally to live in north-west Wales, but apart from his own failing health there were powerful forces that helped weaken his inherently distant relationship with Welshness. The interests of the London publishers, for him so strongly mediated through Edward Garnett and Mary Webb, were a decisive factor in making this gifted writer ultimately offer little to the project of writing Wales in English apart from some classic moments of female Welshness and some caricatured sketches of a distinctly first-contact kind.

But if Vaughan and Goodwin moved in both physical and literary ways away from Wales, a reverse trajectory was possible. Peggy Whistler (1909–58), distantly related to the famous American painter, was born in Uxbridge, in outer suburban London – a context like the one in which Allen Raine had lived. When her professional father died, the family became mobile. She visited relatives near Hereford, spent a year there when she was eleven, and then the family settled near Ross-on-Wye where she went to school. Through these moves her love of the border area and a fascination with Welshness became a positive force for stability, and she wrote under the consciously Welsh name Margiad Evans, drawn from her paternal grandmother, Ann Evans, who was 'believed to be of Welsh extraction'.[127] Her younger sister, Nancy, wrote a small number of fine short stories under the name Siân Evans, but they do not deal as directly with Welsh issues as Margiad did in her novella *Country Dance* (1932),[128] which she illustrated, very finely, herself, as Peggy Whistler: the title-page makes no connection between the two. Margiad has been felt by some to be a false form of Marged, but in fact, as Ceridwen Lloyd-Morgan notes, it is a Gwynedd variant; Evans spent time at Pontllyfni in north-west Wales working on this

book and even had the help of the famous literary scholar Ifor Williams
with the Welsh phrases she used – which did not prevent some
misprints.[129]

Country Dance, in its four coloured illustrations, cyclic form and
courting structure, values the authenticity of folk activities, a view very
common in music and art at the time. The story is also historical, yet
not for the nostalgic purposes of most Welsh historical novels in
English of the early period. A frame story claims that Ann Goodman's
narrative has been discovered, and a final comment explains what
happened to her. Ann is 'a country-woman to the backbone' (vii), living
in a cottage that Evans actually found in ruins. Her mother Myfanwy
dies; this well-known name need not link Evans to Raine, but as
Evans's most-used Welsh phrase is Raine's favourite oath, *Caton pawb*,
a connection does seem likely.

Ann, like many land-symbolizing women, has rival suitors and the
mood created is much like that of Vaughan's *The Battle to the Weak*,
which Evans, a voracious reader, probably knew. Ann's father is
shepherd to 'the master' (another Raineism), Evan ap Evans, a strong-
willed, even bullying somewhat stagey Welshman (Ifor Williams, if he
saw it, would have corrected the name to Evan Evans or Evan ap
Evan). Evan clearly admires Ann but, angry at his pressure, she tells
him she is English and hates the Welsh 'and their shifty ways of dealing'
(24). She is also admired by Gabriel Ford, an English shepherd, who is
himself liked by a willing Welsh girl herself called Margiad. There is a
Bronte-like mood to the story, full of sudden feelings and strange
events, all amplified by emotion. Much as Heathcliff's power is partly
topographic, so Ann eventually gives herself, suddenly, to Evan just as
his harvest is being brought in.

If that sounds like a simplistic reverse of first-contact romance, a
native Welsh victory in the war of fertility appropriation, Evans has a
surprise: the cool note at the end, acting (but not named) as an
epilogue, tells how Ann was found dead in a pool with a head-wound.
Evan was suspected but Margiad acted as witness for him; Ford is
agreed to be the murderer, but has disappeared unpunished. This
powerful ending both constructs a Caradoc Evans-like set of malign
implications (is Margiad's motive finally racial? why did Ford kill Ann
and not Evans?) and also elevates the sense of the strains that come
from living between two worlds, again in a Bronte-like way. Having to
make a choice between two such ferocious male forces killed Ann
Goodman: both men are violent, and the novella finally brings a

feminist dimension into the type of story that – like *The Heyday in the Blood* – usually sees young women as instruments of narrative and indeed of reproduction, personal, social, racial. If Ann is a sovereignty figure, it is only as absence that she has meaning: Margiad Evans conceived the story and the heroine on the basis of the ruined hut she saw, and Ann, like Welsh power, has been destroyed between an arrogant Welshman and brutal incursors. While Evans is subtle enough for such a theme to be clearly suggested, it is not one to which she returned. Like her wish to rebuild the hut for her own habitation, the story of Ann's divided destruction is a means of emotionally positioning herself, the author, as a sentient person on the borders of England and Wales, mundanity and imagination. As Clare Morgan has commented: 'she is fantasizing Welshness; she is also mythologizing herself.'[130]

More than Goodwin could manage, Margiad Evans made considerable artistic use of the hybrid position she had created and the personal myth she had shaped, but she did not return to the issue of Welshness in any detail. Her short stories, collected in *The Old and the Young* (1948),[131] deal with some Welsh characters in a border context, both social and psychological, rather than exploring their meaning in national or colonized terms. Her later novels are semi-autobiographical and have, like her poetry, a rare subtlety and verbal incisiveness. Margiad Evans felt herself to be a Welsh writer and there is no doubt that such a feeling positioned her to write powerfully. It was not just a fancy: she married a Welshman and until, like many born in Wales, his work took them away to England she busied herself among the border people whose lives and nearly hidden feelings are so well epitomized, even ethnographized, in her stories. A writer capable of adapting the first-contact romance to her own purposes, primarily feminist and artistic, and someone who gave, especially in her stories, the long-hybridized society of Powys an ethnographic treatment less highly coloured and less audience-oriented than did Vaughan and Goodwin, Margiad Evans is a constant reminder that colonization is dialectic, that not every incomer chooses to be an exploiter, and that at least some of the most interesting Welsh writing in English has been produced by people who were Welsh by choice.

Section 2

The Industrial Settlement

2.1 SITUATIONS

Industries based on natural substances mined from Welsh soil and exploited on a colonial basis have a long history. The Romans found gold, silver and lead in mid Wales; the coastal strip around Swansea was busy from the seventeenth century with metallurgy, mostly funded from England for profitable export; from the eighteenth century on, mines for coal and ironstone served the growing industrial culture in England and also international export, both from the Flintshire area and especially from the booming region around Merthyr Tydfil; the slate deposits of mountainous north-west Wales were developed to roof the houses of an empire, especially by the Pennant family as a follow-up to their lucrative slave-trading out of Liverpool.

Dramatic as these developments were – and artists seeking romantic sensation often recorded the shapes and sights of these new industrial locations – they did not have a massive impact on the structure and the self-consciousness of Welsh society: they were basically amplified versions of the long-established colonial trading posts that the Vikings, Normans and finally English had set up, mostly along the Welsh coasts and border, to exploit local resources like cattle, sheep, fish and timber. While the engineers, surveyors, technicians of many kinds who developed these early industrial sites were mostly English trained and English-speaking, the workforce was Welsh and the social life that flourished was not substantially different from that of a busy Cymraeg market town.

All this was to change radically, especially in south Wales, when coal went from being a secondary element in the iron-making process, merely a better fuel than timber, into a major strategic feature of the development of the maritime empire of Great Britain. The change was based on steam technology: railway trains and steam-ships, as well as the stationary engines that powered industrial development throughout the world, became dependent on the high quality coal that was first found beneath the narrow valleys that ran through the rising land between the Bristol Channel and the Brecon Beacons, from Monmouth in the east right across Glamorgan to Carmarthenshire. Lightly populated because most of the land was only fit for sparse sheep farming, traced by tracks rather than roads, heavily wooded, watered by fast-flowing unnavigable streams, the region had been by-passed by previous colonists. The Roman and Norman roads, which the English still used to reach Ireland and the strategically important western Wales, ran to the north and south of the region through Brecon and Bridgend.

This whole peaceful, rural area was to undergo a literal upheaval under the forces of colonial capitalism, just as gold and then oil would devastate the natural world of California. In Wales the social, cultural and linguistic upheaval was to be as great; coal-mining was, in its early days, massively dependent on human labour and the work, though difficult and dangerous, was very well paid. Men and their families flooded in to create one of the industrial world's most dramatic boom areas. Cardiff, the major port for the coal, would grow in less than a century from a small sea-port, known only for petty coastal trading and Bristol Channel pirates, to by 1890 the busiest port in the world;[1] Newport would grow in the same way; Barry would be built; and the whole region would be covered by a transport labyrinth of roads and, more importantly, first canals and then railways. South Wales would change from being, like north-east and north-west Wales, a peaceful rural area with one industrial focus, to a heavily urbanized region, dependent to a risky extent on a very limited range of industrial activity,[2] containing two-thirds of the population of Wales. The changes generated a kind of society and culture that Wales had never seen before, in part through new types of housing, work and enter-tainment, but mostly because the forces of industrial and imperial capitalism ordained that the language of the region became English.

This crucial linguistic change, to be the driving force for a major development of Welsh writing in English, did not occur at once. The language of the Merthyr region, that wonder of the new indus-trial world, was primarily Welsh because the major part of the new workforce came from rural Wales. Like the characters in Allen Raine's *A Welsh Witch*, men and women poured from west and north Wales into 'the works', both to labour in heavy industry itself and also to provide the many services – transport, shops, pubs, religion, education – which the booming metropolis of iron and steel demanded. The distances were relatively short; many walked or pushed carts to what, for all its disease and dangers, would be a better-paid and more stimulating life of greater potential than the poor farms of east and mid Wales. The Welshness of the first industrial settlement was so strong, the language was so much part of work and life in the region, many who came in from England – across the border, across the Bristol Channel – became Cymraeg speakers themselves, often through marrying Welsh women. As has been shown by Glyn Tegai Hughes and Hywel Teifi Edwards,[3] the earliest discussions of industrial life in the region are in Cymraeg, and until late in the nineteenth century much of the social and industrial development was predominantly within the Cymraeg language.

But unlike the slate-mines of the north-west, development was too strong and England too near, for this situation to prevail, and it was in any case an uneven development linguistically. Gwyn A. Williams reports that although by 1841 40 per cent of the people on the coalfield were of English origin, only 9 per cent were in Merthyr and as few as 3 per cent in Aberdare, those early sites of industrial development relying on labour mostly from rural Wales.[4] The newer collieries and ironworks, especially those actually in England – as Monmouthshire then was – were much less Cymraeg in culture. John Davies reports that by the 1870s the population of the industrial south was more than 50 per cent English-speaking,[5] and this was driven by the extraordinary growth of new collieries to provide the Welsh steam coal that the navies, both merchant and military, of the world were demanding. The figures of growth are spectacular. By 1880, 69,000 men were working in coal, but by 1901 this had risen to 150,000, and kept rising, to 201,000 by 1908 and in the maximal year of 1921, 271,516 men are recorded as working as colliers across the region.[6] Wales itself could never have provided such a large workforce, in spite of the severe rural conditions in the 1880s – and there were another 20,000 men working in the north-eastern industrial field, mostly in coal.[7] Between 1881 and 1901, 130,000 people came to work in Wales,[8] and the bulk of them were from England, with a significant proportion from Ireland (like Joseph Keating's family) and some from countries like Spain and Italy with which there was a regular trade from the coal-ports.

Some areas of the coalfield remained substantially Cymraeg-speaking: the smaller anthracite region around Rhydaman (Amman-ford), with smaller pits, further from England, and drawing directly on poor farming country, and some small secluded valleys where collieries were established early indicate this native tradition by today providing islands of nationalist support in the sea, however disaffected, of Welsh Labourism. But the overall effect was a massive, irresistible move towards English. The work, the culture and the orientation of the region were all tending away from the traditions of the Cymraeg hinterland, and a symbolic rupture occurred when in 1896 a meeting of the emergent nationalist movement *Cymru Fydd* (Future Wales) broke up in Cardiff: the central figures were David Lloyd George, the figurehead of northern Nonconformist, Cymraeg-speaking Wales, and D. A. Thomas owner of the lucrative and combative Cambrian Com-bine of mines in the Rhondda area. They could not agree on a strategy, and famously the southerners asserted they 'will never submit to the domination of Welsh ideas'.[9] This was to be a costly failure, at a time when Ireland was shaping a strong anti-colonial position, and supports Gwyn Williams's argument that this new industrial Wales was inherently an imperial construction: men like Thomas felt their true interests lay with London, not Caernarfon. But it would be too easy to blame the bosses alone. As Davies comments, the new unions – the South Wales Miners' Federation was formed in 1898 after a six-month lockout – were themselves 'a powerful factor in the process of anglicising the working class of Wales' and a 'lack of patience with its Welsh language and with Welsh attributes were characteristics of many of the early Welsh socialists'.[10] While international profit, mediated through London, was a driving force for Thomas and his ilk, so the men who would shape the south Welsh miners into a force which Lenin regarded as 'the advance guard of the British revolution'[11] also drew on international ideas which were transmitted in English and through English cities – where both Marx and Engels worked and wrote. Just as capitalism is dialectic and generated both the massified labour that could create major profits and at the same time the masses who could resist capitalist practices, so colonialism brought to Wales both the worst and most dangerous forms of exploitation and also the resistant ideas and practices that would oppose them in some of the most bitter encounters created by imperial capitalism. This newly created English-speaking Welsh working class, with some elements of native tradition such as the *gwerin*-like interest in anarcho-syndicalism (to be discussed later), resisted the new circumstances in which they found themselves and which their own writers were to explore in the industrial fiction which is one of the major creations of Welsh writing in English.

Though the dominance of the English language in south-east Wales is becoming clear by about 1900, it is highly uneven: then only 13 per cent of the Monmouthshire population spoke Welsh, while 57 per cent still did in Merthyr and 51 per cent did in the Rhondda valleys, in part because of migration to this later developed area of Cymraeg-speaking workers from earlier coalfields.[12] As the effect of the English-language secondary schools and continued immigration weighed more heavily, these figures changed quite rapidly and the percentage of Cymraeg speakers in Wales dropped steadily.

It is the language effect, not industrialization or urbanization itself, which makes it clear what had happened, in post-colonial terms, in south-east Wales by the early twentieth century. It was not simply a matter of exploitative imperialist capitalism wrenching profit from a land through native labour. That was the story in the north-western slate-field, and a dire story it was, with the refusal to permit union-ization, a two-year lockout, the destruction of a workforce and an industry – an encounter which has been powerfully recounted in T. Rowland Hughes's novel *Chwalfa* (translated as *Out of Their Night*, but literally meaning 'Upheaval' or 'Disaster'), and made the oppres-sive background to Kate Roberts's great novel *Traed Mewn Cyffion* (translated as *Feet in Chains*).[13] But in the south things were more complex than that brutal battle of capital and labour within a Cymraeg-speaking context. Industrial south Wales had in fact become what post-colonial analysts call 'a settler society'. In Africa, Asia or the Indian sub-continent there was an ample supply of native labour to be exploited for profitable labour and a native landowner class that could be persuaded of the advantages of imperial exploitation, and that was basically the situation in industrial Wales, like rural Wales, Ireland and Scotland, until the mid nineteenth century. In other circumstances the imperialists have to import a labouring class or persuade one to settle in the colonized country. In North America the native peoples were too few, too elusive and too resistant to make an effective labour force and the horrors of slavery were used to make extractive industry, mostly cotton, a massively paying proposition.

The American (or, more accurately, English) importation of African labour into the southern states can hardly be called a settlement, as choice was never involved. But in Australia and Canada – where the natives were even fewer and though not so directly resistant were hardly ever used as labour beyond servile work such as shepherding and cattle-guarding for men and for women forced services, domestic and sexual – there was a major push to bring in white residents both to own land and also to work it. Apart from freed convicts, who, like slaves, can hardly be called settlers, though many chose to stay after being released, Australia attracted large numbers of Irish and English labourers; there were even efforts by English charities to round up suitable young women to prevent the settlers producing mixed race children. By the middle of the nineteenth century a self-identifying class of immigrant labourers did not regard England as 'home' and were, as an exploited labour force, the product of a secondary colonization. The basis for the Australian Labor Party, developed early and, then at least, quite radical, these exploited settlement people came to know themselves, their circumstances and their value through the work of ironic realist writers like Joseph Furphy – his novel *Such is Life* (1903)[14] is a classic settler self-description – and, most importantly, Henry Lawson whose many short stories for the Sydney-based but very widely and rurally read *The Bulletin* created the image of the hard-bitten, anti-authority, rural worker who is still, however inappropriately, an Australian national myth.[15]

The settler cultures of Canada, New Zealand and South Africa were less productive than Australia of a powerful self-realizing literature, but they too had a 'rural romance' tradition that is parallel to the first-contact romances of Wales and did to some extent follow this with an imported workers' literature. Not a great deal has been written about the culture of the settlements as such, partly because most post-colonial analysts are more concerned with the oppressions in non-settler countries, which focused on more dramatic events like slavery, the Indian Mutiny, apartheid and European exploitation elsewhere in Africa. But in the settler countries, there is little enthusiasm among those who see themselves now as true Canadians, Australians and New Zealanders to accept that their ancestors were in fact part of an oppressive imperial process – both against the natives and from the land-owning colonists. Guilt at imperial complicity and embarrassment at having been colonized can combine to make people very wary of accepting that they are part of a settlement which is effectively a secondary colonization. It seems clear in the light of the events and the literature written about them that the great adventure of the Welsh industrial writers in English was to parallel the Australians and, with much of the same wit, radicalism and hostility to authority, and with a greater range of responses from semi-romantic to stridently political, to create a rich, potent, memorable and culturally dominating account of the new world in which they had become settled.

The Welsh context was, like the cold prairies of Canada or the stark bush of Australia, an environment full of harshness, that their constructed communality had to work very hard to counter. The colliers' work itself was very difficult: the profitability of Welsh steam coal meant that many pits were deep, with very narrow seams: men walked, or crawled, enormous distances underground to work, went home exhausted and filthy, and suffered injury or death. Davies records that in 1880–1900 while 2,328 miners died in Britain in major accidents (ones with more than twenty-five dead), no less than 48 per cent of them were in Wales (p. 472). There were eight disasters with more than 100 killed in Wales between 1856 and 1900 and the great tragedies ring through south Welsh memory: Cymer, where 114 died in 1856, Cilfynydd in 1894, with 250 dead, the worst of all at Senghenydd in 1913, with 439 dead – and 100 had died in the same pit ten years before. North-east Wales was no refuge: 246 men died at Gresford in 1934. An even more horrifying statistic is that the major disasters only account for 20 per cent of the deaths: most men died alone or in small groups and the grim procession of a body carried home by workmates is one of the deepest images of the dangers of industrial society, and of the new resistant community of the coalfield.

The miners' resistance to their circumstances was both recurrent and difficult. As profits grew and they claimed more of their labour-value there were strikes in 1871 in the Cynon and Rhondda valleys; in 1873 the colliers working for iron companies struck in the Merthyr region; in 1874 there were lockouts across the coalfield. From 1875 to 1903 the 'Sliding Scale' linked wages to profits, but it did not prevent major clashes like the hauliers' strike of 1893 and the six-month lockout of 1898 over the miners' demand for a new sliding scale, which led to the federating of the previously separate, often pit-based miners' unions. With increasing organization the miners' power grew and as profits began to drop when coal as good in quality as the Welsh product was available from America and continental Europe, the coalfield erupted in its most dramatic turbulence with the Cambrian Combine strike in 1910 where D. A. Thomas, by now Lord Rhondda, faced a newly militant workforce and Tonypandy was the never-forgotten scene of violent encounters between miners and police supported by soldiers.

There was another major dispute in the same year in the Cynon valley and disturbances continued right across the coalfield, which led to two miners being shot at a distribution yard in Llanelli and in 1912 a major national strike over the miners' insistence on a minimum wage.

Interwoven with these direct encounters between the newly settled miners and those who had settled them in south Wales was the powerful development of political organization. Early unionism had been linked to the liberal ascendancy in Wales, and the 'Sliding Scale' was supervised by the long-serving miners' leader William Abraham, a Liberal MP who was widely known as 'Mabon', his bardic name as a Cymraeg speaker and poet. He brought many of the values of *gwerin* culture to the industrial situation and basically sought a coalition of interests between miners and mine-owners, but that cooperation became unacceptable to the growing number of younger miners who supported the more radical Labour Party which had great strength in Wales: in 1918, ten of the fifty-nine Labour members of the Westminster Parliament were from Wales and they commanded a third of the Welsh vote. Labour came to be the main voice of south Wales and ultimately much of rural Wales, but there were other voices on the left. The Independent Labour Party was a substantial force until after the Second World War, and more direct impact came from even further left. The Communist Party, formed in Wales at the same time as in England in 1921, played a significant role in the 1930s, producing in Lewis Jones one of the major international writers of industrial fiction. Perhaps because of his central role, and the dramatic events of the 1930s, including resistance to Franco's seizure of power in Spain, the idea remains that the extreme left and the heart of resistance in south Wales was in the hands of the Communists, but this is something of a backward-looking interpretation. An earlier and potent part was played by the syndicalists. Often called anarcho-syndicalism, especially by its enemies, this movement sought direct workers' control of the workplace whether it was a colliery, a factory, a fishing fleet or an agricultural community. Syndicalists believed in direct, if necessary violent, action to seize the forces of production in the names of those who operated them. Both the radical miners and their opponents recognized the force of syndicalism – it is a favourite term of abuse in the *Western Mail* and the word rings more positively through the pages of Dai Smith's *Wales: A Question for History*[16] as he describes the resistant forces on the turbulent coalfield; Davies calls Wales 'the stronghold of syndicalism'.[17] The crucial document *The Miners' Next*

Step,[18] which in 1912 laid out the strategy for a determinedly radical thrust against capitalism, has been described as 'the syndicalists' manifesto'.[19] There were syndicalist groups and magazines through south Wales; D. K. Davies has shown that syndicalist thought coloured much of the thinking and activity of coalfield resistance.[20]

Syndicalism was an international phenomenon: it had a Marxist premise about workers' control of the surplus value they produce, but believed that central organization and fidelity to an overall party line was a debilitating and unfree system. In Wales, however, the syndicalists drew not only on international theorists: the principle that the local community had the right to seize power in its own terms, and answered to nobody, neither a coal-owner nor a union or party leader based in Cardiff or London, was an industry-adapted version of that fierce and strong communality that was itself the basis of the *gwerin* culture. Although the new leftists used English, and often scorned Cymraeg traditions, especially those of the Liberal establishment, the syndicalist traditions that, as will be argued below, are much stronger in Welsh industrial writing than has been realized,[21] are one of the contradictory ways in which this new and Anglicized settlement was, in mode as well as location, in some ways deeply Welsh.

With a massive workforce, organized resistance, the emergence of cultural identity through chapels, choirs and rugby, a defiant stance towards the entrenched power of mine-owners and their allies in the press, government and religion, the south Wales industrial settlement as Britain went to war in 1914 must have seemed a turbulent but potent place. As Alfred Zimmern famously said, it was more like America than England, and a comparably triumphant future must have seemed possible.[22] As the British navy multiplied massively its order for steam coal, and the war disabled many of the competitors, profits and wages surged upwards together and the dream of a wealthy but also democratic workers' paradise must have seemed possible.

As history knows, and as the industrial writers have told, the future of the settlement was very different. Prosperity continued until 1921 and there was a brief recovery in 1923–4 when the coalfields were disrupted in America by strikes and in Germany by the French post-war takeover. But from then on, the change was sudden and drastic: in 1921 only 2 per cent were unemployed in the Rhondda, but by 1929 this had become 20 per cent and by 1937 a staggering 40 per cent.[23] A group of negative forces created the beginning of a slump in the fortunes of the coal industry that, with some minor improvements from time to time, has continued to its present almost complete extinction. The old, often difficult and relatively unproductive pits that had flourished when Wales had no competitors were now, in the face of better-equipped, better-capitalized rivals around the world, seriously unprofitable and needed to be closed or reduced in activity. The more profitable collieries were themselves faced with challenges: the reparations that Germany had to pay France were partly in coal, so reducing that large market, the government's return to the gold standard in 1925 weakened competitiveness, and as a last and most damaging blow, ships were beginning to be converted to oil. By 1924 the good years were over and the owners sought both wage cuts and a longer working day. The miners responded angrily and in 1925 an alarmed government paid a substantial subsidy to avoid trouble while the Samuel report appeared, but as that basically supported pay cuts, with some concessions like pit-head baths, major trouble loomed. In May 1926 the miners went on strike with, for the only time in British history, complete union support, but after nine days of General Strike the other unions withdrew from the action. The miners stayed out through a famously hot summer in the most myth-making of all the Welsh industrial strikes, under the slogan 'Not a penny off the pay, not another minute on the day'. But they returned to work after six months' hardship with reduced wages and an hour extra to work each day for them. Many activists were not re-employed, and the 'non-political', that is owner-serving, South Wales Miners' Industrial Union was created as a powerful rival to the Federation.

Things grew worse. By 1929 national unemployment reached 19 per cent, and the following world slump made the situation even more grave: by 1932 42.8 per cent of men in Wales were unemployed. The north-east was the worst hit, but Merthyr was the most damaged community with 13,000 men out of work. The situation was worse in Wales than England, and many people left to work in the relatively prosperous south – light manufacturing in Slough, car-works in Oxford, service jobs throughout England saw an influx from Wales as the population of the country fell by quarter of a million – and that figure allows for 200,000 incomers in the period, mostly retired people or holiday-home owners from England. The real diaspora from Wales in the 1930s, from the equally slump-hit rural areas as well as the coalfield (33 per cent of labourers left the farms), was close to half a million, with a massive impact on a country that was in many ways in a desperate condition. Illness and malnutrition were the direct result of unemployment, and women's health suffered especially, no doubt through self-sacrifice: at least injuries and deaths in pits fell overall as fewer men were working.

Communities did what they could to help the workless poor – soup-kitchens in the chapels and charity relief were something, and miners marched into England to protest and to collect money through their choirs and bands. The government provided scanty unemployment relief, and when in 1934 the new Unemployment Act imposed a more severe Means Test the coalfield erupted in local protests and marches that had the unusual effect of making the government back down. In the same spirit of desperate resistance, as owners sought more pay cuts and the Miners' Federation struggled to regain authority in the workforce, individual groups of miners, starting at Nine-Mile Point near Blackwood (birthplace of Gwyn Jones, one of the writers) staged 'stay-down strikes' when, without light or heat and short of food, they denied the owners the use of the pits by refusing to come up from work – an inherently syndicalist action. These, like the marches, had some positive effect, and the Federation was able to regroup. As the international economic situation improved somewhat and Britain began to rearm, unemployment grew less appalling, but there were still 100,000 miners out of work in 1939 and after nationalization in 1947 the mining industry continued to reduce, even through the prosperous 1960s. After the fateful encounter between a radical workforce and virulently monetarist conservatism in 1984, the industry was effectively destroyed apart from some highly mechanized open-cut mining and one pit, Tower at Hirwaun, which was, in another version of syndicalism, bought by the sacked miners from their pay-outs.

In one of the most striking international examples of boom and slump, one of the largest long waves of capitalism had dumped on the shore of south Wales a large, densely packed, English-speaking community, a settlement which no longer had any reason to be settled there but which, unlike gold-miners or whalers, lacked the family-free mobility to move on. Not without stark parallels elsewhere in Britain, the south Wales industrial settlement had undergone one of the most extreme, most strife-ridden and also, through its writers, most closely described sequences of events in the history of imperialist exploitation. It was never a silent suffering. Deeply poor as Wales has always been in financial terms, the riches of speech and song, which need no expensive instruments, have long been fostered, and, in their choirs, their media performers, their speakers, their historians, their poets and especially their writers of fiction, the people of the Welsh industrial settlement continued in their very different circumstances the national tradition of making themselves heard.

Industrial fiction is an international phenomenon, though not one that has been widely studied. The subject hardly invites pleasant trips to Rome or California or leisured stays in gilded libraries, and the high-culture canon of English literature and the self-serving interests of most literary scholars have been equally negative to the topic. But those few who have studied the genre agree that Wales has made a contribution to international industrial fiction out of all proportion to its size or population – though perhaps proportionate to the intensity of the Welsh experience. The writers have very strikingly come from the working class itself: most have written from inside their communities not produced reminiscences from a comfortable distance. Raymond Williams, himself a railwayman's son become Cambridge professor, has stressed the class internality of these writers, and also the actual physical difficulties of producing fiction from such a situation;[24] a novel takes a long time to write both in itself and in terms of acquiring the skills in the first place; paper, pens, typing are expensive; even having a desk and a bookshelf is not easy in a cramped, economically harassed community.

What is perhaps even more striking than the numbers of south Welsh who did write about the settlement in fictions is the fact that almost all of them were first-generation English users, as Glyn Jones, who knew almost all of them, commented.[25] Like the settlement itself, especially in its early years, they are both close to and separated from a Cymraeg inheritance, and one of the recurring features in this section will be how often native ideas and traditions are deployed as responses to the situation of this secondarily colonized settlement people, how coal-owners, managers, scabs, police, unemployment clerks, and all the agents, direct and indirect of distant government are criticized and, in fiction at least, defeated in ways that link traditional Welsh attitudes and values to the combinations and resistances that the south Welsh developed on the coalfield itself – even, as in the case of syndicalism, joining the two forces.

The writers, like the people, do this in very varied ways: the point needs stressing because it is easy to see the region as a simplistic whole – by using the outsider's term 'the valleys' for example – and miss the intensely local nature of the experience as the people knew it and the writers realize it: the difference between a massed industrial area like the Tonypandy region in Lewis Jones and an isolated pit village in Menna Gallie. Any account must generalize to generate a description, historical and political ones most of all, but it is important to bear in mind the insistence that Chris Williams makes on the 'divisions, complications and contradictions which belie the received image of a homogenous, organic whole'.[26]

H. Gustav Klaus, one of the very few scholars to make a lifetime's study of working-class fiction, has noted that the Welsh writers were somewhat later than other nationalities to write in this mode;[27] the reasons are in part because it was an in-class production, not the 'sympathetic visitor' fiction produced by Elizabeth Gaskell, Charles Dickens or Emile Zola, and so had to wait until the working class could generate such authors itself. Others, like the Australians managed that a little sooner: and in Wales such a development was hampered by the lack of a tradition in Welsh or English of any self-descriptive fiction and, indeed, by the relatively late development of the industrial coal-field itself – the South Wales Miners' Federation was one of the last major industrial unions to be formed in Britain.

If the combination of language, tradition and history made the self-description of the Welsh industrial settlement relatively slow to emerge, there is also the question of where it would be published. None of the small Welsh publishers, mostly booksellers and newspapers who had produced first-contact material in the late nineteenth century and were still operating, were interested in industrial material. As is clear from the work of Raine and Keating, London publishers, active enough in Welsh romances and contributionist material, were not publishing worker-based industrial fiction in the early twentieth century, even as late as 1917. Both the genre and the audience were major difficulties, and it was only when in the 1930s a sympathetic left-leaning English audience, served by publishers like Martin Lawrence and Victor Gollancz, was willing to buy novels to discover the situation in Wales that writers could work to find a form and a voice to describe the strange new world in which the south Welsh found themselves. Once publication was possible, the flood of material was remarkable, and remarkably varied.

2.2 FROM A DISTANCE: RHYS DAVIES

Rhys Davies (1901–78) seems anything but a likely author of fiction about the industrial settlement of south Wales. The son of a grocer in Blaenclydach, in a small valley leading up from Tonypandy, he left what the main character in his first novel calls 'this sordid mining region'[28] to be a writer in London. Always smartly dressed, a friend of D. H. Lawrence and well connected in London literary society, he became best known for his sensitively modelled short stories and novels which often focused on the feelings of mistreated women. Clearly gay (though like many in the period reticently so), insistently respectable, he seems, and has often been taken as, a fairly conservative aesthetically inclined semi-modernist, interested as Glyn Tegai Hughes says 'in the individual rather than the community' and for Meic Stephens 'unconcerned in his writing with political or social comments'.[29]

   While both comments have force, and Davies avoids taking political sides or speaking collectively about his period, he is always elusive, like the hare he chose as his image in his autobiography,[30] and he does in a usually indirect way engage with the nature of the society and culture in which he grew up and which he continued to visit. In terms of content and setting he actually wrote more fiction about the south Wales industrial community than anyone else – Gwyn Thomas is the only challenger[31] – and he wrote both in occasional factual prose and in many of his fictions about the relations between the Welsh and their colonial masters through time, including the present. A major obfuscation of this in the past was that he often condensed issues of class with issues of gender and, as will be argued below, his most searching accounts of settlement south Wales and its connection with the rest of the country were made through the focus of the women characters that, after his early writing, he favoured.

   It is true, as Dai Smith notes, that he left Wales early,[32] being in London by 1921, before the downhill career of the coalfield had clearly started, and this made his experience of the catastrophe on the coalfield less personally felt than was the case with other writers, but he was not cut off from events in Wales. He often visited his family and the essay published in 1937 on the miners in *My Wales* shows he knows about 1926; he speaks of 'the brutal ruin that the Rhondda is today'[33] and always thought of himself as a socialist. Davies's representation of the miners' actions in 'the savage Tonypandy riots' as the work of 'slavering and barbaric-eyed' colliers[34] has been criticized by Smith as the comment of a moralizing shop-owner's son very unlike that other local author, Lewis Jones.[35] It is a fair point, but Davies's responses are multiple and Smith himself has also called Davies 'an incomparable guide' to the intimate reality of Rhondda life in his short stories (Davies in fact often said they were closely based on reality),[36] and refers as an example to the woman-focused story 'The Pits are on the Top'.[37] The same affectionate if apolitical understanding is found in 'The Two Friends' where colliers' wives pick for coal on a tip and, when wondering who really owns the coal, come up with neither a coal-owner's nor a unionist's answer, but conclude 'Why, God of course'.[38]

Educated sufficiently and with a class background to suggest he was not bound for a collier's life, Davies confirmed that in his description of a visit to a pit where he found 'nothing but the gigantic silence of unshifting death' brooded over by 'the great throbbing power-house . . . unceasing as the mills of God'.[39] The same range of chapel imagery recurred in 1937 when in *My Wales* he described the collieries as 'black galleries of a real hell'.[40] But industrial dismay and decay were neither the real nor the fictional reasons for his leaving Wales: his aspirations were literary. Like Caradoc Evans, he first found work in London as a draper's assistant, and also like him he fashioned a deeply hostile account of the world he had left in the gesturingly titled *The Withered Root* (1927). The hero's father, a collier wavering between drink and religion, and his mother, firmly on the side of drink, are both elderly and have something of the character and the language of Evans's Manteg grotesques. The community is uniformly ugly in setting and behaviour and an oppressive sexuality is often encountered by the sensitive hero – an addition to the Evans range of feeling. Yet Davies appears to have other literary sources: Reuben Daniel – the initials are suggestively autobiographical – becomes fascinated with religion (Davies himself was for a while, and always retained an interest) and becomes the charismatic leader of a south-east Wales based version of the Revival that Raine had dealt with in *Queen of the Rushes*.

This fable enables Davies to sweep his hero, passionate for god and the natural beauties of the landscape (again like a Raine character), into a revival that is really a vulgar performance, speaking to the shallow, spiritless, deracinated, falsely eroticized people that Reuben finds around him. Losing his faith in the revival and himself, he lurches off to Cardiff's dockland, to be rescued by a sympathetic prostitute. He staggers home through the snow – an objectification of his chillingly hostile environment – to die from a fall as his mother tries to welcome him. Though this might seem a young writer's sentimental self-justification through rejection, not all is negative. Rural Wales is genuinely beautiful; Reuben finds value in 'the mystic harmony of the religion that is the glory of the Welsh' (20) as well as the intelligent, tuberculosis-ridden English-educated and highly literary Philip, and a more complex admiration and fear for Philip's beautiful cousin Eirene Vaughan, the first of Davies's many strong troubled beauties. More psychoanalytic confession than novel, *The Withered Root* exhibits both Davies's sense of separation from his unstimulating environment and his already developed interest in D. H. Lawrence (Philip must be some sort of version of him), whom he was to meet and become friends with in 1928. Lawrence liked Davies's writing and favoured him with homilies on the virtues of Welsh primitivism – an overheated version of contributionism. This connection, combined with Davies's talent, determination and evidently engaging personality, was to lead him to establish by the early 1930s a substantial career as a London-based professional writer.

The career not only established himself: Glyn Jones felt that Davies single-handedly made south Wales a topic of interest to English readers and publishers,[41] though no doubt Caradoc Evans had prepared the way for a Welsh writer who could add sophistication to regional curiosity. Davies had the looks and the style for it: his early 1930s novels have an elegant author's photograph on the jacket, far from the austere snap used for Caradoc Evans, and the Welsh writer in London was a role Davies accepted for himself. In a short statement that appeared in 1932 (in the company of contributions by luminaries like Lascelles Abercrombie, Edith Sitwell and M. P. Shiel, and with a foreword by Viscount Esher) under the title 'Writing About the Welsh' he spoke of the difficulties for such a course both with English publishers and the uncaring audience back home. Nevertheless, he committed himself to the role, through 'my passion for Wales, her beauty, her individuality, her quality of perpetual youth, her struggle to keep herself uncontaminated of industrial blights'.[42]

An attack on industrial contamination no doubt pleased a Bloomsbury audience and English readers still enjoying first-contact narratives, but gender played a large role in Davies's self-construction as well. Before he left Wales he avidly read Flaubert's *Madame Bovary*: no doubt this released the potential of Eirene Vaughan, and his second novel, *Rings on her Fingers* (1930),[43] takes a young woman out of an industrial setting to lead a Bovary-like life. But the influence went further: Davies was to say of himself 'I am Madame Bovary',[44] and would often use a woman as the focus and intelligence of the narrative. The stage might have seemed set for a good career with a woman-focused series of sub-Lawrentian novels, but in the next years Davies moved in quite the opposite direction, and made his own claim through the 1930s to be the first serious ethnographer of the south Wales coalfield. He was never without some element of distance between the author and his subject: some traces of romance suggest Raine was a greater influence on him than has been thought, and a Welsh version of Lawrentian vitalism remained with Davies through his writing career. But throughout this work he presents a coalfield society that can indeed be ugly and oppressive, yet can also be a warmer and more positive community that he offered in *The Withered Root* or Caradoc Evans showed in any of his stories, a community that was aware of the deforming pressures created by imperialist capitalism, and could find value in the main theme that Davies had to offer, a sense that the courage and values of these Anglicized modern Welsh were connected back to the struggles of earlier Welsh history. He conceived of the coal-owners as being like the Romans and Normans, exploitative invaders of his homeland, and the industrial proletariat as being essentially continuous with the fugitive, wily, enduring Celts of an imagined native past. The young Davies is very likely to have read at school Owen Rhoscomyl's *Flame Bearers of Welsh History*, a classic nativist text-book, and while it is certainly true that, as Daniel Williams argues,[45] he thought consistently in racial categories, he did so in the reverse of Matthew Arnold, and had a lifelong interest in native traditions, broadly understood. He gave them a personal focus: the fact that he spelled his first name Rhys, after having been christened in Anglicized form Rees,[46] suggests in itself an individual identification, or recon-struction, in terms of native culture. There is no clear sign that he could speak Cymraeg, though in *My Wales* he does suggest he could at least exchange a few phrases. Daniel Williams comments that racialism is 'a collective entity that does not jeopardize the integrity of the individual',[47] and this is a great advantage to Davies: he can write with sympathy and some national feeling while focusing on the sensitive individual central to the kind of novels and stories he and his audience preferred.

His fourth novel, *The Red Hills* (1932),[48] is a curious reworking of industrialism to catch this nativist theme, here fairly heavily Lawren-tian as Jeff Wallace notes.[49] The hero Iorwerth – a princely name like

Rhys – works a private drift-mine in the hills, outside the modern-style colliery village. Both an isolated Lawrentian hero, communing with nature, and an image of an older pre-capitalist Welsh productivity, he is also sexually attractive, to both the village beauty, Ceinwen and an English visitor named Virginia. In a melodramatic climax that reads very like one of Allen Raine's resolving crises – though she preferred fires – the villagers, outraged by what they see as Iorwerth's amoral individualism, cause the mine to collapse on him and Virginia, but Ceinwen insists on a rescue. Suggesting both Iorwerth's vague nativist continuity, in a 'dark loins' Lawrentian mode, closely connected to landscape, and arguing that the best of the industrialized proletariat recognize these antique values, the novel reads as a first step towards the historicist nativism to which Davies was to return regularly, especially through his fascination with the figure of Dr William Price, who appears in several novels and has a dominant place in Davies's autobiography – appearing, as M. Wynn Thomas has remarked, just where 'one would have expected an extended portrait' of the writer's father and mother.[50] Dr Price had an extraordinary career: a leader of the Pontypridd Chartists on their march on Newport in 1839, he escaped to France dressed as a woman. He lived on for many years, to provide medical services to the poor, to criticize the mine-owners, and to father a number of children by a number of women. Most famously, when a son born in his own eighties, named Iesu Grist (Jesus Christ), died, he cremated him on Llantrisant Common, was arrested, successfully defended himself and so instituted legal cremation in Britain, as is warmly remembered by the Cremation Society. They provided a handsome portrait of the doctor, in his usual robes and fox-skin cap, for Davies's *My Wales,* which featured an essay on this exotic hero, a hybrid of modern radicalism and medicine who also was for Davies a focus of his own need for a link back to native values that was not limited to modern politics: he said that the 1930s hunger marchers were 'direct descendants of their forebears who fought locally for the means to live'.[51]

But while that nativist myth of a pre-colonial society was of great use in both *My Wales* and his own autobiography, and is prefigured in Iorwerth, Davies, showing both a professional energy and a commitment to the industrial settlement, now set himself to produce a trilogy which would describe that exotic world from its inception to the present. He produced a full, fluent and powerful account of the coalfield in three books which, however romantic they may at times be and however they may obscure the real thrust of the miners' political challenge, were a very substantial contribution to the project of writing the consciousness of the industrial settlement in south Wales. True to Davies's interest in locating the core of the settlement's values in Welsh history rather than a conflicted present, the first book, *Honey and Bread* (1935),[52] tells for the first time the story of how a simple rural valley became a storm-centre of industrialization. It is his own Clydach valley, which he calls Glan Ystrad. Davies's identity is invoked: the first edition features on the jacket a full-page drawing in woodcut style of Davies as London celebrity and Welsh writer, sporting a rakish urban trilby against a distant green mountain. The valley's landowners have an older type of value: the squire is Tudor Llewellyn, combining in name, quite ahistorically, the ancient prince of Wales and the Welsh-derived English royalty who first subjected the country to purposeful colonization: the extra 'l' in the surname, now common in Wales, seems to be an excess of nativeness.

Here, from peaceful prosperous farming – an over-positive history for the thin land of the south Welsh hills – all is upheaved: 'The old reposeful life was forgotten . . . a tornado passed over it, chucking out in its journey a commotion of fractious men, engines, pieces of grinding machinery, clouds of dust.'[53] The emphasis is on the change to people's lives and their environment, but *Honey and Bread* is also a piece of historical ethnography, explaining for the people of the Rhondda the origins of their present situation: as Michael Dixon comments 'Rhys Davies's geographical setting and historical timescale are not altogether accurate, but nor are events at Glan Ystrad distorted beyond recognition in respect of Blaenclydach specifically and the Rhondda more generally.'[54]

Unsurprisingly, given Davies's own interests in personal matters and the romance tradition of Raine and Keating, the novel focuses on a love affair. Owen Llewellyn, tubercular and intelligent older son of the land-owning family, loves the beautiful village girl Bronwen, but he dies before their child is born and Bronwen marries an incoming mining engineer. Davies may indeed be strictly speaking apolitical, but his plots about love and loss also realize social forces: this is a historicized and socially astute version of the almost caricatured plot of the much anthologized early short story 'Blodwen', where the village beauty is competed for by an Anglicized and undersexed solicitor and – success-fully – by a lusty, mountain-dwelling native. *Honey and Bread* also uses in the eighty-year-old hermit Robert ap Gruffydd a clear version of Dr

Price: he opposes industrialization but, as Dixon comments, not in any practical sense but as a symbol of 'the original ethos of the valley, and the spirit of resistance'. He is ultimately 'a Glyndŵr-like figure who poses an unseen and threateningly permanent challenge'[55] to the forces of colonial capitalism.

If the first part of the trilogy sketches the process to an industrial settlement both historically and impressionistically, the second, *A Time to Laugh* (1937),[56] has a more direct engagement with actual events and is as close as Davies gets to an ethnographic, even radical, account of industrial south Wales. Set around the turn of the century and including a good deal of close proletarian realism, it nevertheless uses a focal figure who is outside the collieries, though, being the local doctor, he is not simply the sympathetic visitor often used by self-distancing industrial commentators like Gaskell and Zola. He also creates continuity. Tudor Morris is the grandson of Owen and Bronwen in *Honey and Bread*; his father was also a local doctor, a rather timid figure who plays little part. Tudor's romance is politically aligned: he rejects a rich bourgeois woman and marries a lusty, but also intelligent, working woman and chooses to settle and practise medicine among the poorest people – his career is the opposite of Rhys Davies's, and may essentially be a modernization of Dr Price himself.

Tudor becomes directly involved in events: in part through his friendship with Melville Walters, a tough agitator, who spends time in jail (it is his sister Daisy that Tudor marries), but also through his own involvement as speaker at the vividly realized mass meetings where the colliers plan their actions, against the bosses, towards a federal union and specifically against the 'Sliding Scale'. While the action is not tied to history – Dixon calls it 'deliberately haphazard'[57] – there is still a strong sense of how things happened, including from the miners' point of view. The detail is closely derived from reality, mostly focusing on the strikes of the 1890s but also using material from Tonypandy in 1910, while the position of the radicals, including Morris, is close to the syndicalism of the leaders of that later period, as Dixon comments.[58]

But Davies holds back from complete support of the colliers. There are strikers who prefer violence to politics, and Davies adds from his own knowledge a sympathetically portrayed account of the difficulties faced by the local tradespeople. Most strikingly, the Tonypandy events are used not as part of a purposive resistance but more as random violence as the strike 'runs out of control' (391), finally fails and the workers are left not, as happened in history, organized for further action, but as no more than 'an aboriginal race dispossessed of any dignity it may have held' (431). The phrasing, especially the race-based epithet 'aboriginal', reverts to Davies's idea of a Celtic continuity of struggle rather than a present historicity, and the doctor himself withdraws, though not completely: he decides to 'stay, struggle and go among them with an intent watching' (431) but the final scene shows him and his wife watching the locals celebrating about their bonfires like colonized natives, and he concludes bizarrely, even evasively, that in spite of everything it is 'a time to laugh' (431). The sudden strain of the apoliticized ending is all the more evident against the detail and weight in which in his longest novel Davies has created the dramatic labour history that was occurring about him in his childhood. An exotic and powerful book, as if Allen Raine and Lewis Jones had, with some difficulty, collaborated, *A Time to Laugh* both realizes Davies's own conflicted feelings about the environment he never emotionally left and also stands as a major contribution to the ethnographic description and, to some extent at least, radical, political evaluation of the new world of south Wales.

In the last novel of the trilogy, *Jubilee Blues* (1938),[59] Davies deployed the manoeuvre which had already permitted him to work effectively, and not without some political impact, in his short stories and some novels. In *Count Your Blessings* (1932)[60] he had created a critique of the confines of industrial society and a pattern of escape and return through a woman, Blodwen, who becomes a successful Cardiff prostitute before returning to her pit village to marry respectably and also, elsewhere, find sexual satisfaction. Cassie, the central figure of *Jubilee Blues,* adds to this extra-political freedom an origin in the rural west Wales that was consistently of symbolic value to Davies. For her small inheritance, she is married by the roguish Prosser Jones and they set up in a pub on the coalfield. One of Davies's many competent, even cunning, wives who find their way to freedom, Cassie's own story is a major part of the novel, but the action also observes with pity the condition of Wales in the 1920s. Politics is realized mostly through Tudor Morris's son David, a confirmed Communist and schoolteacher. He rejects the daughter of a colliery manager in spite of his desire for her, but is less active and successful than his father: Dixon judges that the young Morris is 'alienated', 'a product of the modern mechanized world',[61] and no hope is seen for his own activism or the miners' struggle – Davies clearly, and understandably, did not feel that gains had been made by the mid 1930s when he was writing. His empathy with the situation leads to some powerful scenes, notably when a starving unemployed miner, overgenerously fed by Cassie, can only vomit in distress, but overall his skill in framing the story through Cassie enables him to avoid the strains, as well as the political impact, of *A Time to Laugh*, and the novel ends in a reductive mode consonant with Davies's own overarching nativist simplification of the whole situation as Cassie, free finally of both Prosser and the distressing industrial environment, returns to the rural fastness of the west.

That escape was mirrored in Davies's next novel to deal with south Wales, *Tomorrow to Fresh Woods* (1941),[62] where he gives a full account of the nature and problems of industrial society, including Dr Price again, and towards the end of the novel describes how a young man's desire for literary fame drives him to leave. The character is called Penry: Mitchell suggests Davies refers to John Penry, a Welsh Puritan martyr who in *The Story of Wales* he refers to as an early, and more religious, Dr Price.[63] The religious connection links Penry to Reuben of *The Withered Root* and indicates that now Davies felt able to write the personal narrative of escape which underlies the earlier novel but cannot there find expression. *Tomorrow to Fresh Woods* is the composed work of an established author – an author in England, using a quotation from Milton for his title – who can feel he has paid his debts to his environment. Penry recognizes in Lawrentian mode the vigour and drama of his context – 'He felt the richness of this physical life of the miners and their families' (188) – but also like a working-class Lawrence character he has to move on. Davies now reads the Welsh situation from the comfort of the somewhat bland nativist historicism focused on Dr Price (and perhaps John Penry) and expressed clearly in both *My Wales* and the shorter, less industrially concerned, *The Story of Wales,* published in 1943.[64]

But if Davies's politics and his encounter with colonial capitalism had become simplistic, his fiction remained subtle. He had shown in three novels and many short stories that when he used a woman as persona he was able to deploy a real empathy without it becoming, for him, disturbingly political – and yet the women he writes of always operate in a real social world. This is the basis for Smith's sense of Davies's power to realize the Rhondda emotively, if not politically, and Katie Gramich has suggested that 'the depiction of gender may actually be taken as an encoded representation of class issues'.[65] Just as Bronwen in *Honey and Bread* is involved in love and marriage that are themselves historically meaningful, so Daisy Walters in *A Time to*

Laugh and Cassie in *Jubilee Blues* are themselves to some extent agents in the conflict of the industrial settlement: while Davies evidently empathizes with these figures as women he does not, unlike many male novelists, see women as separate from a world of male politics. Clearly he can be taken as an early, if unconscious, recognizer of the fact that the personal is the political – Jane Aaron's essay on his three woman-focused novels of the 1940s outlines strongly his contribution in this way, and she also argues that he empowers women more widely than in terms of gender issues: 'Davies demonstrates that the will to power, as much as the need for tenderness and intimacy, is equally shared by both sexes.'[66]

Davies most effectively uses women to explore his sense that Wales is a colonized country. Linden Peach has argued that the vanity shown by the leading woman character in 'The Fashion Plate' is precisely a form of frustrated colonial mimicry,[67] and Davies explores the connection of colonization and gender most strongly in what many have felt his finest book, *The Black Venus* (1944).[68] This is a natural sequel to the moves made in the late 1930s novels in that it not only realizes a strong and independent woman but also through her brings to a harmonious conclusion and fictional elaboration the ideas about Wales, its conflicts and values, that have been, with some difficulty and inconsistency, worked on in the previous novels. Another Davies novel that, like his trilogy, cries out for reprinting as the literature of Wales is reconsidered, *The Black Venus* is focused on Olwen Powell, the heiress to a rich farm in 'ancient Ayron', presumably in the rural west, but only forty miles from the nearest coal-port, who decides to choose a husband by reactivating in feminist terms the ancient native practice of 'courting in bed'. In this highly practical ritual, young men would visit a chosen woman, gain admission by throwing a stone at her window (itself symbolic of defloration) and, with a bolster firmly between them (officially at least), the couple would get to know each other and move towards a decision. Ideal in a cold, wet climate when houses had few rooms and the young were constantly observed by family and neighbours, the practice was itself one of the things that outraged the 'Blue Books' commissioners of 1847.

Olwen goes through a lengthy selection process that reads like a liberated version of Jane Austen. She is aware of her political position: 'A woman's testing of a man I am wanting to make it and not always a man's testing of a woman' (33). Davies develops the feminist possibilities: the deacons hold a debate on the matter, but the women themselves hold a parallel discussion afterwards, and he draws attention to the native character of the events: Mrs Drizzle, a miserable English widow who lives in the village, is strongly opposed to the heroine's behaviour. Olwen identifies two possibilities: Rhisiart Evans, an elusive, engaging, deeply native poacher, and Noah Watts, a student from the mining districts, mechanized on his motorcycle, educated and serious – no doubt his first name refers to both Noah Rees and Noah Ablett, the colliers' leaders. Of these two figures, symbolizing the extremes of modern Wales, Olwen clearly prefers the romantic Rhisiart, and it is he who impregnates her during a courting session. He fades into the countryside, and Olwen prepares to bear the child alone, but eventually marries Noah in what is for thirteen years an uncon-summated marriage. But at last the sterile industrial world and the fertile countryside unite as Noah, portly though he now is, climbs in through her window and Olwen finally accepts him in an image of a now integrated and fecund Wales.

The symbolic potential of the story is strongly underlined by the authority figure of Moesen Rowlands, landowner and magistrate, but raffish and lustful, almost certainly Rhisiart's father, who is described in Davies's patriotic historicist terms as having 'the blood of old traditional princes' (28) and one who in the past would have been 'the leader of the horde' (5). This is more than a nativist triumph in reproducing the ancient blood and also incorporating the educated modern values: that in itself would have been a potent enough condensation of Davies's semi-mythic view of Wales. The title refers to a black nude statue (it wears a modest apron on Sundays) belonging to Lizzie Pugh, who clearly plays the role of wise woman or white witch. Symbolizing native freedom, fertility, the natural way of doing things, the figure both connects up the strands of mythic naturalness in the story and also, as Kirsti Bohata has outlined,[69] relates to native peoples in other colonized countries. Inside Davies's displacement of modern industrial conflict through gender and ruralism there remains a stubborn insistence that Wales is after all a colony: the nature of that colonization is not read in terms of economic and industrial forces, indeed they are sidelined and themselves appropriated through Noah but Davies's reading amounts to a far-reaching statement about the situation of the country, its men and, especially, its women.

Like Cassie in *Jubilee Blues*, Davies has fictionally escaped to the west from the traumas of the coalfield, having in reality, like Penry in *Tomorrow to Fresh Woods*, left for the literary London life. Always at some sort of distance from proletarian life, starting with the grocer's shop and ending up in a bedsitter in Bloomsbury, he nevertheless turned recurrently to write about the strange new world into which he was born. As the first Welsh writer of English to conquer London publishing in person, as the first, as Glyn Jones put it, 'to get the valleys across',[70] and especially as someone who turned his own distaste for everyday politics into an early realization of gender politics, Rhys Davies deserves recognition as the first major writer in English from south Wales. Others would write more directly and more politically, and he was never to have real imitators in Wales, but he broke the silence about the Welsh industrial world and almost certainly made it easier for the other industrial writers of the 1930s to make their own voices heard.

2.3 TOWN AND FAMILY FICTION: JACK JONES AND GWYN JONES

It is hard to imagine two writers, even two people, as dissimilar as Rhys Davies and Jack Jones (1884–1970): Jones lived a life of masculine gusto, settled in south Wales after many travels and wrote sprawling, even clumsy, novels that fully accepted everyday industrial life as their topic. He had no long-term view of Wales and Welshness and little interest in literary culture: most of his early work was based on reminiscences – including his grandfather's, born in 1820. He did not start publishing until he was fifty and he did not sustain the energy of his first few novels. But in spite of all those differences from Rhys Davies and his career, Jack Jones is the other initiating force in writing an account of the new world of industrial south Wales, the other of the two figures on whom the rest of the 1930s writers of Welsh fiction in English depended for models, structures, themes and even motifs. Dai Smith calls him 'the most successful purveyor of South Wales realism'.[71] From a Merthyr family of fifteen children (only nine grew to adulthood), Jones had a colourful working-class career. Starting down the pit at 12, he was involved in the 1898 lockout and later branched out as gambler, soldier (in the colonial Boer War) and then both deserter and recruiting speaker – he once shared a platform with Mrs Pankhurst. Back in the coalfield he became a founder member of the British Communist Party in 1921, worked as a miners' agent, a cinema manager and dabbled in theatre: just as restless politically, he moved to Labour and then, having heard Lloyd George, became a Liberal and unsuccessfully fought Neath for them in 1929.

By the late 1920s Jack Jones, like so many others, was out of work, and he turned to writing. Educated in English at secondary school, but still speaking Welsh quite well, like so many of his generation he turned to the informal processes of self-education, especially through Cardiff City library. For all the casual-seeming nature of style and structure in his novels, he worked hard at his drafts and often on his research: there is a clear auto-didactic element in Jones's enthusiasms and his writing. In the first volume of his autobiography, *Unfinished Journey* (1937),[72] he says that when he received a substantial termination pay-off from the Liberal Party, he immediately planned 'a big novel'. By 1930 he had produced a manuscript of a quarter of a million words that described and celebrated the Merthyr district and its people. He named it 'Saran' after his mother, christened Sarah Ann, but it was both too unwieldy and too strange and three publishers rejected it.[73] Always a hard worker and difficult to daunt he would cut it down greatly to become *Black Parade* (1935), the second of his novels to be published, but the most characteristic of his work.[74]

The novel starts with Jones's dramatic flair: two handsome young colliers are bathing after work, singing and squabbling. They are part of a new world; their father was a stonemason who went down the pit for better wages, and as they walk out that evening they observe the 'farm-joskins, hundreds of whom were weekly flooding into the coalfield' (9). The novel will tell the story of this family, focusing largely through its women, but it is much more than a domestic drama: Glyn Jones calls it a 'family-town' novel, Dai Smith sees 'a richly-textured panorama of South Wales from the 1880s to the mid 1930s', and Raymond Williams identifies 'the insertion of a complex political struggle into a local family form'.[75] Recurrently, a character will pause, look out over the town and ruminate on the nature of the environment and how it has changed, with a strong sense of the social character of this strange new world. The ethnographic thrust is strong, and it is clear both from reviews and from personal reminiscences that much of Jones's appeal was that these were the first sympathetic descriptions of the conditions that the people of south Wales now knew so well.

Substantial set-pieces recur and are not always integral to the action of the novel, though when they deal with typhoid and the need for sanitation, changes in transport and entertainment they are directly connected with people's lives. Through this material Jones is deliberately moving towards a social document: he was familiar with the American socialist realists J. T. Farrell and John Dos Passos,[76] and, with whatever difficulty the inexperienced writer might find, he was committed to tell a primarily social story that found its human realization in its characters, not the kind of personalized story with semi-social symbolic overtones that Rhys Davies was to produce. The events and feelings of the characters are dramatic and strong. Glyn's girlfriend is Saran, a vigorous young beauty with strong attitudes and a labourer's hands – she works in the brickyard. Her brothers are from the dark side of the industrial proletariat, drinkers, fighters, thieves – including their own family's money. Between them the characters experience and illuminate the rich, rough life of late nineteenth-century boom-town Merthyr, the foot-races, cycle races, the hectic pubs (Sunday closing has not yet come), a ferocious bare-knuckle fight, the fairground littered with drunken men urinating and drunken women lying in the road. Culture is also available: the brothers, like many others, sing very well, the local eisteddfod is an important event, the chapel is regularly visited, and Saran loves the theatre, though, as Jones's people speak in broad, even erroneous, south Welsh English, she always calls it 'threeatre'. But the culture is marked with colonial impact: the theatre shows companies from England, including *Hamlet* and grand opera, and most tellingly Twm Steppwr, 'Wandering Tom', a pub poet and modern minstrel who is Glyn's brother-in-law, mostly plays English songs. Jones does not make it clear, as Raine did, that the characters speak Welsh to each other, though this must have been the case, as the point is made that the children go to an English school (136–7). The novel is describing, though not confronting, the impact of English industrialism on this inherently Welsh social world.

It is also a narrow world: Saran's fighting brother Harry escapes the police by going to what they feel is the distant Rhondda and few characters travel far. The domestic life of Saran and Glyn is a recurrent focus: she putting up with his drinking, the family constantly growing, and against this background major events in the history of the district occur. The hauliers' strike; the 1898 lockout when Mabon and F. W. Brace come to speak, one in Cymraeg, one in English; Keir Hardie becomes the first British Labour MP for Merthyr; the Boer War – their son Benny joins up; the Revival of 1904 in which Harry is converted and never drinks again. Other features chart the south Welsh industrial experience. The sons are much more radical than their Mabon-faithful father, and Meurig is injured in fighting in the Rhondda in 1910; another brother, Hugh, dies at Senghenydd. In the war Meurig makes a fine soldier and dies bravely; Benny loses an arm; one brother-in-law is blinded; another is a conscientious objector. So Jones realizes the emotional impact of history and context in a compact, dynamic novel, and he does not fail to record in acute detail the decline of the once triumphant economy. Sam, shrewdest of the children and to be a Communist, foresees the impact of reparations; rates are identified as a real problem; Saran's savings, built up through the war from the good wages coming in, rescue the family from the worst effects of the slump. But not from social disintegration: Tom goes to a car factory near Oxford, Ben's children go to college and off to teach in England, and the novel finally notes an English report that recommended simply shifting the surplus labour of Merthyr elsewhere en masse.

Throughout the novel, Saran is the intelligence through whom the passing milestones of south Welsh life to the present are recorded. Evidently based on Jones's own mother, she is not the downtrodden mother of some industrial fiction, largely because very little is made of the heroics of male work. There are scenes in the pit, and the damaging effects of the work are noticed, but Glyn, as both collier and father, becomes a rather marginal character. It is one of the characteristics of Welsh industrial fiction to give women a strong role as coordinators, and this seems neither a product of early feminist urges nor yet the influence of Rhys Davies's focus on women (though the latter may have had an impact), but rather a simple realization of a world where men were away for long hours at work, and sometimes at drink, and both heavy physical labour and the bonds of social connection were the inevitable lot of the women.

Black Parade has been criticized on technical grounds: Glyn Jones said the author's 'concern for language and style [was] obviously nil', and G. F. Adam called the book 'often shapeless and discursive',[77] but these are judgements that assume the mode and form of the classical novel: Adam is closer to the truth when he says that Jones's 'books are social documents rather than fictions'.[78] With his American models in mind, Jones's thrust is to combine real reportage with dynamic narrative of the sort that the characters themselves might speak and enjoy. The modes of theatre and self-education are never far from the text, and this indicates Jones's response to the problem of how to find a literary form, a genre, appropriate to describe this industrial settlement. Romance, as Raine and Keating reveal, will not do; the classic sensitive novel can, as Rhys Davies shows, go so far provided the theme is subtle and non-confrontational: for a mode that could realize the partly oppressed, partly dynamic world of south Wales with the vigour required, and also could give a historical account of this new society, the mixture Jones devised was by no means unsuccessful. As Raymond Williams comments, 'it includes the many-sided turbulence, the incoherence and contradictions, which the more available stereotypes of the history exclude'.[79]

It is not surprising that *Rhondda Roundabout* (1934)[80] found a publisher where 'Saran' was rejected. Even compared to the pruned version, *Black Parade*, it is shorter, uses much less digressive information, and is focused on one fully admirable character and his experiences, with a romance a major part of them. Furthermore, it occurs in the modern period, not over a historical sweep, and the use of the widely known Rhondda as its basis may also have given it added attraction. It is much more obviously a novel, and a good deal less aggressive in tone and theme: Dai Smith found its ending too steeped in pity for credibility.[81] The effect of these differences is that *Rhondda Roundabout* is less powerful and wide-ranging than *Black Parade*. Set in the late 1920s, Dan Price BA, a young preacher trying out for a post in a Rhondda chapel, is staying briefly with his aunt and uncle: she a respect-conscious chapelgoer and he, though also religious enough, a Labour Party stalwart, who likes a drink with his ex-service friends. The novel will tell how Dan does earnestly well in the chapel, frustrates the more vulgar plans of the businessman who wants to develop its activities and income (he is a Liberal of course), meets and with remarkable ineptitude courts an attractive draper's assistant.

This heart-warming story – notably lacking Rhys Davies's ironies and gender uncertainties – is enlivened in one direction by Mog Edwards, the valley bookmaker, generous, apparently honest and devoted to his assistant, a war-damaged officer. In one way a friendly giant reaching back into native folklore, Mog is also a figure who stands in for the wealthy and boss class, and enables Jones to avoid any substantial criticism of such forces in the narrative: there is sentimental caricature rather than realistic analysis hovering about the figure of Mog. And when the novel is enlivened in the direction of actual politics, by lengthy scenes at meetings, here too comedy emerges as an emollient. The most active Communist is a huge man called Dai Hippo who can hardly be taken either as a red menace or a spokesman for the people: he ends a meeting with the cry 'Drink up, comrades' (142). With both realism and politics diluted, *Rhondda Roundabout* reads like a novel tailored for nervous English publishers, and the striking thing is that Jones was able to place, on the basis of its success, both *Black Parade* and the longer, better-known *Bidden to the Feast* (1938).[82]

The last-written but chronologically first part of what is effectively Jones's own trilogy about south Wales, *Bidden to the Feast,* starts in the mid 1860s in a mining family in the Merthyr district. The father is very severe, both against his children and the changes about him; he is 'bitter against the English and Irish who had, in his opinion, come to take the bread out of the mouths of the native Welsh' (9). He is described as 'the Puritan spirit of old Wales' (62) but Jones does not, as Davies might, offer this figure for admiration. The father is shown to be a brutal authoritarian: he drives several sons from the house for marrying out of native Welshness, and when his daughters win a clock for singing he, outraged by this example of public pleasure, smashes it and beats his daughters, causing his wife to have a stroke from which she never recovers. If old Wales has little of value to offer – a strikingly modern position that firmly turns its back on first-contact romance – the new industrial Wales has many problems. The novel, like *Black Parade,* outlines difficulties with health and sanitation and does not always link discussion of them into people's lives and the action. The history of Merthyr (34–5), the sequences on the work and the nature of the hauliers (108–10) move further towards sociology and the very long celebration of 'our horses', their types, work and treatment (116–26) seems, engaging as it is, damaging to the flow of the story. Less disruptive and more directly historical is the sequence of events, not only strikes and disasters but the manoeuvres to elect Henry Richard as the first Liberal MP for Merthyr, with its reminiscence of the Chartists, the Irish-Welsh riots at Tredegar, the Golden Jubilee, the temperance movement, emigration to the USA (two of the sons go), Joseph Parry's achievements in music. Through all this material, as well as in set-pieces on chapels and disasters, Jones acts as a folk historian for his world, amplifying and providing a prologue to the ethnographic work of *Black Parade*.

Here too the family narrative is strong, and woman-focused. Megan and Moriah, twins and singers, separate because Moriah goes off to England with Sion Howell the Cheapjack, seller of shoddy goods and organizer of entertainments (it was his clock they won): he has courted Megan but she is too upright for his dubious charms. Megan remains to run the household and she sees her brothers variously emigrate, die and develop. The developments they undergo seem to fulfil the distinctly unproletarian interest found in Mog Edwards in *Rhondda Roundabout*. There is a good deal of concern with business in the novel, and Jones's fiction in general and his own positions are by no means limited to working-class activities – he sees an easy passage from labouring work into well-rewarded white-collar work. At the start of the story the children's aunt, known in native style as Bopa Lloyd, lives on rents from houses she owns, not as a landowner but through a successfully speculating husband – they both started as puddlers in the ironworks. Sion the Cheapjack is himself seen as far from a capitalist hyena: he is cheerful, even humane, and Megan's rejection of him seems to have some of her father's Puritan spirit. Most strikingly, however, as Bopa Lloyd grows old, Megan begins to manage her houses and then they are bequeathed to her and she becomes quite rich: where Saran in *Black Parade* saved from her menfolk's earnings, here the money is mercantile, even exploitative, in origin. Consistent with that, Joe, the youngest son, who at the start of the novel suffers the boy's first day in the pit episode – a very vivid example of the motif – grows up to be an insurance clerk and eventually borrows enough money from Megan to invest in shipping in Cardiff and marry a Park Place heiress.

The feast to which Jones's characters are bidden is not only one of communal cheer and collective value, it is also one of possible wealth; Megan finds her brothers in America very comfortably off when she visits late in the novel. It is as if Jones gives a narrative to the instability of his own politics, drifting through his life as he did from a founder Communist to a Liberal, then Conservative supporter. It is perhaps not so surprising that the novel is dedicated to Sir Robert Webber, a Conservative Cardiff dignitary, or that Jones's later novels went on to celebrate the romance of business in Cardiff and the mining valleys: Glyn Jones felt they lacked the 'freshness, spontaneity and gusto' of the early novels.[83] But though *Bidden to the Feast* may be finally a financially oriented romance and, as if in a Raine novel, the couple who fail to marry early in the story finally come together after Moriah's death (Sion and Megan settle down together in advanced age), there is never a complete rejection of the spirit and sense of oppression of the Welsh working class.

Jones was always a mobile figure: Kenneth Morgan remarks that his account of Joseph Parry's success in America in *Off to Philadelphia in the Morning* is 'in many respects an oblique comment on the life of Jack Jones himself',[84] and his novels are rarely consistent, with each other, or internally. The effect is very different from the fluent and subtle novels and stories of Rhys Davies, and they seem almost like parallel opposites: Davies does not mention Jones in his review of Welsh writers at the end of *My Wales* and Jones seems not to have been actively aware of Davies's work, though there may be a sly joke in a mean 'Cardi' named Rhys Davies in *Bidden to the Feast* (40). But like Davies, and with a more direct sense of historical and social reality, Jones made a real contribution. Others were to speak with more political rigour and with more subtle insight about the industrial society of south Wales, but Jones has the honour of being the first to tackle head on in a consciously ethnographic way the conditions and institutions of the new industrial community. The variety and inconsistency of his voice, the lack of faith in radical organization and the increasing acceptance of mercantile values, can in themselves be seen as a result of the disorientating impact of the conditions that colonial capitalism brought to his part of the world.

University education was established in Wales by the late nineteenth century and this is envisaged in *Black Parade* and *Rhondda Roundabout* as a form of social and financial advancement for young people from south Wales. Gwyn Jones (1907–1999) was the first writer of fiction about the region to go through this process: son of a Blackwood miner, he went to university in Cardiff and on to distinction as a scholar of Norse literature and history and also a widely influential professor of English literature, first at Cardiff and then Aberystwyth. He coproduced with Thomas Jones the classic translation of *The Mabinogion* and was the first chair of what has become the Arts Council of Wales; he was also a distinguished novelist and wrote many short stories, almost all with Welsh themes. It was entirely appropriate that the first lecture in the series honouring his name was given in 1979 by Raymond Williams, published as *The Welsh Industrial Novel,* because Gwyn Jones's best-remembered novel is a realistic account of a Welsh mining village and the people involved in its activities from the period of the slump, *Times Like These* (1938).[85]

Set in Jenkinstown, a mining village very much like Jones's native Blackwood, and covering the period from just before the 1926 strike to the austerity of 1931, the novel is like Jack Jones's work focused on a family, but one quite unlike the sprawling and chaotic families of his Merthyr settings. Oliver Biesty is a middle-aged miner with a son, Luke, now unemployed, and a daughter Mary, who works in the office of a Newport bus company. Their essence is respectability: Glyn Jones remarked in his introduction to the 1979 reprint that they would be called 'tidy people' (7). Oliver is 'calm, powerful and dependable' (16), Luke is quiet and responsible, even a little timid: perhaps in reflex to these reliable males, the mother, Polly, plays a very restricted role. Oliver is described as 'the best type of miner' (16): this evaluation is internal to the working class, as he is a loyal striker and late in the novel will refuse to organize a collection for a gift for a despised manager, losing his job in the petty processes of victimization that Jones makes very real. An unrhetorical novel, firmly realistic in most ways, *Times Like These* charts closely how it felt to be an ordinary person caught up in the maelstrom of economic chaos in south Wales. Raymond Williams calls it 'the best form of the "working-class family" novel',[86] and this is the calmest, least sensational of all the Welsh industrial novels.

Jones steadily lays out the events: the novel begins soon after the mini-boom of 1923–4 had ended, the miners go on strike in 1926 and afterwards face short time, lay-offs, the brutality of the Means Test, and a desolate future. Resistance is focused through Edgar Evans, fiancé to Mary Biesty and others, including Ike Jones, a schoolteacher's nephew, great reader and radical, locally called the 'Roosian'. But while Jones recognizes the colliers' struggle, and shows the ever-respectable Oliver being inevitably drawn into action, his main interest is to chart more widely the social world around, and even distant from, the pit village. Mary Biesty moves away from home and grows ever more bourgeois in her desire to 'life my own life' (133): her mother sympathizes with this on the grounds that a woman's life in a pit village is 'At best a life of denial and poverty, at the worst, degradation' (135). Most strikingly, though, Jones creates a sympathetic figure from the manager class, Shelton: he respects the colliers as having 'iron in them' (63), is disgusted by the gloating of his directors over their defeat and generally does the best he can to keep the peace and see fair play. It is he who enjoys most the success at rugby of the village star, Ben Fisher, and he does his best to acclimatize his haughty English wife to the industrial context. Shelton is given the unusual power to provide the viewpoint at times in the action, and this is even extended once to Broddam, the upwards-mobile bus owner for whom Mary works.

As James A. Davies has shown, this interest in the agents of industrial capitalism is unusual in the Welsh context,[87] and it is difficult to resolve: Shelton finally inherits his family estate when his brother dies and so he is able to leave the action of the novel he has made more complicated. But that is not the only oddity of tone. At one point the narrator says that as a result of leaving home Mary's 'manners, her clothes and her speech were all improving' (24), and this seems to suggest an absolute value in her moving away from her working-class origin. Davies discusses this statement in some detail and, in spite of his inherent approval of the social range of the novel, involving bourgeois figures, feels there is something 'uncertain' about the moment.[88] Just as uncertain is the effect made when on several occasions through the novel the narrator uses classical imagery to describe the humble pleasures of the industrial environment. The most striking example is when the unemployed miners are swimming in the local river and an extended image treats this as a classical pastoral scene (205), but there are other instances in the book where Jones's learning seems to impose another, more distanced, even disinterested, voice on the narration. This is by no means consistent: at other times the voice can be empathetic as when it says 'Privacy is always denied the poor' (177), but the effect is to suggest that *Times Like These* is at times no more than a visitor's exercise in ethnography, not the deeply committed involvement in the industrial environment that is so clear in Jack Jones and, in his displaced way, evident in Rhys Davies's work.

The final scene is sentimental in its despair: Luke, long out of work, his wife dead, can only say 'Everything do seem so useless, somehow' (319). Smith likens this sharply to the equally despairing, and also externally seen, pathos of Stephen Blackpool in Dickens's *Hard Times* saying 'It's aw' a muddle.'[89] The year 1931 was the nadir of fortunes on the coalfield, and 1935, when Jones wrote, was no better: but there are some features of *Times Like These* that can be described, like its author, as academic. Effective as an account of the period, and bold in its desire to speak about more than the deeply involved working class, the novel is nevertheless itself something of a reverse pastoral, as its occasional classicism reveals. The author never felt inclined to return to the topic and it remains a curious one-off in the sequence of novels about the conditions on the coalfield. Jones's 'short stories of peasant life', as G. F. Adam calls them,[90] are notable for their romantic treatment of rural Wales as a fascinating, dramatic and *gwerin*-based society, from the heroic, even Christ-like shepherd in 'A White Birthday' to his grotesque opposite in 'The Brute Creation'.[91] Jones's treatment of his characters, sympathetic but crucially distant, is consistent with his refusal to permit the teaching of Welsh literature in English – to which he had contributed much as both author and administrator – in his university departments. Aware as he was of the dramatic effects of colonial capitalism, he was in important ways unable to combat it completely, or to identify firmly with those who did. This attitude, so dangerously easy for professional academics and intellectuals, was far from the position of Lewis Jones.

2.4 POLITICAL FICTION: LEWIS JONES AND B. L. COOMBES

Born in Clydach Vale, close to Rhys Davies's home – they must have known each other – Lewis Jones (1897–1939) worked as a miner from 1909 in the Cambrian Combine: a very early experience would have been the dramatic actions of 1910 around Tonypandy. Part of the radical group led by Noah Rees, he joined the Communist Party in 1923 and was selected for leadership, spending 1923–5 at the Central Labour College, the organization set up in London to educate young miners away from the well-meaning but distracting context of Ruskin College at Oxford. When he returned he became check-weighman at the Cambrian colliery, chosen by the miners to verify the tonnage for which they were paid. Always forward in the radical cause, in 1926 he was sent to the Nottingham area to rally wavering strikers, and was in return jailed for sedition: the oppressive power of government and capital was vividly clear to Jones.

He returned to the colliery, but was dismissed early in 1930 for refusing to work with non-union labour.[92] From then on he worked as an organizer, especially of the National Unemployed Workers Union, a bold and often successful idea and institution: Smith describes him as 'a dazzlingly gifted platform orator'.[93] A major figure in the fight against the Means Test and against the 'nonpolitical' union, Jones helped to organize three Hunger Marches to London, and threw his energy into the fight to support the Spanish government against Franco. He became well known in Wales but also found time to write some short realistic stories about the colliers' conditions, which were published in the communist *Daily Worker*. According to his introduction to *Cwmardy*, it was Arthur Horner, the influential Communist president of the Miners' Federation who urged him 'to "novelise" (if I may use the term) a phase of working-class history', as this might be 'expressed for the general reader more truthfully and vividly if treated imaginatively, than by any amount of statistical and historical research'.[94]

Jones was amazingly energetic. He died of a heart attack in 1939 after giving many anti-Franco speeches in a short period,[95] and somehow he found time over four years to complete, almost, two novels. He had planned three – another trilogy: in the unwritten last, the Welsh members of the International Brigade would return to fight for a workers' state in Wales.[96] After Jones's death the last chapter and half of *We Live* were completed by his long-time helper Mavis Llewelyn and seen through the press by D. M. Garman at the left-wing publisher, Lawrence and Wishart. Among all his activities, Jones wrote determinedly – his diaries record how he worked on his book whenever he could – and he had a clear image of the impact he wished to make. His title *Cwmardy* has a general, even allegorical effect, referring to the mining town of Maerdy, recognized as one of most radical parts of the Rhondda, a well-known syndicalist and later Communist stronghold. The story was to be historical, but not so specific or limited as Jack Jones's treatment of Merthyr and much more firmly left wing than either that or Rhys Davies's work – Lewis Jones must have known the first two parts of both trilogies as he started writing.

The characters are as symbolic as the title. 'Big Jim' Roberts, a huge, strong, often comic working-class warrior, is a version of 'The Big Hewer', the Welsh collier's example of the mythic figure through whom, like the Canadian logger Paul Bunyan or the Australian drover 'The Man from Snowy River', working men celebrated their skills and physical values. His son Len is the opposite: never strong – working underground weakens him seriously and his contribution to the cause of resistance is intellectual, political and passionately determined. Len has the role of Lewis Jones, if not the author's robust lifestyle. His first political mentor is Ezra Jones, who has come to the valley after being victimized for his radical actions elsewhere and is the leader of the local union – the Federation is not yet in place. Ezra is a complex figure, seeming to combine aspects of Mabon with Noah Rees, Lewis Jones's own mentor, and a crucial stage occurs when Len realizes that Ezra's cautious approach, seeking settlement where possible and not really wanting to risk all in a major confrontation, plays into the hands of the coal-owners and the imperial government, and he moves, through reading lent to him by an educated friend and the support of the local 'Circle' of self-educators, towards the Marxism that will be a central topic of *We Live*. In this he has the continued support of Mary, Ezra's daughter: she too is less than strong, suffering from an unspecified chest complaint, but although she remains loyal to her father, she sympathizes with Len's growing radicalism and will, in the second novel become an active leader herself. Other women play a role: Len's mother is the archetypal 'Welsh Mam', large, loving, devoted to her family but also free with her criticism. In *Cwmardy* she is named Shane: it is possible that Jones meant to indicate the hybrid pronunciation of the name Jane in the local accent, but in the second book the name is spelt Shan, so Shane is presumably an English editor's or printer's version of Siân. Jane in fact is the name of Len's only sister, older than him; he loves her dearly and there are some unusually erotic moments as he cuddles to her warm body, but her role in the story is to be sacrificed to oppressive power. Made pregnant by the son of Evan the Overman, but abandoned by him, she dies in childbirth, and a vivid scene reveals to Len her hideous, yellowing body before she is buried.

That human destruction by the brutality of power is to be avenged. First Big Jim reveals to the Overman the shame that he only got his job because his wife gave herself to the pit manager (a theme of petty corruption that runs through all this fiction, like people having to bribe their way to teaching jobs), and then, as part of the local riots, Shane leads the women in publicly shaming Evan by forcing him to wear the dead girl's nightgown. The scene reveals Jones's awareness of the native traditions that still existed in the industrial community, and there is a brief reference in the same direction in the opening scene when Big Jim, walking on the hills above the village, talks vaguely of the battle there 'between the English and the Cymro' (3). But these Rhys Davies-like moments of nativist value are few: Jim and Len plunge back into the dirt and smoke of Cwmardy, and the bulk of the action and its meaning are firmly controlled from a modern political viewpoint.

The difficulties and dangers of mining life are shown – there is a major explosion with many deaths and the owners manage to blame a worker for it (another recurrent scene in industrial stories), there are casual deaths in the pit just as there were in historical reality, and Len experiences directly the pressure placed on men to produce coal when conditions are dangerous. In response to this Len reacts, and an important political moment occurs. For all his intellectual and political learning, in addition to his determined radical thinking, Len can also be a man of sudden and spirited action. Faced by a bullying fireman who is forcing the colliers to work without timber supports after a death, Len is inspired, and calls on the men from other parts of the pit for support. It is a syndicalist moment: action is local, instinctive, and completely successful. In the same way, when Len makes his first political speech it just seems to emerge, and he speaks for all the men. In the fighting that follows – a clear reference to Tonypandy – Len is also decisively active, and Mary will react in the same way in *We Live* when she leads the women in an assault on the Unemployment Office. When Len speaks fluently in favour of the syndicalist stay-down strike, Harry Morgan, the Communist leader, based on Arthur Horner, says 'It is anarchy' (289) and Len's final support for him is clearly a moment of reluctant acceptance of the party-line. Communist Party member though he was, Jones was also the protégé of Noah Rees the syndicalist and no respecter of authority: it was widely reported that when he was part of a delegation to Moscow he alone refused to stand up when Stalin entered the room. Even this classically Marxist novel sequence has a Welsh tendency, constrained though it is.

In keeping with his overall symbolic thrust, Jones does not follow history exactly: while the events in Cwmardy clearly follow Tonypandy in 1910, the result of the strike is positive, which certainly did not happen in history. Just as fictional is the fact that in the story the miners learn from the strike that they must form the Federation, which happened twelve years before Tonypandy. The thrust of the novels is to provide a firmly left-wing narrative of the period. It is not always a popular one: Len is one of the few who oppose the war – against his father's militarist enthusiasm. And it is an intensely localized one: in *We Live* Len is sent away for the period of the 1926 strike to organize elsewhere (as Jones was himself), and there is no interest in where he is or what he is doing.

We Live, with Len now in the Communist Party, involves itself to some extent in Jack Jones-like detail with inter-Party disputes that were no doubt Lewis Jones's daily experience: a Party loyalist and miners' leader is shown to be a careerist and leaves for the Labour Party, Mary fights and wins a Council seat. This to some extent muffles the march of a symbolized history, but the narrative does gather itself into potent set-pieces. The impact of catastrophic poverty is realized with one powerful scene, as grim as the death of Jane, when the grocer, previously shown no sympathy in the narrative, kills his wife, with her consent, and hangs himself. The anti-Means Test activity is realized at length, with a climactic scene where Mary is the activist leader. In what Smith calls its finest two chapters,[97] the novel creates a stay-down strike – which, perhaps improbably, is another of Len's instinctive ideas. Finally Spain comes into the story: Len is sent from the valley to fight – there may be some in-party satire in that Harry Morgan, the local Communist whom

Len has at times opposed, chooses him against other advice. The conclusion, written by Mavis Llewelyn from Jones's notes, is a more
sentimental party-line melodrama than Jones might have written himself: as people gather in thousands for the Means Test march, Mary is
given, by one of the Spanish returnees who are being feted, a letter an-
nouncing Len's death. Nevertheless she, and his father and mother, join
the great march that winds its way up the hill and into Communist myth.

The ending is at least true to Jones's pattern that individuals are not
important in their own right: Mary and Len agree that their love must
be subservient to the political struggle and that they must not grieve for
loss – she expects to die first, from her chest complaint. But their love is
as real as their commitment to the Party, and also erotically represented
at times, though when Len encapsulates the amorous politics by calling
Mary 'comrade fach' (168) the difficulty of the manoeuvre is exposed.
But Jones always wants to make human and emotive the experience of
struggle against oppression: this is the effect of Big Jim's often foolish
but always collective opinions, and the emotive and physical engagement of the women has the same effect. John Pikoulis has argued that
Len is also the focus of a personal element running through the novels,
seeing him in the native tradition of 'the wounded bard': he relates this
to Jones's own damaged family life, and generally argues that the
family scenes ground the politics in emotive reality.[98] The contemporary reviewer John Randolph Richards similarly felt Jones 'succeeds
in humanizing the struggle of great forces, for he always resolves it in
terms of flesh and blood.'[99] Both Big Jim and his friend Dai Cannon,
fighter and folk preacher, connect this sense of humanity with earlier
and popular native traditions, and Andy Croft found this vitalistic
element even in *We Live*, seeing it as 'a programmatic novel for the
Popular Front, yet a fully living one, an imaginative mobilisation of the
people'.[100]

That was certainly Jones's purpose, but there have been those who
have felt he failed. Frank Kermode thought the novels were naive and
formally clumsy,[101] a common literary critical way of dismissing
directly political statements. Glyn Tegai Hughes thought Jones could
only inspire the reader's 'incredulity'[102] and James A. Davies takes a
negative view of his lack of interest in character in its own terms.[103]
Even the sympathetic Dai Smith – referring to minor figures, it seems –
felt Jones had 'an inability to make his political characters credible'.[104]
A reverse criticism is by Carole Snee, who felt that the involvement in
personalities in *Cwmardy* moved towards bourgeois fiction and that *We*

Live was, through its clearer symbolic lines, a more powerful political work.[105] Raymond Williams summed up the double impact of Jones's novels by saying the work was 'family-based but with the difference that the class element and indeed the class struggle now have explicit presence in the experience of the Miners' Federation and the Communist Party'.[106]

Collier, orator, class-warrior, organizer of political resistance, a great man for talk, drink and good company of both sexes, Lewis Jones was in many ways an archetypal citizen of industrial south Wales, as colourful as Jack Jones, but more focused in his purposes. That such a figure devoted himself to writing novels about his community suggests both his own depth of purpose and also the awareness – in his case confirmed by Horner as the foreword states – that this was a community that needed to be written about, so new, so remarkable, so much in need of understanding its own origins, its own conditions, and its own ways of coping with the oppressions and the catastrophes that had come upon it. As a Marxist, Jones does not theorize the situation in terms of imperial colonization – indeed Rhys Davies is more consistently aware of the English-Welsh conflict – and as an international leftist he would, like many in the period, have felt that any form of nationalism was against the interests of the working people of the world. His novels use Welsh phrases, but in such garbled form – the spelling 'Argllwyd' for 'Arglwydd' is frequent – that it is clear Jones as a proof-reader, conceivably as a writer, was as ignorant of Cymraeg as the English typesetters; similarly the opening of *Cwmardy* is the only place where native history is involved, and that in the mouth of Big Jim, never a reliable source.

Nevertheless while Jones, like many other Marxists, would not accept a colonial explanation as adequate for the oppressions faced by his people and analyses them only in terms of international capitalism, the account he gives of Cwmardy and the symbolic analysis he provides through his characters and their actions is a very powerful description of a situation that was brought about by the capitalist means of English imperial exploitation in Wales. The people of the valley respond to oppression with the communal allegiance, the courage, the values, the talkativeness, even sometimes the actual practices, of an earlier Wales, and those traces of native value, much more deeply woven in everyday life than Rhys Davies's sometimes tokenish versions of the same phenomenon, are even found in the syndicalism that underlies a good deal of Len's, and Jones's, attitudes. What Jones in fact charts is a transition from a self-aware colonized community – the kind of attitudes realized in *A Time to Laugh* and *Black Parade* – to a more militant community, armed with not only the weapons of instinctive resistance, courage and endurance, but also with the analysis and organization that themselves have been imported as the opposing other of capitalism and which, in the bitter situation of the 1930s, even the syndicalists recognized were now a stronger form of resistance. The Marxist Wales that Jones sees is itself a product of the colonized situation, both in the oppressions it seeks to redress and in the new weapons it plans to use in the struggle.

The novels are consciously far from being polished to the standards of Rhys Davies or literary London. The foreword acknowledges the 'jumpiness of certain portions of the book': but Jones does not offer this as an 'excuse'. With perhaps some pride in his achievement he relates the feature to the conditions under which the books were produced among 'mass meetings, committees, demonstrations, marches'. *Cwmardy* and *We Live* arise directly from the turbulent life of a devastated but undefeated domain, through the vigour and talent of a major Welsh writer, tragically short-lived. Their vivid and direct power, and their occasional clumsiness, are in themselves a challenge to the fluent, sensitive, officially apolitical literature which spread through the world the advantages of English civilization. Against that imperial tradition Lewis Jones produced two novels that remain classics of international industrial fiction and testify to the exotic, oppressed, but resistant and creative character of industrial south Wales.

B. L. Coombes (1894–1974) is remembered as the author of *These Poor Hands*,[107] a fairly short and cool-toned account of a miner's life which was published by Gollancz as the Left Book Club Book of the Month in June 1939 and was a great success, being translated into many languages and taken as a classic statement of the courage shown in difficulties by a working man. On the basis of it Coombes wrote one of the *Fact* pamphlets in 1941 entitled *I am a Miner* and other pieces of autobiographical and politically orientated realism, as described by Bill Jones and Chris Williams in their account of his life and work.[108] Coombes's family came from the English border with Wales and had settled in the coalfield, and he married a Welsh speaker. Always active and curious-minded – he became a competent violinist, a St John's ambulance man and a proficient handler of mechanical coal-cutters – Coombes, like others who described the coalfield, turned to writing in the early 1930s and had several stories published in *New Writing*, edited by the London-based left sympathizer John Lehmann. He was keen to print a novel by Coombes in a new series, but when this fell through Gollancz accepted the book: he had been looking for a worker's autobiography and Coombes reshaped the manuscript, first finished in July 1937, into what he called 'an autobiographical novel'.[109]

Its fictional element is clear from the start: Coombes opens with a vivid image of seeing from his Hereford home the red glow of industrial Wales, and then making his way as an English innocent into this exotic world. Both dramatic and also speaking to an English inquiring reader, this leads him to comment, not unlike a sympathetic tourist from the nineteenth century, on the cleanness of Welsh homes, the willing nature of Welsh girls and, in a more serious vein, the 'great sympathy' (146) of the people. But this newcomer's eye is politicized and the book outlines the dangers of mining work. The calm style gives a moving description of injury and death, and also insistently exposes the deceits and tricks by which the pit officials exploit the miners for profit. The major events of the period are described, lockout, victimization, the 1926 strike, battles over unionism, and the detail is often penetrating: poverty and hunger are vividly realized and Coombes gives a memorable account of how scab miners stole and damaged the expensive tools left in the pit by the striking miners. Often seen as an important document in gaining widespread support for the nationalization of the mines, *These Poor Hands* in tone and title is calm, reasonable, as its title suggests, ideal for rousing the sympathy of English readers. Not only does it alter details of Coombes's own life, as Barbara Prys-Williams has outlined,[110] to make the narrator a stranger to Wales, it also restricts its criticism largely to the petty officials who harass the miners, without the assault on the capitalist mine-owners or appeal to political organization found in Lewis Jones. The narrator's own coping skills – to find a job by his wits, to enjoy music in the depths of crisis – create an image of the better class of working man, far different from Jack Jones's Welsh hooligans, and so likely to appeal to the sympathetic members of the Left Book Club.

While it is aware of being set in Wales, and values the local people and institutions, it does so as part of a wider Britain: the coolness of Coombes's best-known book is in part its deliberate effacing of colonial elements in the situation of the miners, though this is not its only element of euphemism. The powerful story 'Twenty Tons of Coal', published in *New Writing* in 1939 and often anthologized as a classic statement of how capitalism belittles miners even in death, is here not told with a first-person narration and present action, but is recounted in the past, in the third person, from somewhere else and late in the story. As Jones and Williams note,[111] there is no record of how or why Coombes revised his manuscript for Gollancz, but the evidence of his other work suggests that he may well have consciously and under guidance Anglicized it. The earlier novel, 'Castell Vale', which was un-published and only half of which survives,[112] is a much more Wales-focused book, with local language, culture and attitudes, including a distinctly Cymraeg eisteddfod, being richly deployed on what was to be a mining romance like a determinedly working-class version of Keating. Coombes spoke Welsh and valued his neighbours as 'a cultured and progressive people',[113] and it may well be that the limiting of *These Poor Hands* to an effective but basically English-style pro-worker statement was itself generated in the inherently colonial connection between a London publisher and a Wales-based writer.

2.5 HYBRIDIZED RESISTANCE: GWYN THOMAS

If Bert Coombes made empathetic realism an important mode of drawing English attention to the situation in the industrial settlement, a low-toned parallel to Lewis Jones's politicized assault on capitalist exploitation, the work of Gwyn Thomas (1913 81) is far more difficult to describe in conventional literary terms, and this is one of the factors that has led to the general ignorance about the most verbally brilliant writer of Welsh fiction in English – only Dylan Thomas can challenge him – and the writer who made the most complex and in some respects the most powerful response to the conditions in south Wales in his lifetime.

Born in Cymer, a village clinging vertiginously to the mountain above Porth – he frequently remarked that only the excesses of capitalism would have forced people to live in such an improbable place – Thomas was the youngest of ten children, of whom only the first five spoke Cymraeg, and he turned against the native culture because of what he felt were the constraints of the chapel regime. He won a place at Oxford to study Spanish, and a solid learned career might seem to beckon him, to become a teacher at an English school or a university lecturer like so many of the educated men and women who left Wales in the 1930s. But he hated Oxford: in the kind of event that only a Gwyn

Thomas novel could match, his Spanish tutor was so far out of
sympathy with the young left-winger that he later became poet laureate
to Franco. Thomas returned to Wales, out of work, after a six months'
stay in Madrid, in 1934 . Quickly involved in political action, especially
the anti-Means Test action – he spoke of himself, with characteristic
irony, as 'a committee-man and refulgent orator'[114] – and meeting
Lewis Jones among other kindred spirits, he began to write and by 1937
had finished a manuscript which he submitted to a competition run by
the publisher Victor Gollancz for 'the best genuinely proletarian novel
by a British writer'.[115] The novel was *Sorrow for Thy Sons* and famously
it was rejected: as Smith recounts, Gollancz's readers admired the
vigour, found the detail depressing and even repulsive, and felt that it
crucially lacked 'the relief of beauty that Rhys Davies can give'.[116]
Indicating the need of English readers for a light at the end of the
depression tunnel (as well as Davies's standing in London), this
decision had a negative impact on Welsh writing at the time and a
further-reaching and ultimately less negative one on Thomas's own
career. Had Gollancz published *Sorrow for Thy Sons* in 1937 the people
of the coalfield could have read a powerful, intransigent, witty and
deeply confrontational novel that combined the politics of Lewis Jones
– to publish *Cwmardy* in the same year – with the vigorous colour of
Jack Jones and the linguistic poise of Rhys Davies, but more sharply,
even bitterly, focused on the real present condition of south Wales than
any of them. Presumably the reception the book would have had, at
least in Wales and the left-wing English press, would have led Thomas
to move on confidently and the novel 'O Lost', from which only the
short story 'My Fist Upon the Stone' survives, would have been published; it was apparently even more challenging, being a powerfully
ironic study of a complicit pro-capitalist working man. Thomas's career
would have begun long before his first, short and somewhat tentative
works appeared in 1946, and both his fiction and Welsh writing in
English in general would have been different. Such can be the negative
impacts of writing in a colonized situation.

    Eventually published in 1986 – the relation to the final catastrophe of
British mining may well have helped its final appearance – *Sorrow for
Thy Sons* still seethes with power. Eschewing the history, scene-setting
or detailed explanations that the other writers had felt necessary –
Smith comments that Thomas 'did not deign to introduce or explain his
society to outsiders'[117] – the novel starts in 1930 as Alf, the main focus,
loses his job in a colliery and then continues to early 1935 as the Means

Test marches begin. With one brother a contented Tory grocer and another leaving for educational work in England, Alf, with his girl-friend dying in a sanatorium, chooses, like Thomas himself, to stay.

The language is potent: Alf reflects on life in 'the slaughterhouse of South Wales' (65), and the detail is unrelenting: the brothers live in a house that is, since their mother's death, filthy. Hugh and his friend Lloyd are brutally beaten at school; Gwyneth, Alf's girlfriend, en-feebled from tuberculosis, nevertheless has to give her body to a shop manager to retain her job. Worse yet, because not passive, when Alf is about to be paid very meanly by a boss-loving worker for filling his coal shed with a load of coal, he has vengeful sex with the man's subnormal nymphomaniac daughter. This was not the meekly respectable working class that Gollancz and his readers – at the publishing house and at large – were seeking to make them feel good about the plight of Wales, and the politics of the novel are equally aggressive. The founders of the church hall, a colliery manager, grocer and bailiff, are described as the agents of 'coal-capitalism' (67), 'the triumvirate upon whose social activities three-quarters of the community's misery was founded' (66) and the narration glances back to 1900 and 'the great passionate wrong of super-profits in the coal industry' (72). Imperialism is picked up when a visitor to the school, in a flood of Tory 'Primrose catchwords' deplores the local 'trouble-makers' who have caused the 'discontent' and 'industrial idleness' and urges the boys, as 'sons of Empire' to emigrate to find work (105–6).

The details of humiliation are stressed. Alf and his sickly friend Bob walk on the mountains to see men scrabbling for coal: they earn a penny a bag from the tip-owner, and can pick a seventh for themselves. The misery of the Unemployment Office and the smugness of the clerks is developed in great detail – as is the violence with which the non-workers sometimes respond, including eventually Alf himself as he punches the supervisor. The shop people, typified by the unctuous brother Herbert, have no sympathy for their penniless customers. Clothes gathered for charity, Alf discovers, are actually being sold for profit by the well-fed woman in charge and, syndicalist-like, he steals some to give to ill-clad children. He also helps others to some of the miser's coal that he stacked. But politics go beyond this Robin Hood activity: Hugh's friend Lloyd is a Communist before he goes to college and returns to organize among the unemployed – again like Thomas himself – and when Alf attends a Means Test meeting he hears Howells, 'organiser of the unemployed' (219) and obviously an image of Lewis

Jones, speak with passion, frustrate the feeble elderly Labour councillor who urges patience, and urge the Popular Front action that made the Means Test marches effective. However, such positive elements do not lead to a triumphalist happy ending as in *We Live*: the march is attacked by the police; Lloyd is jailed; Hugh feels he has no option but to leave. Alone, without Gwyneth, with no brothers left, but still part of his community, Alf stays on.

Stark as it is, the novel is enriched by verbal wit, sometimes surreal – Alf jokes 'you could always tell the age of a horse by the price it paid for its toothbrush' (45) – by its driving narrative, and by flashes of human warmth, between friends, with women. Thomas avoids using the beauty of the country as a value, but with his characteristic mordant wit sees even the trees outside the labour exchange as mutilated and depressed-looking, like the clients inside. Though the story is so contemporary, there are still connections made with the depth of native tradition. Alf's sickly friend Bob speaks of his father walking to the colliery from Carmarthen (76), Hugh feels the presence of the ghosts of the women who once toiled in the mines (87–8), the brothers' great-grandfather was a Rebecca rioter; Annie, the wretched victim of father and men, including Alf, is envisaged as an absence of Welsh sovereignty – like the valley she is 'aggressive, ignorant, loose' (16–17). The efflorescent wit that Thomas would later display is almost always under ironic control, but it testifies, as his rich version of valley culture always intended, to the spirits and the possibilities of this deeply oppressed people, and the novel's closure, with Lloyd stubborn in jail, with Howells still at work, with Alf's obdurate strength unweakened, expresses that sense of unyielding resistance that the south Welsh community was able to offer still. *Sorrow for Thy Sons* presents a challenge that reaches beyond the somewhat sentimental title to indicate that the suppression of the book was itself an act of a colonial authority: a way of silencing a colonized voice that was too demanding, too aggressive. The final publishing of the book not only restores to availability one of the major works of the Welsh tradition in English: it must also draw attention to the others that still lie unknown, like Jack Jones's complete 'Saran', his two rejected novels of the early 1930s, 'Behold They Live' and 'Shadow Show' (the former, like *Sorrow for Thy Sons*, was judged 'too gloomy' by the publisher)[118] as well as Thomas's own missing novel, 'O Lost', B. L. Coombes's unpublished manuscripts and 'Collier Boy' by the poet Idris Davies. It is in the nature of a colonized voice to be fragmentary, under pressure, mediated through inherently hostile channels, and while it is true that the sympathy of the English left sympathizers was the only means by which these authors were to be published – there was yet no means of publishing substantial English fiction in Wales – it did not leave the writers free, but the remarkable thing is how much did in fact come across, with the notable exception of the powerful, condensed and archetypal narrative of *Sorrow for Thy Sons*.

Gwyn Thomas kept writing, though little is known about his activities. He spoke very generally about his writing, and always ironically, in his autobiography, characteristically titled *A Few Selected Exits* (1968),[119] and even Michael Parnell – to whom a great deal is owed for his work as a collector and republisher of Thomas work and especially as his biographer – was not able to disentangle the literary history of the next years. Thomas did some work in education, including at unemployment camps, and then became a schoolteacher, briefly in Carmarthen and until 1962 teaching French and Spanish at Barry Boys' Grammar School. But he clearly never stopped writing, and it was, by all accounts, his wife Lyn who at the end of the war gathered together three manuscripts and sent them to publishers where – both the brilliant style and the deeply democratic themes must have caught the eye – they were all accepted.

These were not full-length novels like *Sorrow for Thy Sons*, and they had moved away further from realism as a mode: the rejection of that novel seems to have turned Thomas towards the fanciful, whimsical mode of writing that came easily to him. It is noteworthy that such realism itself was not a native tradition, had been only awkwardly used by Jack Jones and in a specific politicized form by Lewis Jones, and basically only for scene-setting by Rhys Davies. M. Wynn Thomas has noted that even *Sorrow for Thy Sons* is hyper-realist – he calls Thomas 'a Rhondda expressionist' – and Dai Smith saw it as 'an attempted break with the naturalistic convention that has usually dictated the structure and intentions of the working-class novel'.[120] The work that now appeared was basically in allegorical form – Thomas subtitled the short-story collection *Where Did I Put My Pity* (1946)[121] 'Folk-Tales from the Modern Welsh', and it seems that he now realized a capacity, which had been obscured in *Sorrow for Thy Sons* by the expectations of the London market, for writing the hybrid stories characteristic of colonized writers, where some aspects of native tradition are interwoven with the modern situation of the society, in the language and the techniques – with some appropriate hybridizing revisions – of the colonizing culture. That may seem a surprising account of Thomas, as

he was, especially in later years, so well-known for his hostility to the
Cymraeg language and the Nationalist movement, and because *Sorrow
for Thy Sons* is so easily assimilated to leftist Welsh realism of the
1930s. Yet if his work is looked at in the terms of post-colonial analysis
many of its features become comprehensible, and the importance of his
contribution becomes clearer.[122]

Not only are the short stories 'folk tales': *Where Did I Put My Pity?*
has a dedication to 'Iolo of the Scarlet Fancy, an ancient minstrel of
Mynydd Coch', and Thomas continues 'This book goes out to all who,
like Iolo, hummed a little in harmony with desolation.' There is even, in
an accompanying quatrain, a briefly Rhys Davies-like sense of continuity with the past, but it is expressed in Thomas's sharply distancing
ironic language:

> My fathers tell me through the night my pain is just as theirs
> So the caper must be ages old and hardening in layers.

Connections are made with Cymraeg – 'Hen wlad fy nhadau' (Old land
of my fathers) from the national anthem and 'ar hyd y nos' (all through
the night) from the folk song – but the language ('caper') and the
apparent reference to coal ('hardening in layers') indicate an ironic
distanced modernity. That mix of tradition and the painful present, the
archetypal move of the hybridized writer, will recur through most of
Thomas's fiction.

The stories are varied in length, though the dedication and the fact
that the title does not belong to any of the stories must suggest that
Thomas had prepared this for publication as a book before Lyn
Thomas dispatched it to a publisher: Thomas and his myth often prefer
casualness to the actual great care that lies behind his writing. They are
a varied group of stories: 'The Hands of Chris', about a tough miner
who fights against local fascists, looks back in mode to *Sorrow for Thy
Sons,* but the dominant tone is an ironic treatment of desperation and
near-impotence. The shorter stories tell of confusions and embarrass-
ments among the people of Thomas's symbolic Rhondda village,
variously called Mynydd Coch or Meadow Prospect. Ironies lie beneath
both names. Presumably *coch* (red) is for politics and the Meadow is
definitely anti-pastoral: it becomes clear that 'The Black Meadow', the
graveyard, is the local prospect both for eyes and bodies. Characters
and features that will recur first appear: Milton Nicholas the Marxist,
usually given a minor role, choric but subtly evaluative; a narrator who

is often anonymous and merely observes the antics and obsessions of people; there is no mining work as such in the present; the combination of sparkling wit with a desolate situation of 'people hungry, people in debt, people caught and spun to a sickened dumbness'.[123] Two of the shorter stories concern figures rather like Lewis Jones's Big Jim Roberts, Uncle Gomer in 'Dust in the Lonely Wind' and Uncle Cadwallader in 'Add a Spoonful of Grief to Taste'. Both are large and violent: Gomer almost meaninglessly assaulting a cinema manager and wrecking a grocer's shop, but Cadwallader, as heroic as his name implies, attacking the police on behalf of a woman who is being evicted. These giants who are basically friendly (a native folkloric tradition), from the narrator's viewpoint at least, are a good deal less developed than the figures who dominate the two longer stories.

One, 'Simeon', is a fairly straightforward though skilfully developed account of a farmer living with two daughters. The narrator, here named Ben, goes to work for him, sees his brutality to his daughters, learns that he molests them, realizes that one of their admirers has been murdered and buried in the garden. He finally rescues and runs away with the beautiful third sister: Simeon attacks Ben for shielding her from his lust, but the elder daughter kills her father. This is a modern version of a native unfriendly giant fable, with some resemblance to *Culhwch ac Olwen*: the giant always attacks his daughter's suitor. The main story of the book 'Oscar' works this theme up much more power-fully by combining the giant's sexual and authoritarian oppression with an allegorical account of coal-owning.

Dai Smith has called 'Oscar' 'a masterpiece of European literature'[124] and Alun Richards ignored its novella length to include it in his second collection of Welsh short stories. Both had good reason: this is Thomas's most condensed and uniformly powerful piece of work, and it combines a striking range of the features of hybrid resistance. Where Ben just worked for Simeon and observed his brutality, Lewis is closely involved with the viciously exploitative Oscar. He waits while he uses prostitutes, helps him home when drunk and, in a sequence that elaborates a scene from *Sorrow for Thy Sons*, guards Oscar's coal-tip to check the productivity and honesty of the coal-pickers. Lewis exhibits the complicity that is a recurrent feature of colonized fiction, expressing the pain through which people live under and cooperate with oppres-sion, and even write in the oppressor's language. Isolation is also realized: this is a non-family story. Lewis's father, once a striker, has died, and his mother is largely silent. His friend Danny is notably weak

– he cannot sustain a job delivering coal, and he falls to his death on the tip. For his own interests with Oscar, Lewis lies at the inquest to conceal that it was Oscar's shooting at Danny that made him fall. Inquests are common in coalfield fiction, but Thomas seems deliberately to rework in ironic and complicit form the final motif from Coombes's 'Twenty Tons of Coal'.

Lewis eventually turns on his master, but for complex reasons. Danny's widow, the perhaps improbably beautiful Hannah, is spotted by Oscar at the inquest and he desires her. She and Lewis conspire to kill Oscar; she is armed with a hammer. But as Lewis watches – the externalized colonial subject – Hannah fails to kill Oscar, and in fact gives him her body, because, she explains afterwards, 'I wanted to be warm again' (119). That night, as Lewis leads the drunkenly celebrating Oscar home, he does not act directly, but lets him fall through a fence into a quarry to his death. Condensing the ogre who seizes the sovereign beauty with the coal-owning oppressor – and that in a sombre world where colliers are unemployed, the mine is derelict and the only coal on show is slag – is as potent a piece of outraged fiction as Thomas ever wrote, and it draws as deeply on native tradition as it does on contemporary analysis. Smith puts his finger on a key element in the story's status as colonized resistance, calling it 'a disturbing allegory for the whole of coalfield history'.[125] The themes alone enlist native tradition as a form of resistance, and there are matching formal features in Thomas's fiction. The collection's self-mocking title 'Where did I put my pity?' is very close in English to a line of *cynghanedd lusg* – seven syllables, internal rhyme on the penultimate syllable – though Thomas's ear for a Cymraeg harmony is more likely to come from the chapel hymns he was forced to sing when young than from the pages of Dafydd ap Gwilym, that other master of complicit fables in a time of colonization.

Less spectacular than 'Oscar', but also mining the veins of hybridity and resistance are two other long stories, published separately in this period. 'The Dark Philosophers'[126] deploys a foursome of interested observers. This chorus's opinions are articulated by Ben, now a bricklayer, but he speaks always as 'we'. Thomas will frequently reuse this multiple-viewpoint device, and the avoidance of the first-person narration of the traditional novel seems another conscious resistance to the culture in whose language he writes. What they observe is a saga of complicity: the Revd Emmanuel Prees has risen from the working class through the help of the local coal-owner, and in the process has rejected

the woman he loved. Various plot complications occur and the observers note the deformed lives of several local people from their base in
Idomeneo Faracci's cafe, but the thrust of the story is to expose and
avenge the class betrayal and the false positioning of Prees. Walter acts
as the leader of the group – that was the name of Thomas's father and
oldest brother – and he manipulates matters so that Prees falls in love
with the daughter of the woman he rejected, a shadow of Oscar's
appropriative lust. In a theatrical ending – Thomas may well be playing
on the operatic melodrama suggested by Idomeneo's name – Prees is
provoked to preach a sermon in favour of love such as he is now
experiencing and dies of a heart attack in his own pulpit. Slighter and
less justifiably vengeful as a fable than 'Oscar', and perhaps expressing
Thomas's own Caradoc Evans-like feeling against religion, the story
has won few admirers, though James A. Davies thinks it is his finest
work, reappropriating it to the English bourgeois novel by praising its
realization of Prees's tragedy in 'a celebration of individualism and a
bleak reminder that, in the end, external forces are stronger'.[127]

A narrating quartet continues operations in *The Alone to the Alone*
(seven syllables again), the most elaborate of Thomas's early work.[128]
The novel opens strikingly:

> Our group which met nightly on a wall at the bottom of our backyard was
> agreed that never had so little beauty been compressed into so large a space
> as we saw in the Terraces. We took this in our solemn way to mean that
> when men consent to endure for too long the sadness of poverty and
> decline, beauty sees no point in staying, bows its head, and goes. (13)

Thomas would often return to the cultural and aesthetic deprivation
that people suffered in the Rhondda. This is not an evasion of politics:
the novel is steeped in displaced references to exploitation and possible
resistance; it is rather an insistence on the human cost of the industrial
context, a more deeply felt account of circumstances than a merely
political narrative can achieve. It is also, characteristically, a motif that
is treated ironically in the novel. The four – this time the narrator is
anonymous and Ben is one of the others – become concerned with
Eurona, who unrequitedly loves Rollo, a bus conductor, notable not
only for being in work and having money, but also for the smartness of
his uniform (his appeal is implicitly fascist). She is offered a job as a
servant in England – another recurrent motif in all this fiction – and led
by Walter they manage to raise enough funds for her to be smartly

dressed for this opportunity. Seeing her startling finery, Rollo falls for Eurona, and she refuses to leave. But this muted replay of the rape of the sovereign maiden is headed for complications: Rollo meets a welcoming widow and abandons Eurona; in response she tears off her new clothes and takes to her bed, naked.

Foiled in their attempt to be socially helpful, the group now encounter another form of exploitation, Shadrach Sims appears – one of Thomas's gallery of energetic, entrepreneurial, business-orientated valley quislings. He employs the four to publicize his new grocer's shops against the chain-stores coming in from England – a contradiction of capitalism. Sims is a great believer in the will, another fascist feature, and he is amazed at the degraded state of Morris, Eurona's father – the four have by now raised her to her usual level of apathy. So Sims dresses Morris in a new purple suit and employs him. Thomas consistently represents inappropriate conformity to the colonizing forces through grotesque clothing. Worse, Sims wants to train Rollo as a fascist speaker. This fails as Rollo is assaulted by a hardy anti-Franco miner, but the four manage some sort of resolution through introducing Sims to Rollo's appealing widow: Rollo assaults Sims and is jailed; Sims retires to his mansion; Eurona, with new clothes wheedled out of Sims by the four, leaves for the Home Counties, and the group returns to its wall, having failed to bring any more beauty into the Terraces, but at least having fought a holding action against various forces of further oppression.

Highly comic in language – the group's landlady, one of Thomas's many Tory-loving workers, is described: 'Up against Mrs Watts the average doormat had a swaggering air of erect independence' (99) – and rich in amusing detail, *The Alone to the Alone* replays the bitterness of 'Oscar' as ironic farce. If that might seem a lightweight response to the situation, Thomas is ahead of his critics, remarking on 'the Celtic jape of always letting words purge the passionate fluid of his sadness into a vat of revolutionary intentions' (123). Always a brilliant wit, who would later dazzle on radio and television, but always also, as his correspondence shows (notably with the American Marxist Howard Fast),[129] a dedicated leftist, Thomas often chose to clothe – he might have resisted the metaphor – his darkest critique in the most comic of fancies: an aproach not indeed unlike folk tale, and in its insouciant tone itself staking a claim for vitality against the sonority of English culture. The manoeuvre to avoid losing the point in the decoration was difficult, and *The Alone to the Alone* can verge on the self-gratifyingly farcical, though its title, its opening, its grey ending all militate against that as an overall reading. It was a mode to which Thomas would return, with greater effect in later novels, and would vary in a major way in his next completed work *The Thinker and the Thrush*, which combined the multiple plotting and hybrid resistance of *The Alone to the Alone* while using a first-person narrator as complicit as Abel Hicks had been in the lost 'O Lost'. But the new book was not published till after Thomas's death, being held up by the publisher's preference for a novel in a quite different mode in which Thomas was to attempt to establish himself as a full-time and major writer on the international stage.[130]

All Things Betray Thee (1949) was published by Michael Joseph,[131] famous in the Welsh literary context as the publisher of Richard Llewellyn's massively successful *How Green Was My Valley*, to be discussed below as an anti-settlement novel. It seems that Joseph felt that Thomas's fluency, allied to the still popular Welsh regional theme, might be very successful. Thomas changed his style, though not his principles. *All Things Betray Thee* is his least witty and most romantic novel, and is his only Welsh retrospective work, in a sense a leftist version of the historical romances of the turn of the century. Unusually for this genre, it has no precise relation to history, no easy use of place, dates and people to give stiffening to a romantic and individualized narrative as is the norm. Allegory is still the mode and that generality, as well as his insistent radicalism, may have cost Thomas his chance of writing a Welsh *Gone with the Wind*.

The novel combines in freehand form the events of Merthyr in 1831 and Newport in 1839, with some back-dated reminiscences of Tonypandy in 1910, the miners' struggle for federation and a general sense of an embattled workforce: Smith comments that Thomas 'transmitted the 1930s into the 1830s'.[132] The places are also generalized: the main battle is in Moonlea, an iron town like Merthyr, with the English and legal military forces who play a major part in repression making their base in Tutbury, the county town, which must be Brecon. The characters are similarly, and curiously, Anglicized. Alan Hugh Leigh is a very oddly named harper from north Wales – not even Alun – who comes to the town to meet his old friend John Simon Adams (more an American than English name), an ironworker who has become the local leader in conflict with Richard Penbury, apparently a version of Richard Crawshay. Thomas used many English names in his fiction: maybe that reflected the multicultural nature of the Rhondda populace, but in this novel at least it seems more likely to have been meant to make the text more accessible in the Anglophone world of England and America.

As Leigh arrives, conflict is brewing. The price of iron is falling – historically accurate – and Penbury is being urged by his aggressive manager towards the wage-lowering lockout he has previously avoided. The lockout occurs, and Adams deploys the alliances he has made with the men of the 'southern valleys': in the 1830s there were no significant numbers there, and the clear reference is to the colliers' combinations that led to Federation. But this is also the 1830s, the time of Chartism: Adams believes in moral force, but the southern men, also anachronistically led by an Englishman, Jeremy Longridge, opt for physical violence, and Adams eventually admits they are right. When he is arrested Longridge's men storm Tutbury jail, the day after Adams is hanged, but in any case they are beaten off by soldiers (now again like the Merthyr radicals). The revolt ends in defeat and a sense that Adams, Longridge and the others were no more than vulnerable predecessors to reform, just 'leaves in the wind' – that was the American title. The novel ends with characteristically potent Thomas rhetoric about the 'new enormous music' (318) they have struck up, which will resound through the decades to come.

Inside that powerful creation of a mythic history for industrial Wales, a fictional shaping of martyrs to elaborate the legend of Dic Penderyn, the novel contains other themes and motifs, including a potentially disabling amount of romance. As Alan Hugh Leigh arrives he encounters the beautiful but aloof Helen Penbury strolling her father's magnificent grounds   they include enclosed farms and Leigh is later brutally warned off for poaching. But Helen likes him and his 'wild harping' and there is even a romantic passage between them on the grass, rather reticently described in accord with public taste of the time. She will eventually use her influence to free the harper from the jail he shares with Adams, and there is some sense that the colonizer's prized woman actually fancies the rough colonized, but she nevertheless ends up marrying the austerely brutal Lord Plimmon – a name that seems to condense the south Wales landowner, the Earl of Plymouth, with the idea of Mammon.

Adams too has his romance with the beautiful Katherine, wife to a man who is simple, in mental as well as class terms: a sort of blond earth-mother, she will eventually lead the people of Moonlea in an assault on the soldiers in vengeance for Adams's execution, but her main role is to suggest pastoral possibilities outside the industrial maelstrom. If harping and nature and these fair-skinned women cast a spell over some of the text, there is also a stubborn presence of Thomas's themes of resistance to the colonizer. The shopkeeper Lemuel Stevens is a particularly nasty quisling, involved in the murder of a radical by a hired thug. The ministers, church and chapel, are lickspittle servants of the colonial industrial power, and the English soldiers are represented as brutal invaders. Leftist politics is also recognized: the loyal radical who runs the pub where the Moonlea radicals gather sits reading Tom Paine (141); Longridge's tough radicals have made contact with the Rebeccaites (128); guns and ammunition are smuggled in farm-carts in an image of a south Welsh revolution; five thousand armed men march on the English base; a radical lawyer from England, with an Irish name, Connor, offers contacts through Chartist Britain. Colonial history is at times implied: the ironmasters are seen as the Normans of their day (238), and the importance of Tutbury as a base of the military-legal complex is recurrently stressed. Other more subtly resistant themes emerge: Leigh is dressed in new clothes to harp for the gentry; he accompanies a timid violinist whose father longs for gentry approval and a prosperous career for his son.

Opinions have differed strongly on this novel. James A. Davies found the tonal mix 'profoundly unsatisfactory',[133] and the far from unsympathetic Chris Meredith, himself creator of an important post-industrial novel to be discussed below, felt in the same spirit that it was 'a sort of Ruritania with class war'.[134] Others, connoisseurs of leftist fiction, have seen value: Glyn Jones thought it was 'the peak of his achievement in the field of the novel'[135] and Dai Smith has seen in it the story of 'the formation of a proletariat and its struggle to conscious-ness'.[136] Most fully of all, Raymond Williams praised the novel on several occasions, seeing it as 'the most important novel of the whole phase',[137] and specifically valuing its allegorical, non-specific mode as a means of speaking about the whole set of forces at work in south Wales and feeling it represents 'the composition of a history' and 'the par-ticularity of struggle given a general form'.[138] In his introduction to the 1986 reprint, Williams calls it 'a quite exceptionally authentic work: authentic in embodying that historical moment, which continues now to include us'.[139]

This is substantial applause from major critics, especially Williams's well-considered praise of the essentially allegorical mode of the book, though he does not see it in its post-colonial context. In that context it can seem today a compromise too far with the tastes of the publisher and possible audience: the presence of the improbable aristocratic romance, the insistence on non-Welsh names, and the recurrence of stereotypical themes in singing and natural beauty seem to cast the shadow of first-contact romance over the book. Its deep-laid sense of resistance and its recurrent brilliance of anti-colonial phrasing – the ironmasters have 'laid their black fingers on the heads of the field-folk' (8) – cannot fully and successfully combat this sentimental element. Features like its plangent title (for long Thomas preferred the stronger, darker 'My Root on Earth') and its elements of harmonious, stereo-typically Welsh fluency, the restraint of Thomas's natural irony, even the unlikely figure of the notably unCymraeg harper himself, all seem to point to an unsuccessful attempt by a colonized writer to com-promise with the tastes of the colonizing reader. Complex, ambitious, but over-reliant on traditions foreign to Thomas's innate radicalism, *All Things Betray Thee* is ultimately less moving as a historical drama of 1831 than the simpler and determinedly nativist *Angharad's Isle* by Michael Gareth Llewelyn (see pp. 127–8), which may well have been a stimulus for Thomas in his attempt to enter the publishing mainstream. As a result of these reservations about the novel, it seems just, if perhaps unfeeling, to conclude that the relative failure of the novel was appropriate and that it was highly valuable that Thomas, for a while at least, returned to his authentic, complex, hybrid and inherently resistant idiom.

The World Cannot Hear You, published in 1951,[140] is a richer and less farcical version of the hybrid resistance found in *The Alone to the Alone* and this is the novel where Thomas most successfully balances his exotic mixture of playful comedy, verbal wit and underlying anger at the impact of industrial colonialism. There is again a multiple narration, the four now employed as itinerant road-menders, though the forceful Walter has been dropped; the local leftist thinkers Milton Nicholas and, less trenchant in his opinions, Edwin Pugh, are also present as a chorus to the chorus. A focal figure is Omri Hemlock who, like Eurona's father Morris in *The Alone to the Alone,* is a pathetic scrap of humanity without work, money or aspirations: a slightly mocking image of Welsh pathos, he has some elements of the holy fool about him, and it seems no accident that the narrator once reveals his own name to be Peredur, the medieval Welsh hero who is parallel to the French Perceval, the ultimately triumphant, Grail-achieving, classic holy fool. Thomas was very widely read, including in the Welsh classics, and it is probable that somone learned in Spanish literature would see many more of these deepening mythic references in his work. Omri's strong-willed brother Bodvan is also nativist in reference: he is down from the north but, unlike Alan Leigh in *All Things Betray Thee,* he goes home after the failure of a scheme by which a local gentry figure, Sylvester Strang of Grosbras Hall, Norman in his heritage, sets the brothers up as old-style yeomen on a model farm which turns out to be, through his agent's malice, on the worst farming land available. In what Bodvan calls 'a sinister jape' (44), Thomas parodies the schemes for the unemployed in which he was himself involved in the late 1930s.

Strang's next well-meaning manipulation is his 'Cottage of Content', a residential school for the distressed where they will learn 'simple crafts like weaving and woodwork' (32): when the four narrators eventually go they are given a diet of English poetry rather than the 'syndicalism and class-spite' (267) which is their natural bent. But Strang, the image of fatuous colonizing charity, is not the worst enemy in the story. Another of Thomas's destructive entrepreneurs appears in Picton Gethin: his Welsh surname is implicitly qualified by his sharing a first name with an imperial general from Pembrokeshire, and he is 'the most goatish and two-fisted element to be produced in this part of the fringe since Harry Morgan left Bridgend for Jamaica' (53). Gethin's piratical practices include a plan to sell the produce of the alleged model farm, but when this fails he disappears, only to return eight years later splendidly dressed (and so for Thomas deeply suspect) to employ the four narrators as warehousemen in his new commercial ventures. He decides (as yet another implicitly hostile proponent of the powerful will: Thomas still has scores to settle with fascism) to improve Omri's life and make him a leader of men. Clothes are provided, speech training as well, but a Mosleyite visit to Birchtown market – apparently Pontypridd – is a disaster when some right-thinking (that is left-thinking) citizens disrupt the event. So Gethin decides Omri should have a stage career, the grotesque nature of which is described in relished detail. Repulsed but still ebullient, Gethin decides Omri should lead a parade to raise local spirits: he kits the local band in resplendent uniforms reminiscent of Eurona's finery, but this is a total failure when only the four narrators and a straggle of children turn up. Omri, the eternally oppressed, is blamed.

Having mocked plans for self-improvement in the valley, civic and personal, Thomas turns the plot to farce. The four become, to their surprise, employed in a new strip mill – a rare sign of an improving economy, and Omri's fortunes also rise as he inherits £100 from his brother. After some ludicrous episodes, such as the failure to relieve flooding in an ancient boat in which he goes down clinging to the tea-urn, Omri redeploys his newly created will in erratic ways. He becomes a night watchman and is treated as a local sage by the local people; then he learns to whistle – another disastrous concert ensues – and falls in love with Delphine Stringer, the lovely daughter and pianist of the over-intense pastor of an extreme Nonconformist mission: the chapels again come in for Thomas's comic ire. In order to win Delphine's heart Omri invests money in the Mission outing and, in the most elaborate of all Thomas's false-dressing sequences, kits himself out as a lover. All goes wrong with 'the body of Omri's longing' (249) including some gross farce with his new wig, and Delphine, deciding all the chaos is Omri's fault and even feeling he has tried to murder her father, goes off with the ever-present, always goatish Picton.

This brilliant and sustained, if sometimes efflorescent, farce is also a carnivalized bitterness at the antics to which the industrial proletariat are reduced in their attempt to find a way forward for the self and indeed the body. Thomas was later – for English establishment organs like the BBC and *Punch* – to write in a lightly comic tone about the gazooka bands and the costumed follies by which the unemployed tried to raise both money and their spirits, but here, writing more for himself and his local audience, such deformations of a natural life are merci-lessly parodied. The four themselves are not free from such treatment: their party piece as singers is the ferocious and totally inappropriate 'War Song of the Saracens', and to audiences of comfortable colonial agents and bemused locals they roar out 'We are those who come early and late, We are those who beat at your gate, Pale Kings of the sunset beware.' These charades do not obscure the fact that the village is 'the Koh-i-Noor in the crown of world depression' (198), that 'an epochal dandruff had fallen on fortune's pate between our hills' (10) or that all the narrators can really do is organize 'a league table for the reduction in the number of mutilated lives' (141).

The plot resolves itself resoundingly when the narrators advise Strang of Picton's designs to convert his college into holiday homes. Strang, apparently through his gentry connections, finds the money he needs to defeat this and Delphine accuses Picton of attempted murder. Insouciant as ever, he returns in midwinter to the narrators whom he inappropriately calls his 'comrades' (284) and – in an ending that treats him as banally as he deserves – as he re-enters his warehouse, his brain full of more schemes, an icicle falls and pierces his head.

Vigorous to the end, the novel is also, through its angry farce, insistently on the side of those who, like Omri bear a 'modest cross of obscure frustration' (134): the Christian irony, unmediated by church or chapel, is trenchant. And Thomas once expresses his purpose: one of the four, the shadowy Ewart, says that 'Art needs to deal with the misery and discomfort of the normal people' not 'abnormal people who grow up with a god-complex' (271). Thomas's view of the traditional self-obsession of the English novel underlies his democratic comedy. This rich novel – there are other story-threads, other 'mutilated lives' not mentioned here – is a forgotten masterpiece of Welsh writing in English, where the most verbally gifted of the south Welsh novelists held most successfully in balance his power over the English language and his distaste, even hate, for what had been done to the people he so highly valued, and – he uses the word a lot – pitied. The purpose of the novel is, its title insists, to make the world hear these people and although most reviewers found it merely comic, reading it fifty years later, especially with the insights of post-colonial analysis in mind, makes it clear that this is a carnivalized masterpiece of colonized resistance.

The novel that Thomas had completed before *All Things Betray Thee* dealt with many of the same themes in an equally powerful way and without the occasional overelaboration that is evident in *The World Cannot Hear You*. This is partly because, unusually for Thomas, *The Thinker and the Thrush* (1988)[14] is written in the first person: but this is not to realize the 'god-complex' of the usual individualist fiction. Stobo Wilkie, grocer's assistant, is a classic unreliable narrator as he steadily tells of his plans to oust his boss and own the shop, to gain the lovely Angela Lang and get even with the forces that frustrate him, including a choric group who are versions of Thomas's usual narrators. It is as if Thomas had here decided that mocking the colonial quislings like Herbert in *Sorrow for Thy Sons* or Shadrach Sims in *The Alone to the Alone* from outside was too easy, and as with Abel Hicks in 'O, Lost' the pattern of complicity with the oppressor in south Wales is too strong not to be explored in painful detail.

The self-interested first-person voice controls Thomas's tendency to swerve off into farcical digressions and imposes a deeply negative tone, but the novel is not entirely without positives. One of the few concessions to an unironized nativism in Thomas is his consistent use of a beautiful rural pub as a base for his valued characters, a haven of peace and positive forces. He gives these pubs unashamedly romantic names like 'The Leaves After the Rain' in *All Things Betray Thee* or 'The Moon for the Stones' in *The World Cannot Hear You*, and here the novel itself is named for the pub, 'The Thinker and the Thrush'. That this connection had ultimate value for Thomas, his own concession to the beauty and the native values that he elsewhere found so elusive, is confirmed by the fact that his own ashes were scattered, at his wish, by a tavern of just this kind at Llanwonno in the hills near his birthplace.

Little else in this novel is positive: rescued by Michael Parnell for publication in 1988, it is Thomas's darkest work, in part through its restrained humour and language, in part through its insistent focus on complicity. It may be no accident that Thomas wrote his fullest account of the treacheries and lack of personal shame that attend those who seek to get on in the mercantile world just as he was also planning to make his peace with English publishing by producing a hopefully saleable historical romance. Like Conan Doyle writing his plangently named 'The Man with the Twisted Lip' as he faced real market success with Sherlock Holmes and London publishing, Thomas may be presenting through Stobo Wilkie not only his account of the cowardly accommodation that many south Welsh made, or were forced to make, with the colonizing forces, but also his sense of his own difficult position as a Welsh writer in English. Only he has, through Stobo, seen so fully the embarrassing implications of that role, but then only he has so fully explored and so powerfully – and also vivaciously – realized the 'mutilated lives' that colonization brought to south Wales.

Thomas continued as a writer, especially in theatre, a form that seems natural to him, though his plays tend to be wordy rather than dramatic. He also gained great and justified fame as a speaker in 'The Brains Trust', and his radio speech after the Aberfan disaster was widely acknowledged as the voice of a nation. For a man of such capacity and such achievements in his major novels, it is somewhat sad to record that even after he gave up teaching in 1962 he never produced work to match his best. The novels and stories that regularly followed his peak with *The World Cannot Hear You* have the wit and the comedy, but not the intense mythic and hybrid power of what went before. *Now Lead Us Home* (1952)[142] shifts its critical focus to American incursion, as it reworks the purchase by William Randolph Hearst of St Donat's Castle in the Vale of Glamorgan (nor far from Thomas's Barry) as the arrival of a millionaire, not unduly exploitative, who is variously fawned on and tricked by the locals. Playful rather than searching, perhaps because the enemy is now not the English forces that Thomas knew so well, there is still clear sign of his biting power. As the locals finally play a charade of their lives for the newcomer's entertainment, he foresees the humiliation of tourist-entertaining through inauthentic re-enactments that has now become a standard practice in modern Wales.

A Frost on my Frolic (1953)[143] returned to the old valley themes, but with reduced power. There is now a dual 'we' narration, but the second is really straight man for the witty schoolboy lead – only here and in some short stories like the moving and much-anthologized 'The Teacher' does Thomas deploy his educational experience. But the novel accepts colonization: in the opening pages Welsh stereotypes, modern versions of the eighteenth-century Taffy approach, are clustered – the hills, the talk, poverty and poetry, the rain, rugby and religion. There seems a continuity between this material and the entertainments that Thomas was now publishing in *Punch*, and that effect is as strong in *The Stranger at my Side* (1954)[144] where the characters with farcical names – such as Hicks the Bricks, Burge the Urge, the cinema employee Lush the Ush – who used to play a role as marginal fun now, with their ludicrous antics, become central.

Both the ready acceptance in England of his work as a regional comedian – the speed of his publishing in the early 1950s testifies to that and must itself have militated against matching the complexity of the earlier work – and also Thomas's own declining health, as well as the fact that the comic journalist and media work earned him far more than the moderate royalties on even his most popular novels, all meant that he became a less serious contributor to Welsh fiction in English as he became more famous. But there was also sheer misfortune. At least some Americans could read the politics in his work – or perhaps his friendship with Howard Fast alerted them to it – because his work was blacklisted in the USA between 1951 and 1958, when *The Love Man* (partly euphemized as *The Wolf at Dusk*) restored him to the trans-atlantic lists. If that had not happened, the financial rewards of that market and the critical support of American liberals might well have strengthened his hand and nerve for more major work. Equally, the long-planned film of *All Things Betray Thee* which might well have released him from the need to be a Welsh puppet for *Punch* and the electronic media, never came about after many frustrations. And perhaps saddest of all, the biographic teleplay on Aneurin Bevan, which Richard Burton was extremely keen to play, was never made in that form. If his authorial fate had been kinder, rather than an entertainer or depoliticized valley writer, Thomas might have become a major figure whose early work would be read for the subtlety that is in fact quite patent.

In another sphere he did not help himself to gain national status. He became notorious during the Welsh-language campaign of the 1960s when he repeatedly derided the movement: the impact of his wit, in this case often waspish, was deeply felt, and led to a position where he was widely seen as hostile to the national interest and his work was thought of little interest. The influential Harri Pritchard Jones, in reviewing Glyn Jones's *The Dragon Has Two Tongues* dissented from his praise of Thomas, saying that while some English-language writers have at most a 'chiefly social' value, he could 'hardly credit even that importance to much of Gwyn Thomas's work'.[145] Glyn Jones had tried to explain Thomas's hostility to Cymraeg and nationalism as being the product of his lifelong leftism, suspicious of all nationalisms.[146] This is no doubt as true for Thomas as for many other leftists, especially those who thought, simplistically, that Saunders Lewis, through his European and religious interests led Welsh nationalism towards fascism in the 1930s, but it is likely that Thomas's virulence on the topic stems from a sense of that familiar theme, complicity. There is enough contact with traditional and nativist Welsh themes in his work to indicate that he saw the value of such a tradition, though he definitely did not want, unlike Rhys Davies, to lose sight of the recent world and its urgent needs by escaping into sentimental nativism. His distance from the language seems compulsive: there are almost no Cymraeg phrases in the novels and the names of characters seem improbably English, at least until Thomas moves toward stereotypical caricature in his later work. Such an obsessive rejection of the language was not uncommon. The austerity of the chapels did not help, but there is more than that: this kind of rejection always seems to occur among men, and can be best understood in terms of the strains on the personality which are created in the colonized situation in the case of those who aspire to succeed in circumstances where native culture is seen as a disadvantage.

The least appreciated of the major writers of Wales, though the one who has also left a memory of a warm personality and a mesmerizing presence, Thomas is best summed up by Glyn Jones, who called him 'the supreme poet of the industrial valleys, the *cyfarwydd* of the working class' (116). Ever generous but also ever acute, Jones deliberately uses a term that links Thomas to the native tradition, a move which in the dedication to *Where Did I Put My Pity?* he had ironically suggested. The word *cyfarwydd* means both story-teller and historian (as 'historian' once did), a combination that modern historiography fully appreciates. In his stories Thomas did in fact tell in allegorical, trenchant and also vivacious form the history of what he felt to be his people, the people that, like Alf in *Sorrow for Thy Sons,* he did not desert. Critics have sometimes commented that he makes all his characters and his narrators use the same language, as if this is a fault in realistic fiction. Thomas denied the implication that some characters should be limited: 'Some of the most magnificent speech I've heard has come from the plainest and commonest people', but he also answered in more than democratic terms saying that he wrote at a level that the people deserved.[147] Aware that he was fictionalizing a society that had faced crisis, celebrating the vitality of the south Welsh, even in their worst situations, and yet also aware of the strains that led many to despair and compromise and complicity in their colonized situation, Thomas has left a complex, rich and powerful body of work that in its varieties and its failures, as well as its successes, testifies to a heroic and memorable effort to realize in writing the inner forces at work in the industrial settlement of south Wales.

2.6 THE RETURN OF ROMANCE: RICHARD LLEWELLYN

Of all the novels, plays and films about industrial south Wales, one stands out as the internationally known version, 'the most pervasive and influental fabrication of Wales and the Welsh ever invented', as Ian Bell puts it.[148] This is *How Green Was My Valley?* by Richard Llewellyn (1906–83).[149] It was a bestselling novel in Britain from October 1939 and America from June 1940 and has scarcely been out of print since, but it became even more widely known from 1941 in the Oscar-winning film version directed by John Ford. Born Richard Llewellyn Lloyd – though some sources add Dafydd Vyvyan as extra forenames – with parents in the hotel business, he spent time as a child with his grandparents in St David's, worked in hotels and joined the army: he later said that the first version of the novel was written when he was serving in India, and as he was out of the army by 1930 this would make the draft a very early Welsh industrial novel preceded only by Keating and perhaps Rhys Davies's *The Withered Root.* But as John Harris has shown, the published version underwent major rewriting through the publisher's 'diluting the Welsh idiom to suit a wider readership' and establishing the romantic title, in preference to Llewellyn's favoured 'Slag' or his substitute, 'Land of My Fathers'. Just as there are no place-names in the finished text – though Llewellyn had visited Gilfach Goch and allegedly worked underground for local detail – the title is more general and romantic than Llewellyn's versions, sentimental as they are, but this merely emphasizes a basic feature of the book. It starts as the hero, Huw Morgan, gladly leaves his troubled valley, as his family's house has been covered by the shifting slag that is a recurrent feature of the text and a symbol of the dehumanizing force that the novel finds in modern industrialization.

But industry is rescued from a leftist critique: pastoral reminiscence celebrates industry of the alleged early days when men returned from the pit with pockets full of sovereigns and sat down to tables groaning with roasted cuts of beef and legs of lamb – and in spite of such industrial wealth the river still held trout for the tickling. Much loved in the Hollywood version, this industrial Eden has been lost through the greed of both masters and men: when union activity is depicted it is mostly deplored and the authoritative voice of the Morgan family's father says that with the bosses 'reason and civilized dealing are your best weapons' (45). The topic of strikes and union activity come up recurrently: there is a negative tone in the haste and 'greed' of the activists – even when he sees the need for resistance the father prefers Owain Glyndŵr (spelt in that Cymraeg way) to Marx, but a more effective containment of radical activism is that each sequence of it is followed by a lengthy sentimental episode. The men's hostility to the father as a pit supervisor leads to his wife's impassioned defence of him at a hillside meeting followed by her near death in a river, sudden child-birth and brave rescue by young Huw who is himself bedridden for years as a result. Similarly, a description of the slagheaps moving is quickly followed by a high-tension chapel expulsion of an adulteress; a later strike is euphemized by a contiguous treatment of the religious revival; the involvement of Mr Gruffydd the minister in resistance to the mine-owners is both partial – he basically shares the father's view – and recurrently deflected into treatment of his unsuccessful romance with Huw's sister Angharad. The most striking of these deflections of politics into melodrama is at the end, where the father leads men loyal to the mine-owners against the strikers who intend to flood the pits, and this communally dubious action is validated by the cinematic heroics of the pit disaster, as the father and a brother die, to leave Huw alone.

Recognizing but avoiding the political thrust of the industrial novel, and seeing all modern industry as a destruction of a once pure land, the novel clearly appealed to a conservative, anti-modernity audience, a position with its own appeal as the Second World War began, but it also has a strong romance structure. Unlike Jack Jones whose stories view from a distance the young characters growing up in work and love, Llewellyn uses Huw as narrator and consistent focalizer. From the time when he first goes off to school the novel becomes insistently his story as a clever child, gifted at carpentry and struck with a slowly recognized and never fulfilled love for his sister-in-law Bronwen. The frustrations he faces are familiar: he is constrained at school through an obsessively Anglicized teacher, poverty drives him down the pits and away from his favoured work, and circumstances frustrate his feelings of love. Llewellyn does recognize, even to some extent realize, central elements of south Welsh experience, but where other writers set out this experience in ways which are variously foreign to the tradition of the individualized and moralized English novel, Llewellyn converts the industrial experience into a homily on personal sensitivity and moralized duty. Just as the valley is imagined as green again, so the novel's technique and thematic orientation have erased the structures and approaches and attitudes, especially those which are consciously elements of colonized resistance, that the other Welsh industrial writers had in varying degrees developed through the 1930s. As a facsimile of Welsh radical writing which was actually in the voice and language of the English novel, it is hardly surprising that the novel was welcomed by the establishment press. In England *The Times Literary Supplement* found it 'vivid, eloquent, poetical, glowing with an inner flame of emotion' and in America *The Saturday Review of Literature* saw it as 'a full-bodied, full-flavoured novel'.[150] A dissenting voice in London was the left-wing *New Statesman* where John Mair saw its appeal as basically to the 'emotionally discontented'[151] and the Welsh reception has been far from positive. Dai Smith has seen the novel as a 'panoply of falsification' in its treatment of industrial history, commenting that it is 'a last laugh' on the 1930s because it reverses so much that had gone before and that it is inherently an American-style myth, both Edenic and, in its insistence on the value of Welsh blood against that of incomers, racist.[152] Raymond Williams links it to both business and empire by seeing it as 'the export version of the Welsh industrial experience' and Glyn Tegai Hughes likens the novel to *Uncle Tom's Cabin* as a massively popular, basically bogus account of an exotic society.[153]

In spite of the success of *How Green Was My Valley*, Llewellyn did not continue in the mode. Though an army officer, he produced another novel in 1943, but it was, surprisingly to many reviewers, a fairly tough, but still sentimental, account of Cockney life, *None But the Lonely Heart*. It was not until 1960, seven novels later, that he returned to Huw Morgan in *Up into the Singing Mountain* and told of his life after leaving the valley and meeting up with Mr Gruffydd, no longer a reverend, in Welsh Patagonia. A south American travelogue cum romance with some loose connection with Wales, this was itself distantly followed in 1975 by *Green, Green, My Valley Now* in which a wealthy and elderly Huw returns to Wales, but not to his now completely de-industrialized valley. He settles in north Wales and, as in *Up into the Singing Mountain*, experiences a set of episodic excitements, here involving both the prince of Wales's investiture and time-share housing frauds initiated by the IRA. Eventually Huw, with two dead wives behind him in this series (yet another trilogy, of an erratic sort), marries a young Nationalist, presumably indicating Llewellyn's own stated affiliation to the Plaid Cymru cause late in life. Just as *How Green Was My Valley* opened by leaving industrial Wales, so Llewellyn's writing career never focused again on that world – if indeed it ever really had. Not a native of the industrial south, and only loosely connected to Wales, he offered an account of the industrial settlement that was both the most inauthentic and also – perhaps for that reason – the most popular elsewhere.

The novel is a classic example of colonized writing that serves almost completely the interests of the colonizer, making the Welsh seem quaint but willing servants of English capitalism, fully validating the individualist and moralist imperatives of English fiction, demonizing any resistance beyond respectful persuasion. In spite of its claims to have been drafted before 1930 it seems purposefully to reject and reverse all the self-descriptive and often consciously resistant features of Welsh industrial writing from Rhys Davies to Lewis Jones. Llewellyn's novel and its massive success remain a powerful testimony to the forces at work against the authentic, if varied, voice of the colonized and the way in which part of the hybridity of colonial culture is that a substantial and favoured part of it will be complicit with the interests of the colonizers. Llewellyn was not the last to write about the coalfield – Gwyn Thomas's major work lay ahead – but by caricaturing and depoliticizing the descriptions of the industrial settlement to such an extent, he created an image of Welsh working-class life which later writers were always going to have to negotiate, and which would dominate the thinking of editors and publishers for some time as an account of industrial Wales.

Changed post-war conditions right across Wales would in time make both rural romance and industrial realism of much reduced interest for both writers and readers, and the separate domains which account for almost all of the first half century of Welsh writing in English would come together, as writers increasingly seek integration between Cymraeg and English traditions in Wales and have a stronger sense of the partially existing and increasingly desirable nature of varied kinds of Welsh independence.

Section 3

Integration and Independence

3.1 TOWARDS INTEGRATION: GLYN JONES, DYLAN THOMAS AND ALUN LEWIS

The romance tradition in Welsh fiction in English, from first-contact tales to love, tension and topography in Powys, was inherently passive, providing accounts of Wales primarily for English readers, though the authors, especially Allen Raine, sometimes located democratic vigour and independent value in characters who were incompletely colonized. The other major early formation, writing the industrial settlement, was less passive, more conscious of the values of its own domain and the vices of its enemies, but it still depended to a considerable degree on sympathetic interests from English readers as well as on realizing systems as foreign to Wales as industrial capitalism and its shadow, leftist critique. Though both these early formations of Welsh fiction in English overlapped substantially in time, they had little to do with each other. Romance was rural, the settlement was industrial; the former was mostly written by women, the latter by men, though Rhys Davies did both, and there was also a tendency, early and late, for settlement literature to slide into a conservative romance of its own kind, as in Joseph Keating and Richard Llewellyn.

The third major movement in Welsh fiction in English, which is still thriving, reduces steadily the reliance on English audiences and publishers and also – just as important – lessens the separation of Wales into areas, genres and mutually ignorant, even hostile, domains of life, work and feeling. This third formation, which is best called integration and independence, is not a simple process, and there are movements back to past patterns, but in general from the Second World War to the present Welsh writers working in English have tended to find ways of integrating Anglicized Wales with aspects of Cymraeg Wales, especially through location, language, cultural history and myth. This has combined with an increasingly independent attitude, a developing sense that they are not working for English tastes at all but for an audience which, while not reading Cymraeg, is nevertheless self-conscious of being Welsh. That kind of emotional independence has been in part aesthetic, empowered by formal moves which broke away from the realist and individualist tradition of English fiction, but it also has been institutional: the authors were often educated at Welsh universities, lived mostly in the country and the new position was increasingly developed through the support of public finances for the arts in Wales.

That combination of integration and independence may sound a positive situation, but a final sequence of this section will deal with modern writers whose sense of independence and interest in a move towards integration with other parts of Wales and their culture derive from and emphasize their sense of having been abandoned by the imperial culture that constructed their world. Without the romantic sentiment of the first period or the self-conscious self-boosting of the second period, modern Welsh writers in English often see images of disability as a focal symbol and in both their artistic vigour and their unrelentingly harsh account of the world about them they express their sense of anger at the colonial forces of many kinds that have led to their exploitation and abandonment: but not yet to their silence or their inability to create potent art as a way of realizing the feelings of a people.

A crucial first step in integration and towards independence was made by Glyn Jones (1905–95). He was born in Merthyr and educated at the Cyfarthfa Castle Grammar school: a whole set of constraining forces are implied in an English-language school in a fake castle built by an industrial baron, and the encounter with them led to Jones's love of English Romantic poetry and the partial loss of his familial Cymraeg. He recovered the language but never forgot his fascination with transcendence: Leslie Norris reports that Jones's 'literary hero was D. H. Lawrence'[1] and in his fiction, more than his poetry, he consistently moves away from social realities towards a high evaluation of the powers of the artist, on an international basis and with recurring elements of his lifelong Christianity.

The move from realism is clear in his earliest book, *The Blue Bed and Other Stories* (1937).[2] The first story is a novella, 'I was born in the

Ystrad Valley'. A collier's son goes to university and returns to Cardiff to teach. Because he could see 'no way in which I was able to lessen the sufferings of my class' (49) he becomes part of a left-wing movement: but this is not Lewis Jones-like political propaganda, it is a surreal fantasy. Revolution breaks out, Cardiff is seized, troops arrive, the central figure escapes into a nightmarish natural world. The initial career is very close to Jones's own – he came back to Cardiff from teacher training at very English Cheltenham – but the novella rejects the political engagement of the settlement writers, even Rhys Davies's lukewarm version, for a quite different domain of value in aesthetic fantasy. The other stories in the volume, mostly, if vaguely, set in Wales, are short realizations of surrealist themes, especially the fine 'Porth y Rhyd' and 'The Blue Bed': the latter being the only one not set in Wales and given by the London publisher special recognition in providing the title of the book. Jones's work was encouraged by that great influencer of contemporary fiction, David Garnett, whose father shaped Geraint Goodwin away from Welsh concerns, and his second volume, *The Water Music and Other Stories*, was well received in 1944. The *New Companion to the Literature of Wales* calls it 'his finest volume',[3] and here all the stories are set in Wales; they move away from surrealism and focus on a boy or girl experiencing events and feelings in environments both industrial, as in 'The Explosion', and rural as in 'Wat Pantathro': Jones's locations themselves express his interest in integrating English and Cymraeg Wales.

A move beyond settlement fiction is clear in the two substantial novels Jones published. In *The Valley, the City, the Village* (1956)[4] he develops a young man's story not towards surreal class war as in the earlier novella but towards another transcendent position, that of art. Trystan Morgan is the son of a schoolteacher but has working-class roots: in one vivid scene he watches his grandmother warm her hands on a bitter day by plunging them in the pigswill. He speaks Cymraeg, but his only interest is to be a painter, not to encourage 'religion, socialism, freedom for Wales' (286). The relative lack of plot relates to Jones's strength as a mood-creating short-story writer, and the book might have been more effective at novella length as it slowly charts Trystan's conversations, partial relationships, eventual failure at university and a final, rural dedication to his art. M. Wynn Thomas has seen a link between Jones's 'Christian moral values' and the Cymraeg tradition led by Waldo Williams and Euros Bowen,[5] but the spiritual element is not as intense as in those writers. The limits of this novel, and those of *The Learning Lark* (1960), an educational satire with a thin plot,[6] are surpassed in Jones's major work, *The Island of Apples*, which he published in 1965, the year he took up his long and busy retirement.[7]

In this novel, as so often in Welsh fiction by male authors, at first we share a young boy's consciousness. But this is to be no plod towards self-knowledge and sensitivity: behind his father's disused factory, Dewi Davies sees in the flooded river the near-drowned body of Karl Anthony. With the initials of King Arthur and an arrival reminiscent of medieval romance, this exotic boy is to pitch the whole story at a level of fantasy. He is daring – he climbs the lofty tower of a ruined viaduct; he is weirdly bold – he may have burnt the headmaster's house; he is also beautiful, with wavy golden hair. To diminutive Dewi, called 'Ginge', for whom a country visit to the family is exotic, this princely figure with his strange European connections, or fantasies, or both, is a revelation: but he is a myth, not a model. When Karl finally joins Dewi at Abergarth (which appears to represent Carmarthen), the police are after him for the headmaster's murder; he steals a boat named 'Tir na n'Og', the Irish otherworld or 'Land of Youth', but as he comes to pick up Dewi, the storm overtakes him and he disappears, like many an early mythic hero, to a mysterious seagoing end. The book enacts, rather than argues for, the value of aesthetic transcendence: what Trystan endlessly discussed, Karl embodies. Glyn Jones creates without embarrassment and with remarkable conviction an image of the visionary possibilities of ordinary life in Wales. Rhys Davies deplored the ugliness of his childhood world; Gwyn Thomas lamented the loss of beauty but could only imagine it ironically; Glyn Jones by taking a firm hold on symbolic narrative, claims aesthetic splendour for Welsh fiction.

His model here is European; Dewi's discoveries do not look towards Welsh tradition, and *The Island of Apples* is, like *The Blue Bed* stories, more a separation from settlement fiction through the instrument of European symbolism than an integration with a wider Welsh world. But Jones did not cut himself off: as Norris notes, he always wrote about Wales and Welsh topics,[8] and M. Wynn Thomas comments that 'the different life of the rural past and of Welsh language culture remains accessible to him'.[9] As well as writing poetry in English, Jones also translated Cymraeg poetry, including the difficult, gnomic 'Llywarch Hen' poems. But he remained close to settlement writers like Jack Jones and Gwyn Thomas, and wrote generously and insightfully about them in *The Dragon Has Two Tongues*.[10] Norris describes Jones as 'a vastly unjudging man' (21) and he worked hard to support other writers and develop the funding of writing in Wales in both languages. This work was as integrationist as his writing itself, and his consistent pressure to link the rural and the industrial worlds is an important move away from the self-defining topographic delimitations of most settlement writing. A wider Wales is often the scene for his writing: in *The Valley, The City, the Village* the places cover all of Wales – the city is apparently in the north, and the village is in the south-west. In his languages, his sympathies and his themes Glyn Jones was not restricted to the industrial settlement of his upbringing, and his instincts for the broad possibilities of Welsh fiction in English were to be developed in many of the writers that, even in great age, he applauded and supported.

It is striking to compare Glyn Jones's career with that of his friend Dylan Thomas (1914–53): the latter is remembered vividly as a great master of almost bardic poetry in English, and also as a recorder of south Welsh folly – equally acceptable in England. He did, however, have another, forgotten identity, as writer of powerful, serious non-realist prose: Walford Davies calls his early stories 'demonic'[11] and they are a sort of Welsh gothic deriving in large part from Poe, the French romantics and the more modern surrealists, but also seeming like a much stronger version of Rhys Davies's darker stories, and themselves a strong influence on the early Glyn Jones's stories. In 1939 Dent, who were to do so well with his work, published *A Map of Love*:[12] it included a number of the famous poems, but more than half was prose. From very young Thomas had been producing dark fantasies, superbly written, dealing in the same imagery of passion, obsession and the interchange of physical and spiritual values that dominate the early poetry: both Walford Davies and Leslie Norris have provided valuable introductions to these stories.[13]

In 1934 Thomas wrote to Pamela Hansford Johnson about working on his 'novel of the Jarvis valley',[14] and many of the dozen or so pieces published separately in the mid 1930s are located in a 'Jarvis valley' which is, from the occasional names of people rather than any specific localization, clearly in Wales. Some, like 'The Tree' are primarily, though very freely, religious, others, like 'The Horse's Ha', read like a surreal version of Caradoc Evans's rural darkness. They range from savage, like 'The Burning Baby' (which seems to be inspired by Dr William Price), to austerely surreal like 'The Mouse and the Woman'. Thomas evidently offered a collection of sixteen of these stories to Dent under the title 'The Burning Baby', but Richard Church, the firm's reader, judged some to be 'obscene',[15] and those chosen for *The Map of Love* are the least powerful. Church also recommended that Thomas should write about his youth in Wales, and it is clear that he did so from the stories that, starting with 'The Peaches', first appeared in collected form in *A Portrait of the Artist as a Young Dog* (1940).[16] No doubt Church was confirmed in his view that Welsh writing should be child-based and sentimental by the fact that *How Green Was My Valley* had appeared soon after *A Map of Love*. It seems clear that, like Gwyn Thomas with *Sorrow for Thy Sons*, what a Welsh prose writer chose to produce was not smiled on by a London publisher, and a career was changed as a result. Thomas's prose grew lighter in tone, ending with comic colonial entertainments like 'A Story' in which the south Welsh industrial world is reduced to a sort of black and white minstrel show for an English radio audience. In 'The Burning Baby' Thomas writes of 'the sourfaced woman Llareggub who had taught him the terrors of the flesh' (25), but this ironical name will become the setting for his major piece of harmless Welsh whimsy, *Under Milk Wood*.

Thomas's 'Jarvis' stories and their like are, and deserve to be better known as, a powerful Welsh version of literary modernism, a projection of D. H. Lawrence's interest in a sentient world in a more rigorous and indeed Rimbaud-like form. If not themselves positively a way of writing Wales in English, it is nevertheless clear that their suppression (and Church's influence, at a time when Thomas was newly married and eager for good commissions, is nothing less than that) was based on a colonially inspired view of what was interesting from Wales – naive entertainment. It is clear from reading the wealth and richness of these stories that Dylan Thomas was potentially a major prose writer as well as a great poet, but the complex and often negative relations with England and its publishing market put an end to such a development.

Not all Glyn Jones's contemporaries enjoyed so long and fulfilled a career. Alun Lewis died in Burma in 1944 but had already created a major reputation as a war poet and received substantial success with short stories. He would undoubtedly have had to negotiate the pressures of London publishing, but his real commitment to Welsh themes, on a much more serious and socially attuned level than Dylan Thomas, and his remarkable versatility promise that he would have brought both international and Wales-wide interests to his writing and would have been an absolutely major figure in the decades after the war.

Born in 1915 at Cwmaman, near Aberdare, the son of two school-teachers, Lewis was educated on a scholarship towards being a member of the colonial elite at Cowbridge Grammar, studied history at Aberystwyth and went on to research at Manchester University – he published several academic papers in his field. This trajectory towards colonial respectability was disrupted by his strong literary instincts, in part towards a reflective poetry strongly imbued with a sense of social responsibility, as in his famous poem 'The Mountain over Aberdare', but also towards fiction. His first collection, *The Last Inspection* (1942),[17] combines stories of army life with others set in pre-war Wales, among them a story ironizing the first-contact romance tradition, 'The Wanderer', dealing with a gypsy, a family, and an onion-seller in west Wales. There are briefer sketches of a man and a girl on a train ('The Lapse'), some boys on a railway bridge reflecting on a funeral ('Interruption'), and, the most searching of all, 'The Housekeeper', taking the viewpoint of the wife of a man on the dole.

The stories indicate that Lewis was interested in both the industrial world and the wider world of Wales. The novel he drafted before the war, 'Morlais', is described by John Pikoulis in his biography as synthesizing 'the industrial novel and intellectual-aesthetic novel'.[18] The young hero, a sensitive boy (called by another version of Dylan Thomas's second name, Marlais), is separated from his original environment, yet remains attached to it. A second, uncompleted novel, 'The Wanderer', takes its hero on to academic research in London. Writing later from India, Lewis confirmed his commitment to his origins, not to the several paths of escape that were offered to him, saying in a letter to his parents: 'When I come home I shall always tackle my writing through Welsh life and ways of thought; it's my only way.'[19]

By disposition anti-war, but, unlike Glyn Jones and several other major writers of Wales at this time, not quite willing to register as a conscientious objector, Lewis volunteered as a docker, drifted into the army and – his education coming out – became an officer in the South Wales Borderers. His best-known stories from the period deal with military life, and the Welsh experience is part of his material: the *New Companion* notes that 'Welsh characters, portrayed sympathetically, figure prominently throughout the book' (424). 'Private Jones' deals with a Welsh peasant at war making friends with an anarchist from the valleys. Pikoulis describes this as 'probably his most neglected story' (146), and its coupling of two regions of Wales normally separated in fiction is a key sign of the way in which Lewis, like Glyn Jones, seeks to speak of Wales more widely than had been usual. In other stories the Welsh are depicted without being quaint or sentimental – the soldier who sings in memory of his wife in 'Ballerina', the simple Taffy Thomas who finds his wife dead in the Swansea bombing in 'Acting Captain', and the same heroic figure in the much-admired story of soldierly stoicism that concludes the volume, 'They Came'. This story ends with Taffy making a commitment that seems Lewis's own: ' "My life belongs to the world," he said, "I will do what I can." ' (213) Even closer to the author himself is the officer who visits his pregnant wife in 'the enfolding mountains of Mid-Glamorgan' (63) in 'It's a Long Way to Go'.

These stories all come from *The Last Inspection*. Lewis's later and more famous stories, posthumously published as *In the Green Tree* (1948), are set in India where the army took him. Reference to Wales is rarer, and can seem sentimental, as in 'Night Journey' where on a remembered British train journey 'The Welsh soldiers were singing their national anthem in harmony, softly and most tenderly' (24). But it is also at this time that Lewis wrote to his parents about Welsh themes and, even more revealingly, said 'I regret my lack of Welsh very deeply. I really will learn it when I come home again' (51). Tony Brown and M. Wynn Thomas argue that in India Lewis was 'made powerfully aware of the predominantly English imperial character of this British-ness'.[20] In the major story 'The Orange Grove', the officer-narrator first loses his driver – apparently Welsh – murdered by native rebels, and then, escorting his body, finds himself stripped of English authority and merging with Indian gypsies whom he finally feels to be in some way like his own ancestors, the nomadic Celts: a sense of integrational independence permeates this fine story.

Recognized as a new poet of real importance, strongly committed to a life of writing, with fiction a major element in his own ambition, Lewis seems to be constructing his own version of transcendence, one more strongly rooted in Wales than Glyn Jones's and more politically radicalized than Rhys Davies's mystical values of Welshness. But there the story tragically ends, with his own enigmatic death, either a weird accident or an equally strange suicide, and no more came from this superbly gifted young writer, committed to realizing in both fiction and poetry a Wales wider than had seemed possible for earlier writers.

That ideal was to be pursued and to a substantial degree achieved by at least one of the successors to Jones and Lewis, Emyr Humphreys, but there were also some writers who reworked familiar forms of Welsh fiction to suggest ways of integration which were closer to home than Jones's aestheticism or what seems to have been Lewis's movement towards an epic stage for his Welsh fiction. These writers' rejection of traditional romance and equally traditional industrial realism played some part in elaborating the range of Welsh fiction in English towards integration and independence.

3.2 ECLECTIC INTEGRATION: MICHAEL GARETH LLEWELYN AND MENNA GALLIE

A Cambridge-educated army officer who was Director of Education in Kent seems an unlikely candidate for writing integrative Welsh fiction, but Frederic Evans (1888–1958) was born in Llangynwyd, Glamorgan, the son of a blacksmith who was also a local historian and antiquary. After rising to be a lieutenant-colonel in the First World War, Evans became a schools inspector in Glamorgan, then left Wales. But he revisited the country in fiction under the pseudonym Michael Gareth Llewelyn, with a name and a writing style apparently owing something to the author of *How Green Was My Valley*, and his work had real success in the post-war years. The first book, *Sand in the Glass* (1943),[21] is an autobiography that also includes a range of native material, including the story of Twm Siôn Cati, and his first novel, *Angharad's Isle* (1944),[22] like a rambling and highly coloured version of Rhys Davies's *Honey and Bread,* tells how the Maesteg region slowly and then drastically became industrialized in the first half of the nineteenth century. The speaker's father is a harpist, there is a strong sense of *gwerin* values – 'the ancient instincts and sense of the worth of real things' (23) – but this is an idea-based story: Iolo Morganwg, the re-imaginer of Welsh tradition, appears in the action, and Tom Paine, the early socialist, is also discussed. Evans leaves little out that belongs to Welsh tradition, rural or industrial – education, fighting, singing, and radicalism are all here.

The style can at times seem self-parodic, especially in the insistence on syntactical reversals to resemble Welsh speech as in 'Wrote my father a letter to say . . .' (106), and the novel becomes a picaresque ramble – the hero fights alongside Dic Penderyn at Waterloo as well as meeting Mrs Siddons. The effect is to combine romance and radicalism in almost equal proportions and also mould a distinctly Cymraeg cultural context into the origins of the industrial world of south Wales. Those inherently integrative elements are better controlled in Llewelyn's best-known book *The Aleppo Merchant* (1945).[23] The title is the name of a rural pub, though there are mines nearby, and the central figure's brother will die in the Gresford explosion of 1936. Other Welsh traditions are evoked in Rhys Ffeiriad, an unfrocked Anglican rector who is the intelligence of the story, and Shaci, the crippled boy whose education and development as a writer, mentored by the ex-priest, is the core of the story. Once again fragments are gathered – the story of Llyn y Fan Fach is retold by Rhys (also used by Hilda Vaughan's *The Fair Woman* published in America three years before),[24] there is a rugby player and a union official among Shaci's brothers, and the young women range from a dark native beauty to an English lady who, improbably, loves the left-wing brother: he gives her a corgi called Taffy.

This mix of motifs could as easily be described as touristic as integrative, and Evans certainly had an English audience in mind – the novel ends in wartime with King Arthur appearing to Shaci to report that 'in the people of Britain we live again' (211). But unlike Richard Llewellyn, the author does not seem to betray the traditions he transmits but rather seems, sometimes clumsily but with real enthusiasm, to be asserting the equal relevance of Cymraeg tradition and the developed values and practices of the industrial settlement: the *New Companion* appears a little austere in calling Llewelyn 'sometimes crudely didactic' (232). At the end of the more tonally and structurally uniform *To Fame Unknown* (1949)[25] (perhaps better organized because it deals with the school life the author knew so well), Mark Beynon, an unemployed unionist miner and older brother to Shoni, the focus of the novel, marries Blodwen, a hard-working schoolteacher and enthusiast for the Cymraeg language; in his own person and family Mark shapes a literal integration of the two elements of Welsh tradition that so often had seemed so strongly separate.

More subtly integrative, and also having wider connections with later women's writing, is the work of Menna Gallie (1920–90). Born at Ystradgynlais in the largely Welsh-speaking coal-mining Tawe valley, after university education at Swansea she travelled widely and lived around Britain with her academic husband. A fluent, witty and always imaginative writer, she was published by Gollancz along with Gwyn Thomas, but her work is both more realist and more open to Cymraeg influence than he could countenance, and it is clear that she is consciously turning away from the genre of valley political realism, however radical and indeed moving her stories can be. Her first novel, *Strike for a Kingdom* (1959),[26] deals with the period of the General Strike in 1926, yet it is in generic form a mystery about two deaths in a mining village in that famously fine summer. In Cilhendre, a fictional mining village on the upper Tawe, the pit manager is found dead. He is called Nixon – in 1959 the name of the already widely despised American vice-president. Expected sympathies are expressed for miners – 'poor devils living a raw deal' (20) – and the area is seen as having been 'raped by the mine-owners' (30). But such sombre treatment is by no means all that Gallie has in mind: there is a hilarious village carnival and many vivid, comic sequences of women's interactive dialogue.

The sense that a world of life and feeling, especially women's feeling, needs to be integrated with the serious business of industrial politics is generically paralleled by the way the novel tends to move away from the sort of treatment expected of 1926 towards something more like a classic murder mystery – a genre dominated by women writers like Agatha Christie and Dorothy Sayers. The strikers' march in Chapter 8 is interwoven with evidence about the murder and the sequence when the police assault the strikers ends with a woman character thinking about the murder. That generic displacing of male politics is surpassed in its integrative effect by a very striking figure. The local justice of the peace and informal miners' leader is also a poet who, as the men march back from Neath after being briefly arrested, thinks about both Cymraeg poetry and the use of English for reformist purposes. This is all effectively integrative, but his name clinches the point. He is called D. J. Williams, and though he was apparently based upon Gallie's uncle, W. R. Williams, the new initials must be a deliberate reference to the famous writer, originally a collier, who produced the *gwerin* classic *Hen Dŷ Ffarm*[27] and, most significant of all, was one of the three who made the major Nationalist statement by setting fire to the Penyberth bombing school in 1936.

D.J. is the consistent focus of the novel: he traces the double-death mystery to its tragic origin, and as the novel closes he is developing with confidence a poem – undoubtedly a Cymraeg one. In a powerful combination of plot variation and thematic focusing, Gallie brings together the traditions of both her native language and the industrial world in which she grew up. When the Gollancz cover blurb offered the novel as a mystery in the spirit of Gwyn Thomas (they also published Dorothy Sayers), it did not mention the novel's title, probably thinking it a little too political. Gallie, often more subtle than she chose to seem, may well be thinking of a coherent Welsh nation – its own kingdom – that was significantly greater, and more independent, than the principality to which it had under colonial power been reduced.

Jane Aaron finds Gallie's other Welsh-set novel *The Small Mine* (1962) more powerful,[28] because here Gallie emphasizes the gender element that was part of the multiple effect of *Strike for a Kingdom*. Again, mining politics are deferred for a mystery about a death, and again, and more fully, the women's viewpoint is of consistent value – there is no D. J. Williams figure to claim the novel for either masculinity or the Cymraeg world. Having established how the traditional industrial novel can be reshaped in her first novel, Gallie here completed the displacement of industrial politics on gender grounds. But it is also a later politics, and a less fraught one. This novel is unusual in being set under nationalization. The time is the mid-to-late 1950s, the mines are owned by the people, there are German visiting workers and the H-bomb is a major concern. Smart young colliers like Joe Jenkins wear Italian-style suits and go to Spain for their holidays. The plot is simple: Joe, a grammar-school boy and easily able to pass his fireman's exam, leaves a large public colliery to work in a small private drift mine where the fireman, known as Link because of his primeval tendencies, has been sacked. On a Sunday when the mine is not working Link, out of malice, sends a journey of coal-trucks crashing down into it, not knowing that Joe is working inside on his own. This death provides the mystery – though not to the reader.

Gallie emphasizes the demasculinizing of her fiction by making only the children able to work out what has happened: they have spotted Link on his way to the mine, and they even conduct a mock trial, itself an anti-patriarchal activity. As important as the male action and the comedy, of which there is plenty, are three women. Joe's mother Flossie, in her efficiency and focused spirit, as Aaron notes, relates to the usual big sentimental Mam, but becomes 'a living monument to the tragic history of coal-mining';[29] Sall, divorcée, pub-goer and occasional lover to Joe and other men who take advantage of her and, brutally, know her as Sall-Ever-Open-Door; Cynthia, or Cyn, Joe's recognized girlfriend, who reacts to his death with a mixture of sorrow and annoyance, refuses to mourn in the traditional, sentimental way, and says '"I'm alive, Mam, I'm going on, see"' (102) to explain both her impassivity and her decision to leave the district for another job with the Coal Board in England.

Raymond Stephens felt the novel 'never really recovered' after Joe's death, but he missed the point of its rewriting of a masculine mode.[30] In the very first scene Joe's face and body are seen from a stimulated feminine viewpoint; men are not much more than disposable – the villagers think that the old Communist Joe Kremlin has been accidentally burnt on the Guy Fawkes bonfire. Even Cymraeg tradition seems now of reduced interest – the children throw an old wooden bardic chair on the same fire. Masculine conflict and masculine disregard of women are major themes in the novel, and Aaron argues that it expresses through Cynthia's final departure Gallie's own sense of her need to leave a constraining environment where women are themselves colonized.[31] That is also a possible way of reading Gallie's other Welsh-connected novel, *Man's Desiring* (1960).[32] In spite of the religious connotation of the title, all the young male hero desires is not Jesu but a successful job in an English university. Close to plotless but sharply, often amusingly, written, the novel locates a clever but naive young Welshman close to a wiser English woman and the two characters together shape something like the Gallie of her later satirical books, who has moved away from Welsh issues, though still writing with wit and a strong sense of a woman's role in the modern world. Always lively, always bringing something new to the patterns of Welsh writing, Gallie has been unduly ignored in recent decades but, now in reprint by Honno, is winning new admirers for her modestly subtle and clearly independent voice.

3.3 A WIDER WALES: EMYR HUMPHREYS

Emyr Humphreys (b. 1919) was part of the new generation who were university educated and committed to Wales. His writing, like theirs, broke with the patterns of the past, but he substantially widened their impact as forces for integration and independence in Welsh writing in English. He must, in terms of productivity, seriousness and versatility rank as the major Welsh novelist writing in English, the only one whose effort, quality and dedication to writing about his country could place him in the Nobel-winning class. He first published in London and twice won establishment literary prizes in England, the Somerset Maugham Award for *Hear and Forgive* in 1952 and the Hawthornden Prize for *A Toy Epic* in 1958, but that success did not prevent him returning with energy and great success to his original chosen role as a 'serious Welsh novelist'.[33]

The first element in Humphreys's widening of Welsh fiction is his birthplace: he comes from Flintshire in north-east Wales, where a smaller version of the southern industrial area is very close, as are English-orientated seaside resorts and also the mountainous Cymraeg-speaking heartland. Humphreys's own *bro* is in itself an epitome of the whole of varied Wales and its closeness to England: as a child he could see from a hilltop both Liverpool and Snowdonia.[34] Born in the seaside town of Prestatyn and brought up in more rural Trelawnyd (Newmarket), where his father was head of an Anglican church school, Humphreys went to Aberystwyth to study history and English. In a curricular version of his developing politics, he disliked the Anglo-Saxon element of English literature and (like Alun Lewis a little before) concentrated on history. But he also moved politically deeper into Wales: he was strongly influenced by the growing Nationalist movement at Aberystwyth and he learned the Cymraeg that had become disused in his family. The influence of Saunders Lewis and the impact and implications of Penyberth were strong – the latter has been called 'a conversion experience' for Humphreys.[35] His response was not a simply nationalistic one, but typically complex. He considered training for the Anglican ministry, as if continuing his father's inherently imperial connection, but when war broke out he registered as a conscientious objector. Here too his experience was multiple: for the first four years he worked on farms in Pembrokeshire and Caernarfonshire, and, then, moving physically in the sort of way that Glyn Jones had done artistically, went to London and southern Europe working with the Save the Children Fund, also having strong contacts with the Quaker Ambulance Unit. But while he was still abroad, his marriage in 1946 to a Cymraeg-speaking Nonconformist, Elinor Jones, strengthened further his commitment to Wales. After the war he trained and worked as a teacher, became very interested in drama and worked for ten years in the BBC as a radio and then television producer, afterwards lecturing on drama at Bangor.

M. Wynn Thomas has remarked that Humphreys is 'one of the most versatile writers who have ever been produced by Wales'[36] and his great variety of themes and – less often noticed – styles rises from his ability to make use in his writing of his wide range of experience as a developing artist. Characteristically, his earliest work was not the sensitive, even self-indulgent, autobiographical fiction of most male writers, but a more austere and critical treatment of the context, both social and personal, in which he grew up. As Thomas describes in his introduction to the reprint, in 1940 Humphreys drafted what would become *A Toy Epic*.[37] At first it was a novel in verse, and then, in prose, it was sent to a London publisher who had expressed interest. The reader was Graham Greene and he disliked it, saying it was 'badly written, unoriginal, oddly novelettish and pedestrian'. Not surprisingly Humphreys set the novel aside, but returned to it later, after his first successes in London and in 1958 the project was made public as a six-part Cymraeg radio series entitled *Y Tri Llais* (The Three Voices).[38] Then it was published in English, and was welcomed by the English establishment, praised by Lord David Cecil and awarded the Hawthornden prize by the committee he chaired.

This is a strange set of events. One literary authority, a Christian moralist Humphreys admired and, in his non-Catholic way, would attempt to match,[39] rejects the book while another, a Bloomsbury-linked aristocratic aesthete who also represented the conservative Oxbridge tradition with which Humphreys had nothing in common, admires it devotedly. Thinking post-colonially can help to explain the situation. The terms in which Greene dismisses the book – 'badly written, unoriginal, novelettish and pedestrian' – seem to assume, via their reverses, that a Welsh novel should be like *How Green Was My Valley,* flamboyant in writing, unusual, epic and romantic. Humphreys was in fact very conscious of not writing in the valley mode, but working more closely to a native tradition. He discussed this in a radio interview, and gave two reasons: one is negative, avoiding what he calls 'the golden endless eloquence of the south Walians', the other positive, 'partially reflecting the great glories of the epigrammatically terse Welsh poetic tradition'.[40] This self-positioning might have helped the success of the book in England when it was later published, as will be discussed below.

But Humphreys was not deterred from his purpose by the rejection. By 1944 he had drafted *The Little Kingdom* (1946). Less ambitious than *A Toy Epic*, this can also be read – wrongly – as less pro-Welsh because of its searching critique of violent nationalism, and that might explain its acceptance by the publisher who rejected *A Toy Epic*. A bullying, English-oriented property owner and businessman plans to sell land to the war ministry for a new airfield in Flint. A road to his own colliery will be a valuable result. His nephew Owen Richards, son of a history lecturer at Aberystwyth and being educated in England, has become a nationalist and is opposed to the project. It sounds as if this will be a heart-warming nationalist and autobiographical drama, but Humphreys is more rigorous than that and tends to explore coldly all forms of enthusiasm, especially those that promote self-centred sentimentality. Owen is outraged when the Plaid committee reject the airfield protest as relatively unimportant; he manipulates people, exploits women, including sexually, and claims that 'I believe I am the spirit of Wales' (43).

Not satisfied with such limited satire, Humphreys criticizes a nationalist use of physical violence (he was a conscientious objector to war, it should be remembered), and shows how the pacifist spirit of Penyberth can be profaned. Owen murders his uncle and, in his attempt to destroy the airfield, is himself shot dead. A short book, without the changes of pace and descriptive colour that will empower Humphrey's best work, this is nevertheless an important statement of his seriousness and his insistence on writing for more than one faction in Wales. Owen is one of Humphreys's many false prophets, and other motifs recurrent in his work appear. Owen's friend Geraint is a self-concerned artist, the local MP represents 'opportunism linked with platitudinous idealism' (38), and the town subject to Humphreys's 'twin plagues of secularization and Anglicization'[41] first appears, named Llanelw (church of profit).

In the following years Humphreys operated basically as what Ioan Williams calls 'an English novelist'.[42] In *The Voice of a Stranger* (1949) he includes a conscientious objector from north Wales, who feels he has betrayed his wife, in an Italian-set political narrative, and in *A Change of Heart* (1951) an academic leaves Aberystwyth for England after he is betrayed by a friend. In *Hear and Forgive* (1952)[43] a teacher finally returns to his wife in the English countryside. Separation, betrayal, alienation recur in these novels, seeming to consider Humphreys's own position in addition to the emphasis on personal moral responsibility, which he stressed in his well-known essay on 'The Protestant Novel'.[44] The work from this period has a crisp, condensed strength, especially as Humphreys shows his drama-oriented powers in self-revealing dialogue and rapid switching of action, as well as his mastery of the unreliable hero, but the lack of a social and political edge – especially a Welsh one – to these narratives relates to the individually focused narrowness of the traditional English novel.

But the 'serious Welsh novelist' was not so easily distracted from his purpose: after what Brown and Thomas call 'the first phase' of

Humphreys's work, he set his first major novel in Wales, *A Man's Estate* (1955).[45] Betrayal and alienation remain the major themes, but the setting focuses a new political resonance. Somewhat overlooked, probably because of the range and depth of Humphreys's later work, though the *New Companion* identifies it as 'the most masterly of the early novels' (273), this is a book of great confidence, skill and power, both a cross-section of a contemporary social world and also an exploration of the strengths, weaknesses and uncertainties of the world in which Humphreys grew up. Reviewers were struck by the novel's form: it is told from switching viewpoints so that the 'truth' behind the narrative is only available to an analytic reader. Commentators both contemporary and more recent[46] have felt this was like William Faulkner, and there is every reason why Humphreys should have had in mind the master of complex, dark and localized fables, but the multiple narration that points to an interpretable reality is a basic of dramatic form. A novelist influenced by theatre like Wilkie Collins had done much the same long ago in *The Moonstone* and *The Woman in White* and Humphreys's own interest in drama is also a likely source of the novel's mobility of viewpoint. But he also looks in another direction: his plot brings an observer – objective for all his discoverable connections – to identify just what crimes have been committed in his own family. As Joyce drew on classical myth in the underlying shape of *Ulysses*, so this novel is consciously based on Aeschylus's tragic fable of Orestes returning to find out his mother's murderous crime; Humphreys himself has clarified the connection.[47]

These complexities mesh with a vigorous realism that tells from varied viewpoints how Philip Esmor-Elis, an academic scientist from Cambridge, banished from the home of the landowning Cymraeg-speaking Elis family and brought up by his father's mistress Gwendoline Esmor, visits in quest of what he thinks might be his inheritance. His father, a Liberal MP, died at the age of forty before Philip's birth and his mother, traumatized by her husband's infidelities and, as it finally appears, her own role in hastening his death, sent the child away. His full sister Hannah lives on in the bleak family home: she aspired to be a doctor, but her health, and it seems her gender, restricted her to being a pharmacist. She is Humphreys's first major Welsh woman character, and her life is drastically constrained. This family, blighted by dissemination, physical and spiritual, also lost in the war Dic, the son of the mother and the stepfather.

All these events focus on a bleak mansion called 'Y Glyn'. Nearby is a small town called Pennant (a name remembering the lordly landowner who precipated the disastrous slate-miners' strikes), and there the extended Evans family operate. Winnie Evans, formerly a servant of the Elises, had a daughter by the MP: Ada is beautiful and strong-willed, a vigorous social hybrid. The obsessively moral Nonconformist minister, Idris Powell, loves her, and the town doctor lends her money: both receive some limited sexual returns. Philip Esmor-Elis and Ada Evans are both outcasts and while she will battle on, he will almost certainly go to Switzerland for work, having been rejected by both Cambridge and the daughter of his bullying college principal. Like *The Little Kingdom*, this account of the forces at work in Wales and on the Welsh people is ultimately a dark one. The gentry exhibit a decayed savagery, with a murderously deranged mother, a physically ruined religiose stepfather and a harrowingly lonely figure in Hannah. The lower orders are no better: Ada is fiercely ambitious and the garage-owner Wally Francis is a crass beast.

This is a non-industrial north Welsh story and it operates as Humphreys's powerful rejection of all traces of rural romance. Yet, in several senses, the novel is wider in its dealings than other Welsh non-industrial fiction. One is in its class range: where Goodwin, Vaughan and Evans represented a weakened gentry and a set of lower-class caricatures, Humphreys delineates all of them democratically, comprehendingly, and unflinchingly. Another extension of the Welsh romance is the concern with religion. As Brown and Thomas comment, this is the 'first substantial instance of his ambivalent treatment of one of [Humphreys's] most important subjects: the cultural (and psychological) legacy of Welsh religious Non-conformity'.[48] A further widening of the novel is as a critique of the exhaustion of Welsh tradition in the Liberal Nonconformist culture. Wally's real name is Cadwaladr, but it means nothing to him; similarly the Elises are chapel stalwarts and communal activists, but all for a bleak self-interest that has destroyed their own various children. Except Ada: Humphreys seems to have some sense of faint hope, like Lawrence, or perhaps more relevantly like Rhys Davies, in the vigour of the unconventional female. The title *A Man's Estate* is ironic in its reference to Philip's fantasy of inheritance as well as its reference to the male condition: but it also by negation suggests that only Hannah has the moral and Ada the physical energy to be inheritor of all that has been wasted in this vividly realized, dishearteningly degenerate world of Wales.

The focused power of *A Man's Estate* might have suggested for its author a career of brilliance and negativity, like that of his English contemporaries Anthony Burgess and Kingsley Amis and his Welsh gentry contemporary Anthony Powell. But he turned back to his own resources, and published *A Toy Epic* eighteen years after it was started. The original rejected draft was twice the length of the published version; it took the story of the three boys on until they were about the age of Humphreys as he was writing. One of the three extensions, 'Michael', has been published as an appendix to the reprint edition: the others remain in manuscript. In its shortened form, *A Toy Epic* was recognized by the English establishment, personified by Lord David Cecil, as fine writing and there may be special reasons for this, themselves implicitly colonial. The reduction of the text to the boys' school lives makes it more acceptable as a novel of troubled childhood: the omitted sequences which project the three into the strains and commitments of adult life, including for Michael nationalism, might have seemed uncomfortably close to political analysis. Another feature which may have given the book appeal in England is the sceptical tone in which Humphreys treats the Welsh positions he explores. Albie, the aspirational son of a Flint-shire bus-driver clearly represents the Welsh working class, including those from the south, especially in the year of 1926 when the novel is set, but his early academic promise is mysteriously dulled and he becomes a surprisingly recessive character who finally suits the servile-seeming banal first name he is given (even more emphatic when he was originally called Alfie). In spite of Michael's apparently central role, his own focal interest in nationalism is shown to be in large part bound up with his peacocking personality, an enlargement of Stephen Daedalus in Joyce's *Portrait of the Artist as a Young Man*. The only aspect of Welsh identity that seems uncriticized, though also limited, is Iorwerth as a character of native value, where the values of farm, chapel and language converge in the sort of figure that in the post-war period other Welsh novelists like Richard Vaughan were peddling with great success (see p. 168).

While from a Welsh point of view the novel is searching, especially about Michael, and negatively about Albie, it is not hard to see how its combination of character-based insight and literary experimentation (it deploys the separate narratives of Virginia Woolf's *The Waves*) and a distinctly reserved commitment to anything anti-English (for the best of self-critical reasons on Humphreys's part) might have made it a success in the English market. *A Toy Epic* remains a very impressive first novel; but in the combined analytic power of *The Little Kingdom* and, especially, *A Man's Estate* Humphreys had moved on by the late 1950s – and was to move much further.

Humphreys's major work, and by widespread agreement the most important single piece of Welsh fiction in English from the twentieth century, is *Outside the House of Baal* (1965).[49] At once both deliberately modest in tone and also immensely ambitious, the novel has a double time-scheme. In ten of its chapters it relates the banal domestic activities of J.T. Miles, a retired Calvinistic Methodist minister and his sister-in-law Kate Bannister: they share her house in an Anglicized north Wales seaside resort. In the present they complete domestic tasks – mostly Kate, and they have a number of conversations with their neighbours – mostly J.T. But the sixteen other chapters[50] explore the lives of the main characters, their families, friends and even enemies over the whole of their long lives. The structure obviously owes a debt to the world of European culture embedded in one Dublin day found in *Ulysses*. Jeremy Hooker has discussed the reuse of Joyce's stylistic and semantic methods, including 'verbal deliberation' and 'above all in his authorial invisibility, whereby epiphany replaces comment, and pointed word the art of pointing'.[51] Just as Virgil in his *Aeneid* deliberately offered half of the number of books found in his model, Homer's *Odyssey*, so Humphreys covers only half a day, apparently in respectful honour of Joyce's masterpiece.

J.T. – as a boy called Joe – is a classic *gwerin* figure who has survived into the baffling 1960s. Humphreys based him on his own father-in-law who also had a rural childhood, trained as a blacksmith, then educated himself into being a Nonconformist minister, and who was living with Humphreys and his family in a very Anglicized south Wales town, Penarth.[52] Even in that bland setting there were resonances: the Humphreys family lived in one of the few old farmhouses now swamped by the bourgeois villas of this Cardiff dormitory, and the house was named, in memory of the initiating moment of Welsh nationalism, Penyberth.[53] History and politics permeate the text and the human decisions that, still at heart a 'Protestant novelist', Humphreys stresses: whereas Joyce concentrated on the human subconscious in the context of European culture, Humphreys, as M. Wynn Thomas notes, 'keeps emphasising the part (ambiguous enough at times) that rational thought plays in the existence of each one of us'.[54] The novel traces the intersection of human decision-making and the sociohistorical environment over half a century, across the whole face of Wales, through many momentous and dismaying changes and through the efforts by the characters to organize both their own lives and the world in which they live.

It is possible to see the novel's meaning as separating into the intellectual role of J.T. and the physical role of Kate, as 'head and hands',[55] but Kate is also the last representative of the landed north Welsh, not unlike Hannah in *A Man's Estate*, and this connection is freighted with allegorical significance. At the opening of the novel her family owns a rich farm called 'Argoed'. This is the surviving part of a great landed estate that passes, through the early death of a crippled heir into the hands of the Roman Catholic church – both a symbol of decline and also, it seems, a rejection of the turn towards Catholicism of Saunders Lewis: for Humphreys, no hero goes without critical scrutiny. The name of the farm is richly suggestive: one of the major works of the Cymraeg literary renaissance of the early twentieth century, was T. Gwynn Jones's poem *Argoed*, written in 1926–7,which used the name for a forest in Roman Gaul as a symbol of the mythical resources on which the British Celt could draw for sustenance in difficult times. That idea itself seems ironically, even tragically, treated as the rich farm, once sustaining a large wealthy family, is itself lost through the casual self-indulgence of the father, through the loss in war of Griff, the most energetic son, and through the absorption into commercial concerns of Dan Llew, the eldest son who eventually sells the farm. In the time of the modern story he wanders both through the streets and in his mind across time: he lives in an ugly modern bungalow bitterly named 'Argoed'.

If Kate and her family represent the decline of the Liberal ascendancy, J.T. personifies the energies of the Nonconformist peas- antry who rose from difficult circumstances – his father was an alcoholic schoolteacher who committed suicide and he became a blacksmith. His own probity led him to oppose the First World War, causing him to be beaten up by war-lovers at an eisteddfod and to lose a comfortable ministry. He is always a seeker after a morally just order, however difficult that is personally or socially. Deeply involved in the peace movement in the 1930s, he sympathizes strongly with the striking miners in his south Welsh chapel. By moving J.T. to the south Humphreys makes a major step in combining the issues that he knows so well from north Wales with the very different concerns of the southern coalfield, and so brings the voice of Nonconformist con- science to the industrial settlement – a voice rarely heard among the southern writers except for the young preacher in Jack Jones's *Rhondda Roundabout* and the heroic but eventually defeated Mr Gruffydd in *How Green Was My Valley*. The southern material is not treated at

great length, but the striking thing is that it is treated at all: in Kate
Roberts's *Traed Mewn Cyffion*, although Wiliam goes to the south and
the author was living there when she wrote the book, the focus
remained entirely on the north, and a similar separation between the
two major parts of Wales was observed by the industrial writers even
when (as occasionally happens in Gwyn Thomas) a character comes
from or goes to the north.

But in spite of his all-Wales experience and his evident moral probity,
J.T. is by no means an idealized figure: the opening words of the novel
present him in saintly terms, with a 'venerable head' and a 'halo of
white hair' (5), but this is an ironic representation. His critics in the
novel see him 'self-indulgently to avoid seeing people and situations as
they really are' (133): his wife Lydia, Kate's sister, eventually finds him
selfish in his moral commitment to others rather than his family and his
son Ronnie sees him as living sentimentally in the past. These may well
be self-centred criticisms, but, as M. Wynn Thomas comments, the
novel as a whole leaves it uncertain whether J.T. is 'a charismatic
visionary or a narcissistic bigot'.[56] As with Michael Edwards and Owen
Richards of the earlier Welsh-set novels, the fact that the author shares
some of their positions does not free the characters from his searching
interrogation of their probity.

J.T. is generally valued as a figure of responsible concern for his
fellow humans. He is not unlike Joyce's Leopold Bloom in his
blundering attempts to do good, but he is also constructed as an
archetypal figure: Humphreys has used material from the archives of
Thomas Williams (Tom Nefyn), who was, like J.T., at the Dardanelles
and sought to 'preach a new social gospel' and also George M. Ll.
Davies, a conscientious objector and leader of the Peace Pledge
Union.[57] J.T. represents for Humphreys the continued life through the
pre-war period of the authentic, often uncomfortable, genuinely
protesting voice. With all J.T.'s limitations, he is still predominantly a
positive figure: M. Wynn Thomas describes him as 'hen weinidog
mwyn' (a gentle old minister).[58] As this comment implies, J.T.'s voice is
also authentically Welsh and indeed, though transmitted through the
English language, it is Cymraeg. In his foreword to this novel
Humphreys has written about his decision to write in English. Where
his great contemporary R. S. Thomas often stated that his native
language, English, was the only one in which he felt confident to write
poetry, in spite of his fluent spoken and written Cymraeg, Humphreys
was competent to write Cymraeg, as *Y Tri Llais* shows, but he chose to

write in English, as he says in his preface to *Outside the House of Baal*, partly because of 'the absence of a developed modern tradition in the Welsh language' but also 'to give a wider public a better appreciation of the Welsh experience of the transformations of the twentieth century'.[59]

His choice of the more widely distributed of the two languages of Wales for his fiction is related to his choice of a style. Humphreys is capable of rich stylistic variety, as is clear from his scintillating novel *Jones* (1984),[60] but except for occasional characterization he usually chooses a neutral style. As Brown and Thomas comment:

> He adopted a minimalist style, in an attempt to minimize the power of English to distort Welsh experience, and as a conscious corrective to the flamboyant wordiness that seemed to him to characterize some anglophone Welsh writing.[61]

Humphreys's unmarked style implies that there is nothing at all strange or unnatural about speaking Cymraeg in this country, nor indeed in representing it in English. The integration of the native tradition and the English language is in Humphreys linguistically conveyed, and this validates the insistence that the local, social and moral dilemmas of this part of the world are worth the artistic power and lavish detail that has been given to them in this magnificently detailed and powerfully structured novel.

For all its critique of the debilitation of the natural leaders of the past, both landowning gentry and Nonconformist gurus, and its less emphatic sense that the equally valid labour politics of the south have also nurtured doubtful motives, *Outside the House of Baal* is a searching rejection of the colonial impact of English rule on Wales. The wretched banalities of modern capitalism are epitomized in the huge new pub that overshadows the house where Kate and J.T. live: 'Behold thy gods, O Israel' says J.T. (62). Like Twm in *Traed Mewn Cyffion*, Griff, the finest of this novel's generation, dies in a war in which Wales was involved through its colonized status; J.T. sees imperial folly at first hand in the Dardanelles; and the vividly realized scenes in London under flying-bomb attack in the Second World War continue this theme of enforced vulnerability. J.T.'s children are alienated from Wales in ways that Humphreys had himself experienced and rejected: Ronnie, the older son, becomes a professor of sociology in an English university (a multiplicity of negatives for Humphreys) and has only contempt for his father's Cymraeg language and Welsh values. Thea, the daughter of Lydia and J.T., uses her charm and talent to pursue a trivial acting career around Europe, another field that Humphreys knew well.

Those seem to be bleak positions for a Welsh voice, and the novel has charted many lost hopes and misguided attempts at recovery: Thomas comments that 'Humphreys believes that Wales in the thirties was a country brimming with superstitious, erroneous dreams.'[62] There is, though, a trace of a positive dream in the novel: at the end, in order to attend a funeral, J.T. may take a mystery tour to what in English is called Anglesey, but in his preface Humphreys suggests a mystical interpretation of this possible departure for 'Fôn dirion dir', that is 'Mona (=Anglesey) the gentle land', suggesting it is an Argoed-like repository of dreams of the Cymraeg past.[63] But a stronger hold on the modern positive is embodied in the sense of survival in the book: J.T. and Kate are still there, to cherish their memories, preserve their language, talk to a neighbour about Cymraeg poetry, sustain some network of the now diasporic family. They remain outside the house of Baal, keeping, like the author, an anxious faith in Wales and its traditions.

Epic as it is in scope, the novel still has its limits. Kate's own inner life is only suggested. It seems she had a physical passion for J.T. that has always been sublimated, especially through food, as Thomas has suggested.[64] She lost her eye bringing him a meal and one-eyed Kate, an image of the disabled and restricted woman in a still masculine Wales, has also a sense of an inner wisdom that may ultimately be stronger than J.T.'s verbalized and inevitably ego-related concerns. Equally, the ordinary people of Wales are not realized in the novel: those who are all too readily inside the house of Baal, or indeed work on the farms and in the mines.

For all its lasting power, this highly complex, inherently modernist semi-epic was both too technically difficult for a wide audience and also too condensed in scope to have a broad sociohistorical impact. When he returned to chronicling a wider Wales Humphreys adopted a much fuller form and a much simpler fictional technique. Moving away from the condensed brilliance of *Outside the House of Baal* Humphreys devoted himself to a novel sequence able through its considerable size to deal with its multi-period material in a more elaborated way than a single novel would permit.

In 1971 Humphreys published *National Winner*,[65] the start of a saga which was to occupy him for twenty years. The novel itself carries no general title but the dust-jacket announced it as the first in a series to be called 'The Land of the Living'. During the series Humphreys came to prefer 'Bonds of Attachment' as the overall title but he finally opted for 'The Land of the Living', and *Bonds of Attachment* became the title of the seventh book in the series, which appeared in 1991. What *Outside the House of Baal* did through condensation and symbolism, the 'Land of the Living' series works out in steady and lucid detail, relying on events, character and motivation to realize the central themes of choice and responsibility in the context of the history of Wales for most of the twentieth century. Other novelists who have wanted to relate the history and the meaning of the social forces of an extensive period have used this *roman fleuve* form, the novel series flowing through time like a river – Proust, Zola, Balzac, Musil are major examples.

But Humphreys did not, like those others, begin at the beginning and let his story take him where it would. His central characters and themes are established from the start. *National Winner* is set in the 1960s, with some flashbacks, and the five novels that followed it went back in time to elaborate the situation arrived at with the death at the end of *National Winner* of John Cilydd More, poet and pacifist, solicitor and nationalist from north Wales, who is the father, actual or official, of the three boys who recur through the series and is first husband to Amy Parry, the other focal figure. Humphreys is never one for rounded and resounding conclusions, and it appears that the open, enigmatic ending of *National Winner*, with Amy baffled and apparently losing an argument, may have been his planned last word on the social politics and moral enigmas of this complex narrative: 'With nothing more to say, she left them.' (405) Yet time and change prompted Humphreys with more to say, and after the five novels set before *National Winner* were published between 1974 and 1988, he added *Bonds of Attachment* (1991), which took the story beyond the end of *National Winner*, through the events in Wales of the years since then and up to the death of Amy. History, that is, entered the process of producing the novel series, and Humphreys responded to it powerfully in the additional 'final' novel.

National Winner begins retrospectively: Peredur Cilydd More, youngest of the three sons of John and Amy – and in fact their only physically shared child – is in an academic version of the house of Baal, the sociology department of a poor English university. He suffers from low self-esteem and with no special reason (other than interesting a demanding and unstable English girl) he revisits his childhood home on the Llŷn peninsula, and begins to develop an interest in his father's life, especially his mysterious death in 1952. He makes some headway in his quest – it may have been suicide – but none with his job or the girl, and the narrative switches to equally lengthy expositions of his two brothers: the pace here and throughout the series is that of a Victorian extended narrative, slowly developing a climax of personal, moral – and political – conflict. Here it will be how Amy, now the widowed Lady Brangor and owner of a great mansion in north Wales, resists the idea of a monument to Peredur's father and prefers a plan to develop Brangor Hall as a Centre for the Advancement of Women. This scheme is supported reluctantly by the eldest brother Bedwyr, an architect who will be involved in the project, and enthusiastically by the middle brother Gwydion, who sees potential for a major television project which will bring Arthurian tourism to this part of Wales and profit him immensely: he has already been stealing artefacts from the house to fund his own version of the project. As an end to the planned series, this would have left the memory of the austere poet-pacifist uncherished while his survivors are borne by their own self-interest towards the modern mammon of the media and the peddling of Welsh traditions for foreign curiosity. That grimly satirical reading of the Welsh situation in about 1970 is consistent with *Outside the House of Baal*, but more strongly than in that novel it is given mythic resonance through the names of the three young men. Gwydion links the modern electronic media that Humphreys knew so well to the meretricious magician of the *Mabinogi* tale of 'Math fab Mathonwy'; in the novel Math is named, by the modern Gwydion, as 'the first television producer' (175). The lengthy sequence in Italy shows the novel's Gwydion to be just as slippery, projecting in adulthood the lack of morality that led him to steal from a shop as a child.

Bedwyr is inherently a less interesting figure, an unimaginative man, a capable professional and devoted if uninspired husband and father: he admires but cannot imitate his wife's religious instincts. He lends Gwydion money, gives Peredur general support in his problems and is, without making any clear decisions, steadily drawn into the plans for the exploitation of modern Wales. This involves both semi-criminal international financiers and the briefly but sharply drawn Sir Joshua Macsen Morgan, 'one of south Wales's leading wire-pullers' (391), whose name refers to Macsen Wledig, or Magnus Maximus, the early leader of the British who impoverished his own people through his dreams of being Roman emperor – his story is also found in the

Mabinogi collection. Bedwyr's own name, it seems, refers to Arthur's loyal warrior, present from the earliest Cymraeg reference to (as Sir Bedivere) the enigmatic end of the king in Malory and Tennyson: in tradition and Humphreys's fiction, Bedwyr is always a spear-carrier whose skills are at the unquestioned service of his lord, whoever through time he might be. Bedwyr More has a complicated parentage: he is John Cilydd's son by his first wife, Amy's great friend Enid Prydderch. Her talented Welsh gentry family is in decline, with only the spirited Enid retaining their former vitality and commitment to the enhancement of Wales – but she dies in childbirth. Bedwyr is, like Philip Esmor-Elis in *A Man's Estate*, a relict of familial failure, doing his best to earn a crust and shape a life.

Peredur is quite unlike both his brothers, neither mercurially unreliable nor easily manipulated. His name clearly refers to the hero of the Welsh Arthurian romance 'Peredur', again in the *Mabinogi* collection. A version of, and probably the ultimate model for the Perceval of the French Grail romances: the hero is a classic 'holy fool' figure, both clumsily naive and capable of revealing deep truth. Brought up in north Wales by a dominating mother away from the masculine world of medieval knighthood, Peredur nevertheless adventures forth and in spite of – but to a crucial extent because of – his naive clumsiness discovers deep moral truths both about proper moral and Christian behaviour and also about the maimed king of a waste land. The Orestes myth deepened and empowered *A Man's Estate*, but the Peredur/ Perceval myth is more directly used as an underlying structure to the whole *Land of the Living* series, a key to the wasteland of modern Wales, though unlike the medieval Christian monastic authors of the grail story (and T. S. Eliot more recently), Humphreys does not offer a gratifying discovery of a source of all value and spiritual substance to regenerate the blighted land. Rather, what the reader discovers in the light of Peredur's quest is that his father, another holy fool, did kill himself, that he was in part hounded by imperial loyalists for his pacifism, in part unable to make his wife's accommodations with the banal techniques of success in the modern world, in part overwhelmed by his chosen role as a conduit of the poetic tradition. Being a national winner, Humphreys darkly suggests, is also a way to become a national loser. A fragment of one of his poems is remembered by many people through the novels:

> The hawk descends
> With burning eyes
> And where he strikes
> The singing dies.

An image of violent nature and of fascist bombing in Spain, the hawk is also the portent of bardic death, and in his last period John Cilydd is working on a poem about Myrddin Wyllt: Wild Myrddin (known in Latin and English as Merlin) is a poetic exile haunted by horrors and he is clearly conflated by Humphreys and John Cilydd himself with Lleu Llaw Gyffes, the victim from 'Math fab Mathonwy', he of the 'skilled hand' and unfaithful wife.

Another version of what John Pikoulis has called 'the wounded bard',[66] John Cilydd, though he represents many of the values Humphreys himself upholds, especially pacifism and the poetic tradition, is nevertheless not a model of complete value. He is oversensitive – as any creative writer may need to be. The local doctor says 'He was born with one skin less than anybody else' (309), and the man who knew him best in his last days says 'he died of despair' as 'the last of a defeated tribe' (352, 353). This is Ken Lazarus speaking, the talented musician and handsome school friend of Bedwyr: John Cilydd worked with him to turn his poems into songs, and came to love him; it seems that what he feared were homosexual feelings finally drove John Cilydd to cross England and wade into the sea at Scarborough, returning, however displaced, like the bard Taliesin to the ocean he loved to watch.

More even than with J. T. Miles, Humphreys distances his novelist's approval from this central figure. Through the sequence where Peredur visits Pendraw for news of his father, John Cilydd is consistently called, by the narration, Mr More: the novel sets out how people saw him, mostly mistakenly, not as he could be internally understood. His purism is a position that is no longer tenable, the novel reluctantly tells us; like Myrddin, he is driven mad by what he has seen and how it conflicts with his values. There is no healing for John Cilydd's wound, and the following books will go back and will explore more carefully the bases of his tragedy, the values that he and others stood for, and examine much more fully whether Amy, the survivor of this whole period, is a bearer of more realistic values or a representation of how people in Wales have responded, timidly, even shamefully, to their situation.

Amy dominates the novels that tell the early sequences of the story. *Flesh and Blood* (1974), the next to be published,[67] tells how the orphan

Amy Powell is brought up by her aunt and uncle, poor hard-working people. She takes their name – the first of many changes she will adopt – and experiences hardship. Her uncle Lucas Parry, injured in a granite quarry, aspires to be a Nonconformist minister despite his lack of education, and Amy is sent to a good local school where she becomes friends with Enid Prydderch. If the figures in *National Winner* were to a considerable extent related to early Cymraeg myth, here they link primarily with recent social formations. Ioan Williams comments that Humphreys's characters are often 'typological', that is they combine 'a view of mankind in close conjunction with a sense of particularity'.[68] Lucas Parry is both a credible, striving, ultimately unsuccessful person, and also a dark archetype of the *gwerin*. He never achieves his dream of being a minister, but as the harshness of his life floods into his person- ality, the novel does not permit us to be sorry for him.

Enid Prydderch is also a socially conceived figure: a generous girl, the best of her debilitated family, she will love and marry John Cilydd More for his talent and his dream of poetic values, but she, like most of his dreams, will die. Other figures have more clearly schematic value: Connie Clayton, friend to Aunt Esther, is in service far away with English aristocracy and she is grotesquely imperial in her attitudes and accent, almost like a Gwyn Thomas character, though still a Cymraeg speaker. Equally caricature-like is the Welsh-born Anglican rector, who fondles the adolescent Amy's breasts and even proposes to her in a depressingly materialist way; there are English colonists about like Jack Pulford, whom Amy briefly finds more arousing. More complex figures exist: Miss Vanstrack's originally Dutch family has, with mercantile wealth from Liverpool, bought a nearby Hall and she would like to send Amy to a high-class Anglicizing school, but her uncle refuses. Among the natives, there is also Val Gwyn, romantically handsome, deeply nationalist, with a special yearning for the beautiful Amy, but he soon develops TB. The nationalist cause is more vigorously but less purely represented by Sali Prydderch, a bossy school inspector – a literal Aunt Sali, she is target of a good deal of fairly simple satire – and her elderly admirer, Professor Gwilym, one of the many boring and self-centred professional men who damage good causes in Humphreys's novels; their representation grows darker in the later novels and Jane Aaron and M. Wynn Thomas link this with the failure of the 1979 devolution referendum.[69]

Throughout *Flesh and Blood* and *The Best of Friends* (1978)[70] these characters interact. With a constant sense of motion and transport about her – this is far from a static world – Amy makes her way educationally and politically. In student political action at Aberystwyth she acts decisively, always having a firm hand, as in two moments in *Flesh and Blood* when she throws stones at her enemies. Val, clearly her favourite, is offered a position that will effectively muzzle him by Sir Prosser Parry, a manipulative old politician, but he rejects this to retain his nationalist purity. In *The Best of Friends* he insists to Amy 'we are captives in our own country' (355), and Amy herself is drawn into the world of political power when she becomes secretary to the sister of Lord Iscoed, a Cymraeg-speaking coal baron resident in the north: but she will eventually resign in search of her own 'independence' (415). These moves and counter-moves in terms of nationalism in north Wales are both sociohistorically interesting and also a crucial setting for the development of both John Cilydd and Amy. The events of these early years also occur across a geographic range. Humphreys's ironic place-name Llanelw recurs as the north-eastern seaside resort around which the early action occurs, but John Cilydd comes from further west, where his family has a gloomy mansion like that of the Elises in *A Man's Estate*. Eventually he and Enid, and then he and Amy, will settle in Pendraw, a small seaside town on the Llŷn peninsula. But this move westward, apparently into the Cymraeg heartland, does not have a simple sense of increasing value. There are colonial forces in Pendraw just as there were *gwerin* elements in Llanelw: Humphreys does not deal in unexamined simplicities.

The political geography of the novel-sequence takes a further step with the amount of time spent dealing with issues related to south Wales. The focal character here is Pen Lewis, a vigorous Communist union leader who comes to the north to a conference. The name seems to refer to Lewis Jones: 'pen' means head, and Pen Lewis can be translated as Chief Lewis. But his full name, Penry Aneurin Lewis, refers more widely to the south, combining the Communist novelist's name with the first names of Rhys Davies's autobiographic hero from *Tomorrow to Fresh Woods* and the famous south Wales labour politician Aneurin Bevan. In this character, and the extended treatment of him in the following novels, Humphreys develops the partial integration of north and south in *Outside the House of Baal* and considers both the issues that belong to the south and also how the two parts of Wales can interrelate. Even to involve a character like Pen Lewis in such a novel is a major step, as M. Wynn Thomas comments:

the strength of those parts of the novels which deal with the Rhondda (say) is that they make clear the severe difficulty which faces those who try to draw a complete comprehension of Wales – a comprehension which can encompass the valleys, Cardiff, the rural parts – all of it.[71]

Through Pen Lewis, the situation in the south is realized more strongly than it was in *Outside the House of Baal*. There is a lengthy scene in Lewis's own Cwmdu – an allegorically named 'black valley' – as the Communists successfully resist an eviction. Amy visits the area and goes on a march; later she is present at a demonstration in Cardiff against the Conservative Prime Minister Stanley Baldwin. These sequences both realize the dire situation in the south and the radical responses to it and also symbolize a north-south Welsh combination. But this is not in any real way a political one. In *The Best of Friends*, during a discussion of nationalist strategy Val Gwyn says 'the key to the future is the south-east' (263), but neither the novel, nor the series, explores how such a linkage might work.

Instead, Pen Lewis operates in personal terms as well as – perhaps even rather than – political ones. He is a handsome and sexually aggressive man and Amy, herself very desirable, is bowled over by him, on more than one occasion literally. Roaring about on his motorcycle, striding into meetings, vowing intransigence to the bosses and damn-ation to all half-hearted non-activists, Pen is himself almost a caricature of male power. Lewis Jones himself had a reputation with women, but not in such melodramatic terms. There is some respect for the power of the south Welsh labour movement in this characterization, especially when compared to the tubercular Val Gwyn and the at best nervous John Cilydd More, but there is also an oversimplification of Pen Lewis's figure that ultimately makes him easier to dismiss. Later on in the book focused on him, *An Absolute Hero* (1984),[72] Pen is seen as 'manipulative' and his contempt for the Welsh language is not accepted – Amy says 'if you possess average intelligence why not set about learning it?' (141). The character flaws of his son Gwydion may well be meant to trace back to his flamboyant and somewhat selfish nature. He is certainly a man of action: Amy is swept away by his manly Marxist vigour and he fights and dies in Spain, but not, it seems, as Penry the martyr. Lewis is not a figure whose meaning remains as part of the text's interactive self-interrogations as do the other characters from this period.

The story of Pen and Amy, the further interaction of nationalists and their Liberal enemies, John Cilydd's marriage to Enid and his beginning of a career as a solicitor as well as a poet now regarded as extreme (another year's entry was rejected by the eisteddfod) fill two more novels, but they are surprisingly short, and it appears that a new publisher, Dent, was not willing to publish Humphreys at the length that best suits his slow-moving, thoughtfully developed fiction. *The Salt of the Earth* and *An Absolute Hero*, published in 1985 and 1986 are, taken together, a little shorter than the other novels, and as a unit have a strong developing structure. Throughout the events of these novels, Amy is seen in a more positive light than the spoilt self-enthusiast of *National Winner*. A true friend to Enid, and never jealous of her, working hard to restore John Cilydd to function, treating Val Gwyn with tenderness, even asking him to marry her when he is ill, and responding naturally if not wisely to Pen Lewis, she appears to provide that rare thing, a major and essentially positive role for a woman in a serious Welsh novel. She seems almost like a youthful Jane Gruffydd from *Traed Mewn Cyffion*, and while there are clear traces of vanity and triviality in her – she is unduly taken with a fancy gallery in Cardiff, and she is certainly impetuous at times – she can nevertheless be read hereabouts as a basically positive force, something like a combination of the active Lydia and the supportive Kate of *Outside the House of Baal*. There is no sign that Humphreys is thinking of her as a sovereignty figure: if there is a mythic parallel it may be a supportive maiden like Luned in *Iarlles y Ffynnawn* (the Welsh version of *Yvain*), one of those selfless figures who served the wandering knight and brought him through to success. Yet that is not going to happen to John Cilydd, and Amy will be redirected back towards her characterization in *National Winner*, one of the self-serving political manipulators like Sir Prosser. As a whole her trajectory is not entirely evident, though it may well be that Humphreys shapes her as a symbol of the people of Wales who, during the 1920s and 1930s, did face bravely the major mystifying challenges, in both the north and the south, but during the Second World War and afterwards lost their idealism and dealt mostly in self-indulgence and self-advancement.

The Salt of the Earth and *An Absolute Hero*, drawing on figures established earlier, also make strong statements about some more clearly 'typological' figures. One, entirely negative and a foretaste of Gwydion, is Eddie Meredith, Oxford-educated son of a boorish workhouse-master. He becomes involved in films, and is an unrelieved representation of media corruption. Another seems like a transplantation of J.T. into the novel: the Revd Tasker Thomas, Nonconformist, pacifist, genial conversationalist, recurrently represents the values of these positions, and also the way in which such a figure annoyed the powerful on a local and a national stage. The most interesting of all these characters who delineate specific positions is Nathan Harris, a retired minister, now disabled, who thinks deeply. He speaks about ways of reconciling class struggle and the position of the Nonconformist church; he may be closer to the text's (and Humphreys's) own positions than anyone else.

The four novels that bring the story up to Pen Lewis's death – three novels in terms of Humphreys's usual length – have moved fairly slowly over about twenty-five years. The task of *Open Secrets* (1988)[73] is to move the action on, not to the time of *National Winner* but to the period just before John Cilydd's death in 1952. The war begins; evacuees arrive and so do refugees, bringing aspects of a world wider than Wales itself. The European dimension of Welsh possibilities is something that Humphreys develops, both from his own experience and also, it would seem, following Saunders Lewis's perception of Wales as relating to more than England. John Cilydd remains anti-war: he served briefly in the trenches in the First World War and he uses his family property to shelter conscientious objectors. Even the former nationalist diehards Sali Prydderch and Professor Gwilym are opposed to this, and their arguments with John Cilydd crackle with a tension that presumably derives from Humphreys's own experiences as a conscientious objector. Another antagonist is Eddie Meredith, now commissioning patriotic media material, who has the gall to use a central phrase for his own manipulative purposes against John Cilydd: 'I think I'm probably just as aware of bonds of attachment as you are' (180). Later Eddie will seek John Cilydd's support for a holiday camp on his land, a theme already developed in *National Winner* when it was a locally living English colonel who offered various bribes for such a sell-out.

John Cilydd is not alone: Mabli Hughes, who had been at Aberystwyth with them, reappears as a vigorous nationalist, sounding like Enid's recreated voice. But as he, with her support, separates himself from social approval – he regards the war effort as collaboration – Amy is increasingly implicated in politics as a 'Welsh socialist' (169) and in war management generally. She is in uniform before long and, now being shaped by Humphreys as a much less sympathetic figure, decides that she needs 'freedom of action' and should leave John Cilydd to 'avoid damage to what they call my public life' (205, 204). Yet it is still not clear that she is all bad: at the end of the novel, as eager for self-validating action as ever, and strongly, if shallowly, responding to the refugee problem in Europe, she rushes off to post-war Germany with an ambulance full of medical supplies. There is also work for her in the story and its symbolic structure. Even when she has distanced herself from John Cilydd, he is still vulnerable to her 'compelling beauty' (216). They visit the farm where her foster-parents lived. Lucas Parry is now dead but the area is fertile: they make love there and Peredur is the result. As in myth, the child stems from the fastness of north Wales, and the oversensitized man and the undersensitized woman produce a child who will bear the burden of a quest for truth.

Open Secrets also tidies up some details: Val Gwyn finally dies; Nathan Harris is buried as Peredur is baptized and eventually will take up Nathan's task of seeking the grail of complex truth; John Cilydd's sister Nanw, who has always hated Amy – 'she collects men' she tells him (272) – and like so many of these women, including Sali Prydderch, lost a lover in the First World War, burns herself to death in the family home. Dark events gather as John Cilydd's life is moving towards an end. As the novel concludes, Gwydion's petty theft and Amy's self-centredness look forward to the end of *National Winner* and John Cilydd's increasing distraction relates more closely to the years between *Open Secrets* and the suicide that Peredur's enquiries will in part uncover. The technical task of closing the gap up to the death of the devotedly nationalist and pacifist poet has been completed with great skill. But time has moved on. By 1988, when *Open Secrets* was published, Wales had changed very much from the wasteland of nationalist hopes in post-investiture 1971. Never one to be too optimistic, yet also never one to leave his own positions unquestioned, Emyr Humphreys realized there was more to say, especially about a Wales where the language movement and the nationalist party had made real advances, where voices were not all ones of nostalgic pessimism, and so he used the title he had planned for the whole series, and had first used in writing about Kate Roberts's own condensed national epic,[74] for a new last volume that would both represent and also interrogate the years since 1971 when, it seemed, not all in Wales that was national had in fact been a loser.

In the opening action of *Bonds of Attachment* (1991)[75] Humphreys has Peredur, having left his English university, fail to obtain an academic job at Aberystwyth: an English self-promoter is appointed. But Peredur meets a nationalist librarian who shows him John Cilydd's

diaries and he goes to his father's part of Wales to settle in an empty
Protestant manse (for Humphreys a deeply symbolic setting) to explore
his past. Switching then to John Cilydd's diaries, the narrative goes
back to the past and his First World War and between-wars experiences, but it also keeps moving into the conflict of the present as
Peredur, on an adult education lecture trip, meets a young nationalist
activist, Wenna Ferrario (her father is that recurrent figure of natural
value in post- Second World War Welsh fiction, an Italian prisoner of
war). Already heavily involved in language activism, as it is coming up
to the investiture of the prince of Wales, she is among those planning
resistant action. In the argument of the book she is the opposite of
Gwydion, who urges Peredur that he should 'work within the system':
the narration clarifies that Gwydion's role was 'to contain and tame
that upheaval of protest and political consciousness that had spread
throughout this decade from one end of Wales to the other' (126, 128).
The criticism is emphasized by the unusual use in this novel, alone of
the series, of a judging narrative voice, as Tony Brown and M. Wynn
Thomas have noted.[76]

Amy is pro-investiture; she even has plans to involve Brangor Hall in
this confirmation of colonial continuity, and to include Bedwyr and his
skill. Wenna is clear that Amy is 'one of our persecutors' (141). The
story continues to interweave the conflicted present with John Cilydd's
early experiences, including some darker reading of Amy's early motiv-
ations than had appeared in the books covering the same period – she
was in favour of the holiday homes and appears to have had adulterous
affairs: she was contemptuous of pro-Cymraeg tax resisters and John
Cilydd's support of them, and she placed her 'unflagging hopes of
advancement' in the Labour Party (310). At the same time Peredur tries
to understand and evaluate the forces of his own time. Wenna dismisses
Welsh cultural values: she is against the past, saying 'it will bury you
alive' (223), but Peredur is drawn to love her and support her violent
cause. Yet, in a clear memory of *The Little Kingdom,* she is also a self-
dramatizing figure, and like Owen Richards she is killed in nationalist
action, an attempt at a propaganda explosion. Humphreys, like John
Cilydd, remains opposed to violence, and even Wenna tells Peredur
'you can't recover the Holy Grail or redeem the wasteland by foul
means, can you?' (233). With his brothers' help, and his mother's
knowledge, Peredur escapes.

In a final irony his mother makes one last turn to possess the power
of the present. She says 'Your Wenna was right' and 'You must live

from now on to see that she didn't die for nothing' (356, 357). Stricken with cancer, Amy dies in melodramatic mode espousing yet another new position, insisting that her nurses speak Cymraeg and 'take some pride in your ancient heritage'. In doubt, knowing she 'was trying to please me' (358–9, 369), Peredur can only still ask questions, as the Grail knight learnt to do: it was not asking questions that caused the land to become waste. In the spirit of his father he asks:

> Can anyone stage a revolution without violence? Does it have to be a revolution? Or should you condemn your class and your country and yourself to a condition of permanent grovelling servility and sycophancy? How was one to beat it? (360)

Like John Cilydd, he has no answer: but he is alive, and this sequel that the resistance of the 1970s has imposed on the series raises new possibilities of the reintegration of Cymraeg and English-language Welsh culture, and clearly suggests that such integration might indeed lead towards types of independence.

In the reprint of the series by the University of Wales Press, Humphreys has inserted 'The Land of the Living' as a series title, followed by the last verse of Psalm 27: 'Diffygiaswn pe na chredaswn weled daioni yr Arglwydd yn nhir y rhai byw' ('I had fainted unless I had believed to see the goodness of the Lord in the land of the living': Humphreys's own translation). He adds the note that he 'took it to mean that the poet would give up without the hope of a meaningful destiny for his people' and that this is 'apposite to a sequence of stories drawn from the life of a society under siege'. The overall title was first used by Maxine Hackett, the clever but socially displaced English girl who briefly saw Peredur as a path upwards: she commented that though his father was dead his mother 'was still in the Land of the Living' (63). The irony is typical of Humphreys's sceptical and searching critique, even of his own values. But as when Eddie Meredith hijacks the phrase 'bonds of attachment', the value of Humphreys's titular concepts survives misappropriation. The distance between the practical, even pragmatic, survival of Amy and the grail-like hope of grace in Wales is long indeed but, like *Outside the House of Baal*, this massive account of events, values, betrayals and commitments in twentieth-century Wales seems to recognize the value of both the lowest and the highest forms of survival and for all the impact of Val Gwyn, John Cilydd More, Pen Lewis and Wenna Ferrario it is striking that it is the doubt-ridden, uncertain figure of Peredur who, like his medieval avatar, seems to get stumblingly close to the difficult messages of continuing value. Containing both a deeply negative and a possibly positive conclusion in the two volumes written at different times to end the series, covering an extraordinary range of Welsh social, historical and emotional experience from the twentieth century, the novel series flows powerfully as Emyr Humphreys's fullest contribution to the self-understanding of the Welsh people about their recent experiences under colonial rule, and their still uncompleted move towards integration and independence.

3.4 A WIDER WALES: RAYMOND WILLIAMS

There are both parallels and divergences in the careers of Emyr Humphreys and Raymond Williams (1921–88). Both were politicized at university, had professional careers in England and broader European interests, yet both focused in their fiction on Wales; both used, in differing degrees, a nationally conscious viewpoint as the overall position of evaluation; both chose a plain style far from the self-conscious rhetoric of many Welsh writers in English. But there are also differences. Raymond Williams was born in the working class, not the educated professions, and he went to Cambridge, not Aberystwyth. His politics were communist and then democratic socialist, adding Welsh nationalism only late in life. He fought in the Second World War as an officer in an anti-tank regiment – though for the Korean War, liable to call-up as a reservist, he registered as a conscientious objector as Humphreys had previously. His professional career was as an academic, first in adult education and then at Cambridge from 1961, not in radio and television (though he wrote powerfully on the electronic media), and his European career was not Humphreys's links with the world of refugees and life in Italy, but a position in touch with the leading European leftist thinkers. Though he published fewer novels than Humphreys, Williams's creative career was quite similar. He was writing plays and novels in the late 1940s and had drafted *Border Country* several times before it appeared in 1960. Like Humphreys he was not satisfied with a single-volume approach: the 'Welsh trilogy' added *Second Generation* and *The Fight for Manod* to *Border Country* and at his death he was working on what would have been a historical trilogy.

Williams has been best known as a major cultural and historical critic, but the signs are clear by now that his influence in that direction is diminishing, and the socioliterary approach that was so revolutionary in the 1960s is now regarded as normal, even basic. The fiction was for long largely ignored, though it was very important for Williams (in fact he produced equal numbers of fictional and critical books), but it seems to remain as vivid and important now as it ever was. The fiction realizes in some detail the thoughts about Wales that were, as Daniel Williams has shown,[77] common in Williams's later academic writing, when he became especially interested in how English-language fiction explored and expressed ways in which the Welsh have responded to their colonized status.

Born in Pandy and going to grammar school in Abergavenny, Williams knew as a child the farming and service work of that southern Powys border region. His university training was interrupted by the war and after Cambridge he worked in Sussex as a local organizer for the Oxford adult education board and went to an academic position at Cambridge in 1961, where he stayed until his early retirement at the age of sixty-two. Always interested in drama, and the author of several plays, he also early on drafted novels – one about Alaska, one about a man choosing his own identity and one about a troupe of utopian activists. None of these has any apparent Welsh link, but he also worked on various versions of a novel about a young man's education and move away from home in Wales. When his father died suddenly, he recast what was to be *Border Country*, using the meaning of his father's life as the stimulus for the hero's reorientation towards his origins.[78] Matthew Price, history lecturer in a London university college, is called home to Glynmawr – clearly Pandy. He feels strongly his father Harry's now weakening power, but also the surviving sense of community among neighbours, relatives, fellow-workers, and he appreciates the close, organic relation between this community and the physical world in which and through which they live: the railway workers are also gardeners and his father is at least in part a farmer. This is familiar enough – the emigrant regrets the values he has lost – but the novel also establishes the central conflict of this historical community, the general strike of 1926 when the railwaymen joined the miners for nine days.

Williams vividly realizes the instinctive resistance of the workers: in a distinctly syndicalist way both the stationmaster and an anti-socialist worker join the strike and after it the men combine on a local basis to resist and defeat the management's victimization. There are also strongly felt accounts of women's work in support of their families and towards the respectability that in south Wales is summed up by the word 'tidy'. But a major theme develops about the father's identity as a worker. His friend and co-signalman Morgan Rosser delivers fruit and vegetables to help the still-striking miners and this turns into a life's work for him: not because he is an opportunist, but because, it becomes clear, he was so traumatized by the failure of the strike. He was the local union secretary, and he had faith in the networks of fraternal and democratic support. When they fail the miners, he turns to another inorganic system of distant organization, the world of business. The others, including Matthew's father, who merely had local and organic feelings, are not so defeated. This is a telling account of the deep relationship between major party organization, whether union, labour or communist, and the commercial bourgeois world on which it is inevitably modelled. Both are in fact imports into Wales, both have colonial impact, and both can be resisted by local communality. When Harry repeatedly refuses the offer of a good job from Morgan, and causes some offence, he is opting out of the externalized system and validating his *gwerin* identity.

The other argument the book puts forward is related, but more tendentious. Matthew has moved away, and indeed is a different person: he is called Will at home. This was also true of Raymond Williams, known in Pandy as Jim. But Matthew comes to identify his academic work with the peasant-like activity he sees and values in his father, and feels that he is in fact a projection and continuation of that world. The novel works hard on this point: Harry himself says 'You're my kind, Will, and the men you work with are my kind' (312). Matthew is able to say to his wife, on his return to their London suburban house, 'Only now it seems like the end of exile. Not going back, but the feeling of exile ending.' It appears to be an improbable identification, but Matthew goes on, 'For the distance is measured, and that is what matters. By measuring the distance, we come home' (351). The claim made by Matthew, and Williams, is not that he is in fact one with his father but that through a geographical manoeuvre he can identify with the communal life of the village still. It is the geography that counts: *Border Country*, in its title and in many of its scenes, is rich with a somewhat romantic identification with country that stands in for an identification with a society. Time and again Matthew looks up at the landscape, names the mountains, walks up to see the farms where he and his father have been before. The setting means more here than it does in many Welsh fictions, basically because the author and his viewpoint are a long way away – in Sussex and, later, in Cambridge. Jane Aaron has argued that the emphasis on topography and its meaning in Welsh women's fiction is both the product of and the compensation for their lack of social power and a sense of identity,[79] and the same kind of alienation appears to be behind the specially emotive force of landscape in both *Border Country* and much of Williams's later writing – a form of displaced integration evident also in Rhys Davies, another sympathetic exile, but quite absent from the work of someone as physically and socially located in the country as Emyr Humphreys.

As he later showed in several essays,[80] Williams knew the Welsh industrial writers well and admired Gwyn Thomas especially, but he chose for himself, like Emyr Humphreys, a very different style; in *Politics and Letters* he says that in *Border Country* he wanted 'to be very careful not to write in what had become identified in England as a "Welsh style"' because he felt this was 'a form of cultural subordination, the only – slightly degraded if subtle – way the Welsh could present themselves to a London audience' (279). Partly as a result, some readers have found his novels rather slow-going and lacking in humour, and the identity with landscape is often the major bearer of feeling and colour.

The second novel in this series is the one that least deserves to belong in a 'Welsh trilogy', has least to do with landscape and, perhaps as a result, seems the most stylistically ponderous. *Second Generation* (1964)[81] deals with two Welsh families living in what is obviously Oxford, though no place-name is given. Two brothers have moved from the border area of the previous novel to work in a car factory: before motorways, Oxford, like Slough, was on the direct route from much of Wales to London and had long been a great magnet for scholars, drovers and ordinary workers. The brothers are, like Harry and Morgan of the previous novel, different: Harold is a devoted union organizer, fussy, a man of systems; Gwyn, who lives next door in working-class east Oxford is calm, a gardener, the organic match of Harry Price. Their partners fit: Harold's wife Kate is a Labour Party activist mixing with dons as well as workers and Peter, their son is working on a D.Phil. in sociology at the university end of this bipartite city. By contrast Gwyn's wife Myra and her daughter Bethan are passively feminine, home-lovingly emotive. But the Welsh values of organic calm in Gwyn and Myra and of self-improvement, represented in Harold and Kate, are not here related to their place of origin but rather to what Williams saw in the England where he worked as 'a profound crisis inside the [working] class' resulting in its depoliticization and the decline of real resistance.[82]

The failures of a new world do not validate the older world of Welsh values: at a crisis in his research and his emotions, Peter drives back to the Wales they came from, only to find himself as isolated there, and in any case 'part of the same network' (234) of communications and social bonds that runs through Oxford as well. The thrust of the novel is mostly about the class conflicts of the United Kingdom but there is also an extension of the theme in a post-colonial direction: Peter is finally, and it seems authoritatively, told, by a Nigerian diplomat that

> Nationalism is in this sense like class. To have it and to feel it is the only way to end it. If you fail to claim it, or give it up too soon, you will merely be cheated, by other classes and other nations. (322)

The lesson is one that can apply to Wales, and in later novels Williams will do that, but here his concern is with the British working class represented by the Oxford car-makers, with both the active and the passive element represented by Welsh people. That separation from the main interest of this study does not of itself weaken the novel, though it has its drawbacks, such as the uncertain treatment of both Kate, Williams's first major female character, and the university itself, seen in somewhat caricatured terms – there were active leftists on campus at the time. Both the least Welsh and the least convincing of Williams's political novels, *Second Generation* nevertheless outlines, more fully than *Border Country,* the serious nature of Williams's project, and that came to a powerful fruition in the last of the trilogy, *The Fight for Manod*, not published until 1977 though it was apparently rewritten many times from 1956 on.[83]

As Daniel Williams has shown,[84] the author was long conscious of the impact of English dominance over Wales, a theme to be found in his later work, notably *The Country and the City* (1973),[85] his essays on Welsh industrial writing and the thoughtful reviews he produced of non-fictional writers about Wales, including Emyr Humphreys.[86] But his thoughts about the colonized situation and exploitation of Wales are the main theme of the last of the 'Welsh trilogy', developing the authoritative Nigerian voice at the end of *Second Generation* and the fleeting contact with a Caribbean bus-conductor at the start of *Border*

Country: as Katie Gramich has noted, Williams there indicated his understanding of Wales as a colony.[87]

In *The Fight for Manod* Matthew Price from *Border Country* and Peter Owen from *Second Generation* are both asked to assess a plan to develop a mid Wales valley: with European funding a series of medium-sized high technology towns are to be developed along a mid Wales river now only set with farming villages and small market towns. This new disseminated city will be a model for other developments, and the government has suddenly gained interest in a plan that has been shelved for a decade. The two investigators are chosen by Robert Lane, Peter's Oxford supervisor and an admirer of Matthew's historical sociology, who appears to have an objective position on the project – though his probity becomes less certain by the end.

Matthew, a historian of communities in Wales, goes with his wife to stay in one of the villages in order to assess the impact on site; Peter, ever the alienated but politicized academic, married with moderate success to Bethan and working as an investigative journalist, conducts his researches in the archives and paper-trails that may explain the larger picture – it is intriguing, and perhaps initially surprising, that Merryn Williams, in launching *Who Speaks for Wales?* commented that it was with Peter Owen her father tended to identify.[88] Matthew's investigations, both topographical and conversational, reveal enthusiasts, doubters and some locals who clearly plan to profit by the scheme. But Williams also – again like Humphreys – spends time and chapters outlining the actual interrelating and sometimes conflicting lives of the local residents, giving women a more significant role than previously, though not Matthew's wife. Gwen and Ivor Vaughan, brother and sister, are the survivors of the local landowning family; Trevor and Modlen Jenkins are a hard-working, basically peasant couple; another farmer, Gethin, is a diluted Caradoc Evans figure, austere, conniving, wanting to marry Gwen for her property.

The most relaxed in tone and most skilfully realized of Williams's Welsh trilogy, *The Fight for Manod* creates simultaneously the organically interwoven life of the local community, with its roots in both earth and history – a full development of the limited vision of *Border Country*, and also a clear outline of the forces seeking to disrupt that life and profit massively from the effects: a transfer to Wales of the sense of capitalist exploitation that was basic to *Second Generation*. What Matthew comes to sense locally is proved by Peter's largely offstage enquiries – a fuller draft of the novel gave Peter much more space, with his international detection matching Matthew's local enquiries, but London publishing requirements curtailed that. He discovers that there is an Anglo-Belgian company behind the scheme, eager to use Manod as a test-bed for its Europe-wide development plans, and the government is very keen to accept this windfall and bend the rules to permit it.

In a climactic scene at the ministry, as the civil servants and politicians are forcing through the scheme, Peter walks out vowing to publicize the scandal and Matthew, arguing strongly, has a heart attack. Robert Lane, regretful and still insisting he is not implicated, visits Matthew in hospital and says that the scheme may still go ahead: this is not a happily ending story. Matthew though, and here he must be somewhat like Williams himself, is committed and will work on to turn all his research into a book – a community can operate not only through the emotional living of its people but also through the insight of writers, whether historian or novelist. And though this novel has, like *Border Country,* been filled with the topographic and somewhat romantic details that compensate for Matthew's – and perhaps Williams's – own lack of real connection, at the end Matthew sees, more legitimately than was managed in the earlier novels, the intellectual work of realizing the movement of history as his own contribution: 'What could be heard, momentarily, as this actual movement, had conditions of time, or growth, quite different from the conditions of any single life, or of any father and son' (207).

Ordinary life goes on. Gwyn and Myra, the organicists of *Second Generation,* have themselves in *The Fight for Manod* moved to the rural service station where they used to have their holidays; Trevor and Modlen, their parallels in the action, are moving to a better farm. Intellectuals can also participate. Matthew, when he recovers, will almost certainly accept a job he has been offered to run a centre for historical research in Wales. Williams and his family themselves were by now spending a good deal of time in the house they bought at Craswall, up in the Black Mountains beyond Pandy. This was to influence his last fiction, but before then he produced two more novels which used the idea of Welsh values in the spirit of independence, though not integration, to comprehend, and criticize, the idea of modern Britain and the wider world.

From 1968–72 Williams was the television critic for *The Listener* and out of this came his very influential book *Television: Technology and Cultural Form*, one of the first to engage with the actual impact and inherent nature of television.[89] He was also a life-long enthusiast for future fiction, and the two come together in his unduly overlooked *The Volunteers* (1978).[90] The story is set in a post-democratic future of a coalition government dominated by international businesses like the electronic news provider for whom Lewis Redfern, a former radical activist, works as a specialist on the world of possible resistance. Covering the shotgun wounding of the Secretary of State for Wales at St Fagan's Castle, Cardiff, he uncovers a double trail of radical activity. One is old-style Welsh syndicalism: as the Secretary tried to recover coal stocks from a depot near Newport, the workers, loyal to the striking miners, stayed inside, resisted incursion and one of them was killed by soldiers. This epitome of Welsh industrial resistance through time seems connected to the shooting of the Secretary of State, and Lewis, with a good deal of detection (generically this is a mystery story),[91] traces it to some of the 'Volunteers', long-existent radical moles in the British hierarchy and civil service. Not all the moles have remained faithful: Mark Evans, a high-flying Welsh former MP is now implicated, in part at least, with the international, American-controlled world of scholarly foundations (it is notable how much Williams himself avoided such activities). But Evans's son is a real activist, and the novel ends with Lewis on the run because of his exposure of inter-national fixing. He is hidden among the Welsh workers, but it is conceivable that he will also join the active Volunteers, partly to link up with his former wife, partly through a sense of their political value.

A skilfully constructed and well-paced book – the usual pausing, even ponderous, style is hardly in evidence here – *The Volunteers* testifies more to Williams's life spent on the edge of media and politics than his account of Wales, but the country does provide the value of communality and inherent resistance to hostile exploitation. Wales plays a very similar role in Williams's last completed novel, *Loyalties* (1985).[92] This appears to be the book Williams mentioned in *Politics and Letters* as '*The Brothers* – somewhere between *Border Country* and *Second Generation*' (301). Bert Lewis (the surname again adheres to a radical character in Welsh fiction, presumably still in honour of Lewis Jones, and also found in the hero of *The Volunteers*) is a stalwart 1930s miner who fights in Spain and is later wounded in a tank in Normandy, where Williams himself had fought. A man of deep loyalty to his people and the Communist Party, he marries the beautiful Nesta when she is pregnant and abandoned by the English upper-class Com-munist Norman Braose. Their son's education at Cambridge and his subsequent probing of Braose's background is the core of the novel, which again turns on moles. In this case Braose and his Cambridge friend Pitter, both scientists, have been to some extent involved in spying for Russia, though their real involvement remains obscure. Williams was obviously a connoisseur of the Cambridge spies and the difficulty of establishing exactly who worked for whom, and how much, but the novel also deals in personal betrayals and misplaced loyalties. It was his Moscow controllers who made Braose abandon Nesta, and his sister's devoted support for Nesta and the son appears to come as much from the protection of upper-class blood as from her own leftist sympathy.

More a reverie on British class politics than a book about the Welsh relationship with England, *Loyalties* is a personal novel in that it deals with Williams's experiences in the Communist Party, at war and at Cambridge – hence the 'post *Border Country*' reference, it would seem. But it also shows traces of his growing interest in a more distant history. Norman Braose recalls William de Braose, a brutal Norman lord of south-east Wales, notorious for the mass murder of Welshmen in Abergavenny in 1176 and grandfather of another William who may also be recalled, as he was executed for adultery with the wife of Owain ap Cadwgan in 1230. The historical undertones of the text recur in the name of Nesta, surely reminiscent of the beautiful and fertile Nest, daughter of Rhys ap Tewdwr, who married or lived with a range of Norman gentry in the mid twelfth century, including Henry I.

That faint stream of history was to broaden greatly. In his last years at Cambridge and after his retirement Williams worked on the other project he mentioned in *Politics and Letters*, 'a historical novel of a different kind' about 'continuity of place rather than people' (302). This became the unfinished *People of the Black Mountains*, yet another Welsh trilogy. The first volume *The Beginning* appeared in 1989, the year after Williams's death, and what was finished of the second volume, edited by his widow Joy Williams, came out in 1991 as *The Eggs of the Eagle*.[93] The plan was to tell the story of events, people and conflict in Williams's own Black Mountain area from about 4000 BC until the present: it was written 'from the point of view of the people who were using this often very unpromising land to make a living'. But it was not just a human-scale story: the idea was to trace 'the movement of history through a particular place'.[94] As Williams's comments on Gwyn Thomas's *All Things Betray Thee* indicate (see p. 105), he valued especially history which was not tied to dates and data, but which sought also to interpret its patterns, both social and personal – a Brechtian kind of history that replaced sentimental recreation with analytic comprehension.

A great deal of research went into the project. The interview with John Barnie in *Planet* is rich with Williams's knowledge of a wide range of sources: Joy Williams, herself a historian, gathered materials from many places, especially Cambridge University Library.[95] To link past and present Williams uses the double time-frame of both *Loyalties* and *Border Country*, with a modern narration in which Glyn, studying history at Cardiff – so a student of Dai Smith and Gwyn A. Williams – looks for his grandfather lost on the Black Mountains; in short sections between the historical sequences his progress is charted. Inside this modern story, the historical action gives a sequential account of major events in the developing human history of the region – and so of Wales, and indeed Europe. Sometimes, important events elsewhere which involve people from the area are recounted, as when they are taken off as Roman, or indeed Celtic, slaves. Williams is especially concerned with changes in social and communal culture – the ways in which families become tribes, then meet other peoples, learn about implements, learn to trade. Neither the Celts nor the Romans are treated with much respect, both being stigmatized as early imperialists. Local feeling is strong in the medieval sequences in *The Eggs of the Eagle* which deal with Abergavenny, detailing Norman treachery there, including de Braose, and the town's later role in the rebellion of Owain Glyndŵr.

The third volume would have come up to date, as Joy Williams indicates in an afterword, with stress on social development and communal response. Williams would have dealt with the nineteenth-century resistances he knew much about, and so with writing the industrial settlement. There would also have been resonances across time that looked towards an almost mystical meaning of place: an American airman whose plane was to crash on the mountains was to be a descendant of an earlier emigrant. Glyn would ultimately find his grandfather at a site of special meaning, probably inside the stone circle the Celts had treated as a sacred place and which the 'measurer' – the first intellectual of the saga – had taught the Bronze Age people to build: he had studied at far-off Salisbury Plain, just as Williams brought his abstract learning back from Cambridge to apply it at home.

The opening of *The Beginning* matches the form of the mountains and valleys with the back of 'your hand' (1): the reader is made to identify with the landscape. It is easy to read this negatively as a sentimental personalization of the ambient world. However, Williams meant it in reverse, to suggest that as human society has risen from its material base in the most direct, geological, terms, there is as a result an intensive identity of community, people and place. This was worked out in fuller detail in *Border Country* and *The Fight for Manod* and the broad range of the historicizing imperative of *People of the Black Mountains* leads to a selective shorthand that must lack the depth and conviction of the other accounts because of its very ambition. Yet Williams tries to realize 'the voices' that Lewis Redfern found absent at the St Fagan's Folk Museum – he found there that 'Folk is the past: an alternative to People'.[96]

In the *People of the Black Mountains* Williams's effort is to activate those voices and, in the questing frame, link analytic history and an affective relationship with place through time. It is an ambitious effort – a cross-time version of the epic impact of Kate Roberts or Emyr Humphreys. Tony Pinkney has seen the fragmented nature of the narrative and the questioning of political and traditional certainties – such as the advance of human society and the nobility of the Celts – as postmodern features,[97] but these elements are more recognizable as the far-reaching and formally innovative products of an authorial mind both committed to writing about Wales and also sceptical of received opinions, features which Williams strongly shared with Emyr Humphreys. Had Williams lived both to finish the trilogy and revise it in his usual meticulous way, this would have been another major piece of Welsh writing in English, with its own strength of academic scholarly analysis as well as a range of vigorous scenes and voices.

Williams knew little Cymraeg, though Dafydd Elis Thomas has said that he learned some through his experience in Plaid Cymru,[98] and his real interest was restricted first to the border and then to industrial Wales. But as Daniel Williams's selection of his writing about Wales shows, he was in his later years very sympathetic to the nationalist movement: a key statement, entitled 'Who Speaks for Wales', is a perceptive and favourable review of Ned Thomas's crucial contribution to the nationalist and language movement, *The Welsh Extremist*.[99] Williams joined Plaid Cymru, though retaining close links with the positions of the southern leftists, and it is clear that he was thinking deeply in his last years about types of integration that were both possible and valuable in Wales as part of its increasing independence: like Emyr Humphreys's Nathan Harris he linked socialism and small nation nationalism as a viable and valuable combination.[100]

Both the fiction and the non-fiction dealing with Wales indicate that Williams was a figure as serious, wide-ranging and searchingly thoughtful as Emyr Humphreys, and the two of them, with their difference of foci and their similarity of serious investigative power, combine to offer a rich account of what is lamentable, what is valuable and even what is possible as Wales moves from a traumatic past into an anxious but also potentially successful present and future.

Not all of Wales's major talents have been so productive. Alun Lewis was lost in war and another writer of comparable gifts chose, it seems consciously, not to deal in any serious way with his origins but, like Williams in his earlier academic work, set his sights on international intellectualism. Stuart Evans (1934–94) came from the Swansea valley mining village of Ystalyfera and left Oxford having won both the prestigious Newdigate prize for poetry and a reputation for wit, comedy and theatrical writing. He, like Humphreys, worked in teaching and radio but turned from poetry to fiction. He admired Gwyn Thomas and was himself a notable raconteur of valley life, but his fiction is different. His first novel, *Meritocrats* (1974), is based in London and Europe and though Sylvie Keller, a cultured BBC literature specialist, comes from Merthyr there is no Welsh interest. This aversion seems consciously confirmed in the brilliant and complex *The Caves of Alienation* (1977).[101] Michael Caradock, a major novelist of Welsh origin, whose books are in the novel summarized through reviews and discussed by critics, and who is approached through Idris Lewis (like Evans a Jesus man), wrote one novel about leaving Wales and dealt with some Welsh themes in others. Caradock, born to the Welsh bourgeoisie, rich and clever, but orphaned, is a high European intellectual, but eventually returns to Wales: there he is murdered. As a self-critical self-projection this has some links with Michael Edwards in Humphreys's *A Toy Epic*, but the brilliance of Evans's creation of this prolific, Wales-ignoring author seems to celebrate rather than deplore his own position, and Evans's own later fiction was dominated by a verbally glittering and consciously anthropological account of the *haute bourgeoisie* of London and Europe.

3.5 LOOKING BACKWARDS

Stuart Evans consciously avoided, Alun Lewis was unable to start and Raymond Williams never completed the work of writing a wider Wales, but there is still a very substantial post-war account of Wales and the Welsh in fiction, and the process did not end with the writers discussed so far. Yet if there has been a serious self-examination of their community and its history by some Welsh writers, there has also been a less serious, even exploitative engagement with the country and its traditions. There were writers who thought less deeply, inquired less perseveringly, and tended to historicize their material in a shallow way, either presenting a version of first-contact approaches or combining the setting and stereotypes of the industrial settlement with the excitements and simplicities of romance; instead of exploring a wider world they were content with the narrowness of nostalgia.

London publishers were involved. In his account of Welsh writing in English from 1950 to 1975 Roland Mathias comments, as one who was there at the time, that there was a definite English market for Welsh fiction into the 1950s and Raymond Williams has commented on the phenomenon as well.[102] Where the first-contact authors had relied on an English audience interested in quaint wonders, and the settlement writers had found a substantial hearing among those who sympathized with the situation on the coalfield, the writers of the post-war period had a real but less easily defined attraction for English readers. In part it may have been the massive success of *How Green Was My Valley* generating the hope of similar pleasures. But there might be other elements: during the French Revolution and the Napoleonic wars the difficulty of overseas travel gave visits to Wales at least some enhanced value, and that seems an overlooked cause of the interest in the country during and immediately after the Second World War. There are other possibilities: one of the curiosities of English culture is the approach-avoidance relationship with Germany, that linguistic and to a sub-stantial degree racial kin. It is clear that after the First World War interest in Germanic scholarship and myth faded and phenomena like the apotheosis of the irresistibly Celtic Arthur into the model of an English king[103] as well as the flourishing of modern Celtic writers in England acted as a form of compensation: that may well have also been a factor after the Second World War. But it was a short second honeymoon with Welsh nostalgia: as soon as travel was possible again and the world book market picked up, London publishing became the touristic frenzy it still is, with internationals like Norman Mailer and Saul Bellow and former colonials like Patrick White and Chinua Achebe and then the wider-ranging south American magic realists all providing displaced literary compensations for a former world power.

That short period of interest in Welsh writing certainly helped some
writers already discussed, but it also made publishable a type of fiction
where instead of pushing on experimentally to revise the settlement
novel as did Glyn Jones, Gwyn Thomas and Menna Gallie, some
writers merely replicated the nostalgia of romance or the routines of
settlement. The later Jack Jones exemplifies the latter, and a striking
version of the former is Richard Vaughan (1904–83), spoken of in the
1950s as a major Welsh writer, and one of the best known and at the
time most successful exploiters of the post-war English interest in
quaint and romantic representations of Wales. Actually named Ernest
Lewis Thomas, he was born in rural Carmarthenshire into the middle
class and steadily moved away – to school in Pontypool where his
father had a shop, as a bank clerk in Merthyr, then to London, finally
working as a free-lance journalist there. After the war he was an English
teacher in London and then, as a reasonably successful writer, came
back in 1961 to a Carmarthenshire farm.

His first novel, *Moulded in Earth* (1951), was dated around the turn
of the century, set deep in the country and makes much of rural
practices and, especially, passions.[104] Like the title, the story insists on
the organic value of country life to the residents and the novel is a rural
counterpart to the conservative Welshness of Llewellyn's *How Green
Was My Valley*, with the effect of a new wave of first-contact fiction –
John Harris describes it as a 'revivification of elemental tales' and notes
that it was very successful, serialized on the BBC's 'Woman's Hour'
and a Book Society recommendation.[105] It was followed up as a loose
trilogy by the even more romantic *Who Rideth So Wild* (1952) and *Son
of Justin* (1955). The language of Vaughan's characters is heavily
characterized, or caricatured, as Welsh, much like that of Michael
Gareth Llewelyn and the action is bold and broad – the *Anglo-Welsh
Review* described *Who Rideth So Wild* as 'fornication and fisticuffs'.[106]
The *New Companion* is quite positive about his work, saying he has 'an
unforced, lyrical style which sometimes shows moments of great
beauty' (715), but Tony Bianchi has been more critical: speaking of the
'seductive simplicity of the novels', he sees Vaughan as reproducing 'the
unambiguously alien voices of the early tourist accounts' and links him
with writers who construct 'a compensatory myth based on the past, on
mysticism, or on some other escape route'.[107] Vaughan's response to his
point of origin was the opposite of Caradoc Evans: he revered
Machen's *The Secret Glory* and shares Machen's sense of mysticism
deep in Wales.

More recent and persistent in their success have been authors who have combined what Bianchi calls the 'bodice-ripper' approach to Welsh fiction[108] with historical events and places of importance in the development of the industrial settlement. Alexander Cordell (1914–97), actually George Alexander Graber, was born in Colombo in a military family and after time in the Far East joined the regular army. He published an English war novel, *A Thought of Honour,* in 1946 and after settling in northern Gwent turned his attention to local industrial history. His great success was the sensationally titled *The Rape of the Fair Country* (1959), covering the familiar ground of the development of industry in the south-east but writing in an unashamedly and highly gendered melodramatic tone. The Mortymer family arrive in Merthyr: they are manly men and womanly women beyond the imagining of Jack Jones or even Richard Llewellyn – fists and busts cram the pages, in a repetitive plot and improbable stage Welsh.

Cordell also produced a trilogy: having experienced Merthyr with Dic Penderyn, the family drifts into the rural resistance of *The Hosts of Rebecca* (1960) and then attends the outburst of the coal industry in *Song of the Earth* (1969). Cordell is a master of what Raymond Williams called 'headline novels',[109] and yet his success is not entirely meretricious. As Harris notes 'Cordell took great pains to get his details right'[110] and Chris Williams, an expert on industrial south Wales, has commented on the accuracy of Cordell's history, and argues that some of his interpretations were in advance of historical comprehension at the time.[111] Among other novels – including several using his experiences in China – Cordell went on to write another trilogy dealing with high moments in Welsh radical tradition: *The Fire People* (1972), one of his calmest novels, and one where he used documents he discovered himself,[112] deals effectively with the Merthyr rising; *This Sweet and Bitter Earth* (1977) embraces both the slate-quarry strikes of the turn of the century and the Tonypandy riots of the next decade; while *Land of My Fathers* (1983) returns to the Newport Chartists' rising. A bestseller in his day and popular still in public libraries, Cordell must have contributed more information and sentiment to a wide audience about Welsh industrial history than anyone except Richard Llewellyn, though he is now only published by Blorenge, a small press from what tour-guides call 'Cordell Country'. Always in some way a rebel – his biography includes details of the impressive number of arguments he sustained, notably with publishers[113] – Cordell does at least in his technicolour mode give voice to a sense of exploitation and heroic resistance, and in this respect might be thought of less harshly from a post-colonial viewpoint than writers like Richard Llewellyn and Richard Vaughan who clearly, and presumably consciously, shape their Welsh material to satisfy an English and inherently colonial taste.

If Cordell added something of radical history to his rippling of muscles and ripping of bodices, Iris Gower (b. 1939) has more recently done much the same for the position of women in Wales. Actually surnamed Davies, she was born and brought up in Swansea and after several historical romances took the nearby coastline as a pen-name and as Iris Gower produced *The Copper Cloud* (1976),[114] a female version of the male industrial experience in nineteenth-century Swansea, including a girl's first day at work, not down a mine but with equal horror experiencing life as a water-carrier among the copper furnaces. This and the sequel, *Return to Tip Row* (1977),[115] are fairly short, but with *The Copper Kingdom* (1983) Gower produced the first of the large-scale historical industrial romances that have made her, as Harris comments, 'a favourite of library patrons'.[116]

Using a less melodramatic style than Cordell, Llewellyn and Llewelyn, she gives 'everyday conversations a pleasant rhythm', as Kathy Piehl comments, also noting Gower's 'ability to incorporate history in a story'[117] among the lusty, dangerous life of nineteenth-century industrial Swansea, which Gower called with historical reference, Sweyn's Eye (the Norse name of the city was Sweynsey, the island of Sweyn). The basic structure of *The Copper Kingdom* is a classical woman's romance, but as the bold young heroine is Welsh and the aloof handsome man she wins is a fair-haired English industrial capitalist (appropriately named Sterling), the romance is also a benign account of the colonial process. After six novels in this series, Gower extended her output, and her bestselling success as a Welsh Catherine Cookson, with six novels in her 'Cordwainers' series of novels set among Swansea artisans, beginning with *The Shoemaker's Daughter* (1991),[118] and she has continued with the 'Firebird' series set in what the blurb to *Kingdom's Dream* (2001) excitably calls 'the romantic potteries of South Wales'.[119] Predictable as her plots may be, and limited as their politics inevitably are, Gower's novels do have some social force. She gives a more consistently major part to women than Gallie managed, makes it clear how much their work is part of the societies that are being constructed in industrial south Wales, and she, as a native of the area, has the gift of writing dialogue in a convincing way, not the parodic gabble so common among comparable writers.

There were other authors, especially in the years after the Second World War, who produced novels for London publishers to cater for the public interest, passing as it turned out to be, in fiction about the nearby exotic land. Tom MacDonald (1900–80), born in Cardiganshire to a Irish tinker family, was a journalist in South Africa when he wrote a number of rural romances in the 1940s: after his return to Wales in 1965 he wrote on, including two novels in Welsh. Cledwyn Hughes (1920–78), a pharmacist born in Montgomeryshire, produced two short novels in 1947, both well-controlled explorations of unromanticized Welsh life, *A Different Drummer* and *The Inn Closes for Christmas*.[120] He gave up pharmacy and became a professional writer, producing three more low-toned but thoughtful novels and a set of general books including ones on travel and for children. D. Gareth Owen cherished rural Wales in the tone of Richard Llewellyn with *The Place Where We Belong* (1945), *Spring in the Air* (1946) and, the least sentimental of his work, *Clouds Across the Moon* (1947).[121] Barbara D. Roberts (born Elizabeth M. D. Roberts) did much the same for the border gentry with *Still Glides the Stream* (1944) and *Some Trees Stand* (1945).[122] Mostly lightweight, these authors have a continuity with the first-contact stories: William Glynne Jones not only wrote for children and sentimental rural stories like *Farewell Innocence* (1950) and *Ride the White Stallion* (1951), he even published a book whose title could come straight from the late nineteenth century, *Legends from the Welsh Hills* (1957).[123] Against all this sentimentality it is bracing to read Nigel Heseltine's reversal of the romance tradition, *Tales of the Squirearchy* (1946):[124] with a ferocious wit and a pared-down modernist style Heseltine, also an editor and poet, created brief fantastic satires on Welsh gentry in a small book that was not from one of the London romanticism mills and, in a parable of negative reception, is not held or recorded in the British Library. Sadly, Heseltine moved abroad and never returned to his brilliant satire.

3.6 WOMEN'S WRITING

There have been more socially related publishing trends in Welsh writing in English than nostalgia. Iris Gower's work is not only driven by historical curiosity and nostalgia: it also relates to the major growth in women's writing since the 1960s and the recognition by many publishers that women are a major part of the reading public. That was an implied feature of the early romances, whether trivial or searching, but the well-known fiction of the industrial settlement and the work of the post-war period, both nostalgic and exploratory, were distinctly male in orientation, with a rare exception in Menna Gallie. As part of Jane Aaron's wide-ranging work in reassessing fiction from a feminist as well as a Welsh, and indeed Cymraeg, position, she has shown in her important anthology *A View Across the Valley* (1999) that there were many women writing outside the field of romance, but they gained little recognition, especially because they tended to work in the elusive short-story form.[125]

Aaron's anthology goes up to 1950, so indicating the inheritance of the modern writers. The romance novelists are present, Anne Beale, Allen Raine, Bertha Thomas and Hilda Vaughan prominent among them, though there are also strong stories by largely unknown writers, including Sara Maria Saunders, Ella Lloyd Williams, Kathleen Freeman and Eluned Lewis and a subtle piece by Dorothy Edwards. A clever Cardiff graduate, taken up in Bloomsbury circles by David Garnett but never at ease there, Edwards wrote with incisive elegance and died young – ending her own life in isolated despair. Margiad Evans and her sister Siân (born Peggy and Nancy Whistler respectively) contribute strong stories, but the most enigmatic are more recent. Rhian Roberts, about whom even Aaron can find no data, writes a sharp valley story from 1947, 'The Pattern', in which a boy's viewpoint exposes anti-Italian racism during the war. If that sounds like Menna Gallie's political critique of masculinism, Dilys Rowe's powerful 'A View Across the Valley' (1955), with the darkly surreal flavour of the early Dylan Thomas stories, brings into mythic form the sense of recoil and escape from male industrial society that Cynthia activates in Gallie's *A Small Mine*.

Though the material is not large in amount, it is strong in character, and a pattern is visible of a clear woman's voice, interested in view-points other than that of the dominant male, strongly realizing a sense of domestic limitation, not afraid of either feeling or critique and indicating that romance is a genre that women writers can redirect into thoughtful and even challenging modes which can bear strong elements of both integration and independence. These writers have had a sub-stantial succession. The well-known Cardiff-born writer Bernice Rubens (b. 1928) does not 'fit neatly into any singly category',[126] and her work is mostly concerned with families, often Jewish, around the world, but *I Sent a Letter to My Love* (1975) uses a Porthcawl setting for a wry but also moving account of a plain woman's entanglements with emotion, and *Yesterday in the Back Lane* (1995) realized through a psychothriller format both a woman's anxious existence in Cardiff and a powerful reminiscence of life in the wartime city.[127] More focused on Welshness is Moira Dearnley's novel, *That Watery Glass* (1973),[128] a woman's coming-of-age story about a clever research student in English literature at a mercifully unidentifiable college of the University of Wales. She suffers in her work and her emotions until she experiences a happy ending, redolent of symbolic integration. Not herself a Cymraeg speaker, Gwenda is made pregnant by and happily married to a lusty native with the deliberately symbolic name Dafydd ap Gwilym. Not only is this a novel which imagines a form of integration between the two cultures of Wales – and a fertile one at that – it also bears a crucial sign of independence in that it was published in Wales by the Llandybïe firm Christopher Davies, previously Llyfrau'r Dryw. Close to Caradoc country, far from the English impact of the settlement, a publisher produces a subtly written women's novel imagining a Wales that has learned integration on its path to independence. It is a striking moment, and one that Dearnley supported with a potently allegorical story, 'The House in Builth Crescent', in which two English bourgeois immigrants have been steadily reduced to poverty in the basement of their empty house, and must in the end accept help from the Welsh woman doctor whose mother was originally their servant.

The ebbing of colonial power that Dearnley imagines also clearly happened across the frontier of gender colonialism as well. Though Alun Richards's first Penguin anthology (1976) included the Dearnley story, and one by Kate Roberts, that was all; his second collection (1993) ends with six recent stories by women.[129] Two are translated from Cymraeg, and indicate a substantial upsurge of women's writing in that language. The others were new names, but now well known. Glenda Beagan's 'The Last Thrush' is about a dying woman's aware-ness of the sense of loss and casual treatment that comes from devotion to sons; Penny Windsor's 'Jennifer's Baby', in different but parallel mode, shows a young mother drastically losing interest in both husband and baby son; Clare Morgan's 'Losing' both celebrates and deprecates the process by which a girl grows towards womanhood among male brutality and uninterest; and Catherine Merriman seizes a wider writerly independence for women by writing sharply yet comprehend-ingly about men, brutish bikers, in 'Barbecue'.

Insisting on the right to write as women about their own concerns, but also including the world of men in that purview, the new wave of women writers who have operated from and in Wales in the last twenty years, like their colleagues around the world, have both shaped a new viewpoint and also foregrounded long-held but mostly silent views. In *State of Desire* (1996)[130] Catherine Merriman, an English-born resident of south Wales, deals at first with a familiar issue as a new widow discovers both sexual freedom and a warm relationship with her son. But her energy, and that of the novel, goes further than gendered self-fulfilment: Jenny Parsons and her lesbian friend Sal also become involved in resistance to the planned open-cast mine that will destroy the beauty of the hilltops above their village. Like the feminist detectives of 1980s America or, closer to home, the Welsh women at Greenham Common and those whose radicalism emerged in the 1984 miners' strike, they have a real social politics in addition to a gender position, and they fight successfully to win communal freedom as well as their personal liberties.

Merriman can be seen, in her Welsh-set stories,[131] as a developer of the position crafted in a series of novels and stories by Siân James (b. 1932). Born a speaker of Cymraeg near Llandysul and becoming a teacher after university at Aberystwyth, she spent decades in England, married to the actor, the late Emrys James. She developed a career as a novelist, reshaping English bourgeois romances with a frequently ironic tone – a couple's best friend could turn out to be the wife's lesbian lover, a dead husband could be revealed to have had a surprisingly active and treacherous past. Increasingly she set her work in Wales. Both lyrical and trenchant, *A Small Country* (1979) moves away from romance and the leisured life. On a prosperous family farm the father leaves to live with his pregnant schoolteacher mistress, but after her suicide and the death of his wife he works a mountain farm with the child and a young wife, a former servant; his daughter, the nervously beautiful Catrin, falls in love, sees her lover and brother die in the war and ends up a harassed nurse, her looks nearly gone, married to the older and at least kind family doctor. This sense of coping with the wretched, cruel, or sometimes just ludicrous nature of life runs through all of James's work. *Love and War* (1994) has a similarly bitter and only reminiscently sweet account of an extra-marital affair in the Second World War, while *Storm at Arberth* (1994) deals with older characters exchanging their needs and deceptions.[132]

In the novels James usually focuses on a strong, suffering semi-tragic woman, but this limited if powerful, viewpoint is often extended in her short stories, which were collected by Honno as *Not Singing Exactly* and won the Arts Council of Wales Prize for 1997.[133] Produced over many years and in many places – a few have the tone of an English woman's magazine – about half the twenty-two stories are set in Wales (not all have a clear location), and they often use children as narrators to foreground family tensions and the recurrent theme of the strains faced by women. Their problems may be easily mastered as in 'Mountain Air', where two sisters go on an outing with the children, unheeding of husbands or other men; but they can run deeper as when a mother is sidelined in the house she serves in 'The Rugby Match'; or they can be coolly countered as in 'Love, Lust Life' where a dying woman relishes a long-past affair. Children can observe cruelty from the past in 'Hester and Louise' (another Italian prisoner-of-war story), pains in the present in 'John Hedward', or the agonies of adolescence in 'Luminous and Forlorn'. The narrative can grow colder, expressing a grim if self-sufficient form of coping in 'Not Singing Exactly', and in the final story, 'Happy as Saturday Night', the joyless pleasures of a girls' night out in Cardiff.

James remains a writer on women's issues: her men are offstage, sometimes caricatured, but the newer wave of writers, including the wide-ranging Merriman and the sophisticated Clare Morgan are avoiding the constraints of feminine feminism and some of the most recent writers, especially those found in the substantial anthology *Mamma's Baby (Papa's Maybe)* (2000),[134] cannot be categorized as women writers but take their place beside their male colleagues in dealing with issues of the period. In arriving at that thematically gender-neutral situation, the women writers have for the first time gained their own form of independence and integration, both dissolving previous structures of discrimination and also, by dealing with Welsh people in fully serious terms that are largely uninterested in, even unaware of, colonial constraints, have made their own substantial contribution to a literature which realizes a national independence.

3.7 AFTER INDUSTRY

If the recognition of a female and often feminist voice in fiction is one major feature of Welsh writing in English in recent decades, another has been the normalcy of publishing in Wales itself, aided by Arts Council grants, promotion of Welsh books in various formats and a growing sense of a national community of writers speaking about the condition of their country. Authors have no longer needed to follow the interests of London publishers, and though this has often meant a reduction in income – almost all modern Welsh writers in English, or Cymraeg for that matter, support themselves by other jobs, with the help of occasional grants – it has also given them a much greater independence and capacity to write on topics of local and powerful concern.

Not all the recent fiction referring to Wales has shown the moves towards integration and independence being outlined in this section. Some old-fashioned patterns can recur, as with condescending mockery in Kingsley Amis's *The Old Devils* (1986), touristic sentimentality in Bruce Chatwin's *On the Black Hill* (1983) and the modernized first-contact melodrama of *The Sin Eater* (1977) by Gwynedd-born Alice Thomas Ellis. But now such colonial productions are in a small minority: modern Welsh writing in fiction deals primarily with Wales today; Tony Bianchi has offered a powerful reading of the issues involved in a number of the writers in his essay 'Aztecs in Troedrhiwgair: recent fictions in Wales'.[135] A major topic of recent writing has been the way in which Welsh writers, much more than elsewhere in Britain, have confronted the major single change in the social, economic and cultural life of the country, the decline of heavy industry. By the later 1960s industry in the south and the north-east was much restricted because of international competition and lack of funding to renovate to profitable levels – English capital was by then venturing into empires elsewhere. Pits and factories were closing, support services were being reduced. The nadir of economic run-down, both real and symbolic, was the closure of all the coal-mines in Wales as a result of the political conflict of 1984: the British miners, the Welsh prominent among them, resisted Tory pressure in one last great strike. It was heroic, and like many heroic actions, ill-judged. They were defeated, yet the strike of 1984 showed that even in their last moments the miners of south Wales still stood for the values of courage, community and resistance, and that memory has not faded. One pit reopened, Tower in the Cynon valley, brought back to successful operation by the energy and commitment of its own men. The values of the industrial community continue to be kept alive by writers, even if only as a memory, a Utopian dream, of what was once possible. This post-industrial writing, now by men and women, now published in Wales, and also often reaching out in integrative mode to the rest of the Welsh and Cymraeg traditions, has continued into the twenty-first century and is a major part of the modern voice of Welsh writing in English.

Between the wars writers had responded to the situation by recounting the developmental history of the coalfield and the need for resistance, whether it was political, social or, in the most nostalgia-loving of cases, naively romantic. In the new period of decline, history was restricted to an occasional memory of the glorious past – the glories of both community and conflict – and, the more disturbing feature, there now seemed no credible path for resistance except a withdrawal into the personal routines of escape, compensation or resentful discontent. Standing out among the writers of often bitter fictional accounts of industrial decline is Ron Berry (1920–97). Living in the Rhondda and working in a colliery from the age of fourteen – though he left the pits for good in 1940 – always energetic in thought, speech and body, and increasingly committed to writing fiction, he produced a first novel *Hunters and Hunted* (1960),[136] which celebrates in a driving style the random adventures of three young workers, in the pubs, out hunting, with their women. Their energy, often misdirected, contrasts starkly with the dying industrial world of what Berry calls 'Blaenddu deserta', a characteristically brief deepening reference to the cultural possibilities of this world, in spite of its bleak existential present. That novel appeared in the Hutchinson 'New Writers' series and his next also appeared with a London publisher. The energetic adventures of Hughie Davies are entitled *The Full Time Amateur* and in sport, work and personal rela-tionships Hughie is always promising but never fulfilled. He is 'violent, inconsistent',[137] and this relates to a lack of clear identity arising from the insecure and inherently worthless nature of the work available to him, some of it in mining: his unfocused personality offers a strong con-trast to the well-founded sense of identity of the older miners he meets.

A more fully organized sense of social problems and their historical context is provided in *Flame and Slag* (1968)[138] where with some skill Berry interweaves the story of a new generation and their insecurities, focused on Rees Stevens and Ellen Vaughan, with the memoirs of Ellen's father who helped to start the local pit that is now closing: the novel, like its title, celebrates both the vigour and the aftermath of industry. In the context of history, Berry is able to make action more than casual: Rees's father died in an accident the day before 'vesting day' when the pits were nationalized, and he is himself injured shortly before the colliery finally closes. Though the author tells this story in the spirit of what he calls 'plebeian bile' (45), there is some positive element to be found in the enduring affection of Rees and Ellen, in spite of all their differences, and there is also a clear recognition of Cymraeg culture as still being available to these people whose story is almost benighted, but somehow find the spirit to survive.

Berry's work sustains this double vision of an oppressed yet hardy people largely through the muscular drive of his own language and imagination, but he found it hard to become published after 1970 as London publishers lost interest in his kind of work, being both retrospective and Welsh. He gained an increasing reputation among some Wales-based critics, notably Dai Smith, who praises his account of mining life, John Pikoulis who wrote persuasively about Berry's qualities, and Simon Baker who edited a collection of short stories,[139] and his last novel *This Bygone* (1996) was published in Wales.[140] It has a historical plan from the 1930s to just before nationalization and creates a viable life for its hero Dewi Joshua by permitting him to marry a woman with money and move into ownership of a small mine and, finally, to have a beautiful second wife and a child. That possibly romantic access to an alternative way of life is also found in Berry's emphasis on physical fulfilment, sometimes in love but often in sport or hunting: *So Long Hector Bebb* (1970) is a powerful, complex and ultimately tragic account of a boxer,[141] but Berry can also have a lighter tone as in the short story 'November Kill' (found in Richards's first collection) where two of the young men from *Hunters and Hunted* spend days digging, in an affectionate recreation, rather than cold parody, of a pit rescue, to recover a terrier from a fox's den. The vigour and sense of authenticity of Berry's style – Pikoulis speaks of his 'epigrammatic rhythms' – links him to the 1930s industrial writers and Pikoulis sums up 'Rarely can the valley sub-culture have received such impressive linguistic demonstration'.[142] Berry's verbal power and ironic realism give him clear leadership among a group of other writers who have written both nostalgically and elegiacally about the world of men and mining.[143]

Alun Richards (b. 1929) is also strongly aware of the negatively post-industrial nature of his south Wales settings, but unlike Berry he does not deal with the lost industrial society so much as the impact that the loss has had on the men, and very often the women, of the area: the *New Companion* describes him as 'the supreme chronicler of south Wales valley life in decline' (640). A full-time and widely successful writer, including sea stories and major television series, notably the ground-breaking *The Onedin Line*, Richards has consistently produced short stories that deal with the people of his invented Aberdarren, localized to 'Dan y Graig Street' – the original seems to be Pontypridd. Many of the characters and events remain on site, but a character in the Algarve can suddenly reveal an Aberdarren origin and through this locational focus his two short-story collections, *Dai Country* and *The Former Miss Merthyr Tydfil*[144] have coherence, as well as a quality that makes them, in their often humorous but recurrently deep ways, both searching and revealing as ways of charting the social costs and the human responses to the loss of industry. Some are post-Dylan Thomas and Gwyn Thomas sketches, like 'Bowels Jones' or the London-based 'Dai-logue', but the best stories are quite long and explore thoroughly the situation and feelings of the central character, often a woman – Rhys Davies seems to be Richards's mentor. His characters may fall into self-righteous anger as in 'One Life' or sour irritation as in 'The Scandalous Thoughts of Elmyra Mouth', but through them Richards can realize both the sense of a failing socio-economic world and the stubborn persistence of individuals within it in a mode less masculinist, more ethnographic, than Berry.

It is striking, and presumably the result of the forces of English publishing, that while Richards's short stories contribute strongly to a modern sense of how Wales can be represented in English-language fiction, his novels are different. *The Elephant You Gave Me* (1966) uses a Welsh-trained social worker as hero, but the story is no more than a troubled love affair set in England; the heroine of *A Woman of Experience* (1969) is from Wales and does return home to help resolve her problems, but the context has almost no significance. The only one of Richards's non-maritime novels not to be in some way exile work – and the only one published in Wales – is *Home to an Empty House* (1973).[145] Here, as in many of his best stories, the focus is a woman, a primary schoolteacher of warm nature and low aspirations, with an out-of-work, ill and indolent husband. She experiences success at work, has a desultory and less than integrative affair with a self-made Cymraeg-speaking man, and ends up alone, but with her courage intact and some sense of worth out of all her trials. The novel, like the two short-story collections, uses a sympathetic and only rarely sentimental humour as a means of realizing a sense of one sort of Welshness with great credibility. As Gramich comments, his 'evocation of Welsh speech, places, characters and social relations is invariably accurate, often uncomfortably so'.[146] As a result the best of Richards's work seems further-reaching and more lastingly important than its deliberately modest tone and approach might suggest. As Gramich also observes, he 'allows debates about definitions of Welshness to bubble underneath the comic surface of his texts' (267). The title *Home to an Empty House* in itself seems to express something of Richards's determination to write about his homeland's plight, and there is much about this modest but searching novel and its heroine that makes it read like an allegory of the condition of Wales in the late twentieth century: baffled, disappointed, lacking outlets for its talents and emotive powers, but still on its feet – and still writing.

An author of the same vintage who has only once focused on Wales is Dannie Abse (b. 1923). His creative work has centred on his highly regarded poetry, and his profession was medicine in London, but *Ash on a Young Man's Sleeve* (1954)[147] is a powerfully realized account of growing up in a radical Jewish family in Cardiff in the late 1930s and the war. Ethnic and religious variety is not emphasized: in many ways the hero is a typical Cardiff lad, chasing girls and going to see City play, but part of the richness of this urban coming-of-age story is its location in Cardiff (curiously, until recently a rare setting in Welsh fiction), and its treatment of one of the city's varied ethnic contexts. A well-known book of considerable impact, much studied in schools, this was followed by a thinner novel, *Some Corner of an English Field* (1956) based on Abse's national service but set entirely in England, and, after a period, by the lighter 'Welshman in London' story *O. Jones, O. Jones* (1970).[148] Herbert Jones, who has taken on the name Ozymandias for variety, is a London medical student and has the encounters with women and eccentrics characteristic of these urban novels, but the story lacks the Jewishness and radical context, not to mention the benignly banal streets of Cardiff, found in Abse's major novel.

More directly post-industrial than Berry and Richards, but also more consciously allegorical and integrationist, is *Shifts* by Christopher Meredith (b. 1954),[149] a novel which makes the classic statement about the situation, both social and personal. Born in Tredegar, Meredith is another writer who went from university at Aberystwyth into teaching. As a young man he worked in the local steel mill and in the late 1970s began a novel focusing on the closing of a steel mill, and its impact on the characters. He set this aside and developed his reputation as a poet, but the miners' strike of 1984 led him back to that novel: it is both directly and indirectly shaped by the loss of heavy industry in south Wales. Well received around the world, and widely regarded as a major contribution – an automatic choice on most courses on Welsh literature in English – the novel is both searching and complex. Its narrative involves three major characters: Jack Priday, who returns from England and obtains short-term work in a steel mill which is expected to close soon; his school friend Keith Watkins, who works in the mill; Keith's wife Judith. Jack moves in with them and has an affair with Judith, but neither is dedicated enough to stay together and Jack finally moves on, drifting back to England as an image of aimless Welsh diaspora.

Keith shifts in an opposite direction, though with little more assurance. Through wandering on the hills and linking his own work with its past he resists, however accidentally, alienation. He has become interested in industrial history and he prepares and gives a competent talk on the topic. The focal moment is when he starts to learn Cymraeg so he can understand the language of the initial industrialization of the area. At one point Keith studies some notes for a sermon, found in his old home 'in a language that was his own, but that he could not read' (127). Meredith has, like Humphreys, learned the Cymraeg that was lost in his family and this is a possible future for Keith, one that is described by Aaron and Thomas as 'representative of a popular movement within the valleys community' of the time.[150] The idea of integration with the fuller traditions of Wales as a path ahead for the south-east has also been seen by Dafydd Johnston as the idea behind Meredith's second novel, the vigorous historical fiction *Griffri* (1991).[151] *Shifts* offers more moves in the same direction. One other older worker, Emrys, has interests similar to Keith but he suffers a heart attack; the history professor who shared the platform with Keith also makes a point that looks toward integration – 'the Welsh consciousness was only partly affected by industrialization' (156).

But Meredith is far from offering a glib renativization programme in this powerful novel of post-industrial anxiety. Many other characters are represented as being affected by the closure of the works – one goes back to the army, one, ironically, goes to the mines, while others, especially women, are driven to misery, mechanical sex, drink or even suicide by the wretchedly bleak nature of their lives in an area whose life seems to be running down. A focus of these dismays is Judith, Keith's wife. She does not work: the novel is set just before women's employment was made normal both by feminist expectations and, in south Wales, by massive male unemployment. She has friends who work in the casual, ill-paid light assembling that was to be the future in the industrial valleys, but she would prefer more communal activities; nor is she attracted to having a child with the uninteresting Keith.

Judith's inner life realizes a dream of freedom, especially deep swimming with flowing hair, but when she and Jack visit a lake in a hired
sports car there seems little appeal to her in this version of a television
commercial and she bluntly says to him: 'Neither you or him have got
anything to do with me' (201).

Each with their element of value – Keith and historicity, Judith and
liberty, Jack and his quick-witted imagination – the characters are, in
spite of their gestures towards friendship and even love, unable to shape
new communal relations in a devitalized community. Jack has deserted
his girlfriend in England when she was pregnant; Keith has nothing to
offer Judith; she has only electronic dreams; Jack and Keith work and
drink together without real bonding. With considerable skill, Meredith
constructs this world of anomie in a text itself without the traditional
narrative coherence and development: the novel works by stream-of-
consciousness segments, by juxtapositions and by temporal leaps, and
to this construction of fragmented identity it adds clear elements of
allegory. Richard Poole argues that the character called O, almost
retarded, from the same school as Jack and Keith, who haunts both the
steel mill and the characters, is a figure of nullity who is also the
author's own self-projection as a neutral observer.[152] Both allegory and
complicity, from a post-colonial viewpoint, are ways of discussing the
sense of inherent weakness in a culture, and it may well be that in this
powerful deepening of the text Meredith is relating to the inherently
colonial context that created the steel mill in the first place and then
took it away, so leaving the characters in the newly oppressed situations
that this powerful novel explores in impressive depth.

In his most recent novel, *Sidereal Time* (1998),[153] Meredith has in
part pursued the techniques that make *Shifts* so technically effective,
including the issue of temporality, and he also has explored much
further the possibilities of a central woman character. If Judith was left
something of a mystery in *Shifts*, Sarah Bowen, the central figure of
Sidereal Time is explored in remorseless detail, physical and mental.
Her work as a teacher is always harassed by shortage of time and
energy, let alone success, and the parallel narrative about a clever but
erratic schoolboy, Steven Leyshon, and his own dreams also expresses a
sense of unfulfilled potential. This is in itself another reworking of the
post-industrial theme and a central element of it is the feeling that the
characters are unable to perform, physically and emotionally, in a fully
human way. They may be robotized, as in the mill or the school, they
may be frustrated, as with the intellectual instincts of Keith and Steven,

they may feel emotionally stunted, like Judith and Sarah, but their dominant image – like that of the community at large – is unfulfilment, immobility, betrayal and incapacity.

This position is variously developed in the work of what M. Wynn Thomas has called 'a constellation of younger talents'.[154] Duncan Bush, a poet and essayist who, Aaron and Thomas comment, has 'imaginative solidarity with the whole underclass of workers',[155] focuses in his novel *Glass Shot* (1991)[156] on a man with no pride in his low-skilled work as a tyre fitter, seriously dysfunctional both in his stalking of women he meets at work and also in his spying on his former wife and her new family. Driving a big American car, and fascinated with all things American, he fantasizes that, Maltese-Irish in origin, he looks like a native American. This deracinated and dangerous figure on several occasions makes fleeting contact with the miners who are on strike in the year of the novel's action, 1984. He feels a vague sympathy but no kinship with them: urban alienation has him in its grip as Bush, like Meredith a poet of substantial reputation, realizes with convincing and grisly power what it is to be a man in a world where masculinity has none of its traditional work-focused structures.

Russell Celyn Jones creates a similar figure in *Soldiers and Innocents* (1990):[157] a valley boy has become a hardened paratrooper, and now goes on the run with his son, abducted from an estranged wife. The writing is spare and strong, and the countryside and family is revisited in a dark reversal of the tone of *Border Country*. As with Bush the emphasis is on the alienated individual, not the damaged society that such people comprise. Jones followed this with *Small Times* (1992), a novel about a Welsh pickpocket in London which might have seemed a withdrawal from Welsh themes, but in *An Interference of Light* (1995)[158] he constructed a complex historical allegory, interweaving the emptying village houses of late 1950s Gwynedd with the slate industry in the 1930s through the eyes of an American, Aaron Lewis. Reminiscent of Williams's double time-schemes, the story is focused through two moves, both formally related to post-colonial literature. The quarries are in the grip of a bitter strike – a deliberate relocation of the troubles of the late 1890s – and Lewis is a Pinkerton detective, brought in as an informant by the quarry owner, an updated version of Lord Pennant. But this mixture of allegory and complicity is in fact only the context for Lewis's personal experiences and an elegy for the passing of a rich community. Jones's writing is too powerful to permit nostalgia, but the novel seems to express, rather than explore, the strains of past and present in this context. In more recent work Jones's technical power has been deployed in international thrillers, but he has the capacity to be a major writer of Wales if his career and interests permit it.

A path like that of Bush's anti-hero, in a less extreme form, is traced by the central figure of Lewis Davies's ironically titled *Work, Sex and Rugby* (1993).[159] As building labourer, reasonably good rugby player and passably attractive male, himself named Lewis, he goes through the routines of masculine life without any perspective given by identity. Davies can also write with considerable para-poetic insight, as in his *Tree of Crows* (1996),[160] and like Bush and Meredith he imagines men who are on the edge of dysfunctionality, incapable of normal social process in some ways and some degrees. In his finest novel so far, also written as a play, *My Piece of Happiness* (2000),[161] he follows the imaginative logic of this post-industrial school by creating genuinely disabled figures. George Rees is a social worker, former boxer and soldier, as well as psychiatric patient, who drifts through life in Cardiff; his clients are literally disabled, ranging from the severely handicapped Andy who – not unlike Bush's hero – lolls before a television making incoherent responses, to Sean, physically normal but of low intelligence, whom George helps to handle a paper-round as a way of moving toward social integration. Rich in its creation of this other world of those whose handicap is physical, not sociohistorical, the novel delicately depicts something like a romance between Sean and a marginally disabled girl from wealthy north Cardiff, with a nervous liberal mother. Here, as with the isolated and basically schizophrenic George, Davies suggests that new communities can be made even in the extreme circumstances that he both creates – part of the novel's power is its realization of disabilities – and also symbolizes through the image of the people of south Wales who bear such deep social and historical handicaps.

Another contemporary novelist who works in a more directly narrative way on the same theme is Richard John Evans, a graduate of the Glamorgan University creative writing school, where Meredith teaches, in *Entertainment*.[162] Evans uses a moderately sensitive would-be writer, Philip Mackay, to focus a sequence of violent, meaningless events in the modern Rhondda, from pub life to street fights to drug houses. His memorable friend Jason is confined to a wheelchair, yet is very strong in the arms and extremely aggressive, both physically and verbally. Combining dark social realism with symbolic views of human possibilities – Jason can dance in his wheelchair and has a ferocious wit as a rapper – the novel has more room for fragments of optimism than most in this dark modern school. Philip's sister is devoted to drama and seems likely to follow her talent out of the Rhondda; Philip finds some sort of peace with the eccentric, isolated Emma, who tolerates use of her house on a bleak estate for drug users but also, through her gallery of postcards, can access a wider imaginative world. In some ways it is a young man's book: Philip's sexual success with the gang members' girls seems neither probable nor parody and his enfeebled father, a casual Karaoke performer, adds little to the text's depth. But as a realization of the post-industrial situation, a grimmer version of the world of Meredith's Keith and Jack, the novel writes into recognizable ethnographic form a new scene in the history of colonization and its aftermath in Wales. It is a fictional counterpart to the vigorous films of the same period, *Twin Town*, with its farcically ironic, and to some merely tasteless, escapades in Swansea, and, realizing the tragic aftermath of the loss of industry and work, Ed Thomas's important play and later film, *House of America*.

These fictions bring forward to consciousness the images of disability that have had a covert presence in the post-war imagination: Dewi Davies's father in *The Island of Apples* and Nathan Harris, Humphreys's most trusted figure, were both physically damaged, and this image is recurrent in the post-colonial context as Ato Quayson has argued.[163] Once the image is noted, it seems to be everywhere: in Tom Davies's vigorous novel of 1984, *Black Sunlight* (1996), the figure of central value is a mental deficient who assumes almost Christ-like status;[164] in Desmond Barry's *A Bloody Good Friday* (2002), a tough but also mythic recreation of recent valley life, Davey Daunt the narrator walks with difficulty;[165] among the drug addicts and drifters of Niall Griffiths's *Grits* (2000)[166] social decay and the wreckage of the drug culture have, realistically, reached as far as Aberystwyth and the physical impact of their degraded excesses is very powerfully realized as forms of social disability. In Trezza Azzopardi's novel *The Hiding Place* (2000),[167] about Cardiff's dockland and the human cost of its decay over the past decades, the focal figure Dolores Gauci had an accident in childhood that left her hand a painful, useless, disfigured lump: among these post-industrial writers there is no marked difference of gender.

Along with a sense of disability goes an awareness of social and ethnic variety. *The Hiding Place*, which was short-listed for the Booker Prize and exhibits great feeling for language and a skilfully crafted intercut structure, may use women as its major foci but the failings and

frustrations of the male characters are drawn just as strongly, and the
novel suggests the decline of a great port with as much social impact
and underlying political anger as does John Williams's male-focused,
music-linked *Cardiff Dead* (2000).[168] Azzopardi also deploys the multi-
ethnic nature of Cardiff's past and this can be seen on a wider basis
linking Swansea and Austria in the poet Stephen Knight's *Mr Schnitzel*
(2001),[169] and in Charlotte Williams's prize-winning *Sugar and Slate*
(2002) about a woman who is both Afro-Caribbean and north Welsh.[170]
Further recognition of social and personal difference is the male gay
voice in John Sam Jones's *Welsh Boys Too* (2000) and the lesbian
counterpart in Erica Woof's *Mud Puppy* (2002).[171]

   The most serious version of post-industrial angst is Rachel Trezise's
In and Out of the Goldfish Bowl (2000).[172] Another University of
Glamorgan creative writing graduate from the Rhondda, she has
written a novel that is in some ways familiar: a female version of growing up in a hard world. But here there is neither collective harmony nor
sentimental tragedy: with a vain and mostly thoughtless mother, and a
series of stand-in fathers, Rebecca grows up on the notorious Penrhys
estate in a house that has 'an air of disability' (21). She often lives in the
shed for secure isolation, with only a dog to love and only her lust for
reading to separate her from all the others headed for a life of drink,
drugs, petty crime and random sex. Her goldfish-like meaningless
circuits are, though, suddenly immobilized when at the age of eleven she
is raped, repeatedly, by her stepfather. Child abuse was never so hateful
in its realization or effect. This is an ultimate disability, and it stays with
Rebecca: 'normality would not come . . . the violation could not be
undone' (50).

   She spins into her own desperate behaviour, but after the police bring
her back from England, where she has run off with a boy, her mother,
finally appalled, insists the stepfather is tried for rape. He is found not
guilty – 'he had raped me again' thinks the increasingly dysfunctional
Rebecca (62). Nothing will work now: not going to school or thinking
of college, not loving a boy – he plays in a band called 'Accidental
Homicide' – and she moves into new goldfish circuits of thieving, drink,
drugs, self-cutting, attempted suicide. But like the others in this tough-
minded and ultimately undefeated school of writers, Trezise can find
positives. At her grandmother's death, Rebecca comes to believe she
can imitate her strength in shaping her own identity – as a writer. The
opening and closing of the book are a perceptively written, confidently
imagined frame that suggests the human agent can, even in the

aftermath of colonial late capitalism and its condemnation of so many to be an underclass, still find a way to speak about its situation, a way to write a Wales that is not yet defeated.

3.8 WALES WRITTEN IN ENGLISH

Gwyn A. Williams, at the end of his powerful book *When Was Wales?* (1985), concluded bleakly that the Welsh were 'now nothing but a naked people under an acid rain':[173] weighing on his mind were the failure of the devolution ballot in 1979 and the evident collapse of the industrial life-support of his part of Wales. In the same context Emyr Humphreys, at the end of *The Taliesin Tradition* (1983), saw from the Cymraeg point of view the need to 'preserve the society under siege' but also felt a positive possibility that artists 'anchored in historical reality by their language, their landscape, their history' – that is, integrative Welsh artists – were capable of such resistance.[174] As if to move towards fulfilling his hope, in the last twenty years, the women writers and the chroniclers of the post-industrial world, have found more than dust and ashes. So have the Cymraeg authors: Robin Llywelyn and Wil Owen Roberts have created masterpieces of symbolic fiction that both realize despair and disability – future self-immolation and the historical plague – and also the power of imagining and writing: both have been translated and widely read in English, another form of integration.[175]

The voices of Wales have not been silenced; forms of communality have been reimagined, against what seem like overwhelming odds. In the last ten years there has been a relative flood of new fiction in Wales. A collection like *Mama's Baby (Papa's Maybe)* prints fifty-five different authors, all at work at the end of the twentieth century. New novels and forgotten reprints by women have appeared from the energetic Honno; the University of Wales Press has with Emyr Humphreys moved into classic reprints; novels come in steady numbers from local presses like Gomer, Seren and Parthian, often with Arts Council of Wales support. Aaron and Thomas have described this new, post-devolution efflorescence as giving 'the impression of a newly vitalized Welsh literary culture'. Yet the evidence of the past, of discontinuities and slumps in the success of Welsh fiction in English, suggests this is no time for confidence, let alone complacency: the sales are not huge, the publishing companies are insecure and often depend on massive inputs of committed and under-rewarded work. But just as the Cymraeg speakers and writers can justly say, in Dafydd Iwan's anthem of the language movement, 'dyn ni yma o hyd' (we are still here), the English-language writers of Wales have not been displaced by new colonial fictions, whether from London or New York; in fact in terms of their numbers, their access to local publishers and indeed their aggression, insubordinacy and – a crucial matter – their quality, they are probably going through one of their best periods.

It is a long way from an Allen Raine romance to a Rachel Trezise semi-tragedy, from Jack Jones's industrial boosting to Christopher Meredith's elegy for work and manhood. A century of writing has covered a great deal of ground, but so have the Welsh people and their socio-economic context. It is through their writers that the English-speaking people of Wales are able to look back at a literature as remarkably varied as their experience, and a literature that, like the people themselves, has with difficulty, uncertainty, but also with deter-mination and spirit, moved towards both some forms of integration with Cymraeg Wales and also real forms of independence, both emotional and political. These authors have thought with care, scepticism and a powerfully recurrent integrity about what values are most to be praised and what forms of oppression, deliberate or coincidental, are most to be criticized. The writers of Welsh fiction in English have constructed a monument to their own persevering commitment and skill, and a living memory of a unique culture for the people of Wales and for anyone around the world who might value a courageous, independent and vociferous literature.

Notes

NOTES TO SECTION 1

[1] Roland Mathias, *Anglo-Welsh Literature: An Illustrated History* (Bridgend, 1987).

[2] Moira Dearnley, *Distant Fields: Eighteenth-Century Fictions of Wales* (Cardiff, 2001).

[3] Andrew Davies, ' "The Reputed Nation of Inspiration": Representations of Wales in Fiction from the Romance Period, 1780–1829', Ph.D. thesis, Cardiff University, 2001; Jane Aaron, 'A National Seduction: Wales in Nineteenth-Century Women's Writing,' *New Welsh Review*, 27 (1994), 31–8, and *Pur Fel y Dur: Y Gymraes yn Llên Menywod y Bedwaredd Ganrif ar Bymtheg* (Caerdydd, 1998). Translations from this text have been approved by the author.

[4] John Davies, *Hanes Cymru* (London, 1990), tr. by the author as *A History of Wales* (London, 1993); Gwyn A. Williams, *When Was Wales?* (London, 1985).

[5] *Rebirth of a Nation: A History of Modern Wales* (Oxford, 1981), p. 14.

[6] Davies, *A History of Wales*, p.387.

[7] Gwyneth Tyson Roberts, *The Language of the Blue Books: The Perfect Instrument of Empire* (Cardiff, 1998).

[8] Davies, *A History of Wales*, p. 435.

[9] D. Gareth Evans, *A History of Wales, 1805–1906* (Cardiff, 1989), p. 228.

[10] T. J. Llewelyn Prichard, *The Adventures and Vagaries of Twm Shon Catti* (Aberystwyth, 1828). This was reprinted in London, as well as Wales, several times in the early nineteenth century, and some of the early editions gave a more colonized note by adding the subtitle 'The Welsh Robin Hood'.

[11] James Motley, *Tales of the Cymry* (London, 1848).

[12] George Tugwell, *On the Mountain, Being the Welsh Experience of Abraham Black and James White etc., Esquires, Moralists, Photographers, Fishermen, Botanists* (London, 1862).

13 Benjamin Williams, *Arthur Vaughan* (London, 1856).
14 Roland Mathias, *Anglo-Welsh Literature: An Illustrated History* (Bridgend, 1987), p. 66.
15 Williams, *When Was Wales?*, p. 201.
16 H. Elwyn Thomas, *Where Eden's Tongue is Spoken Still* (London and Newport, 1904).
17 Matthew Arnold, *On the Study of Celtic Literature* (London, 1867).
18 Ned Thomas, 'Images of Others', in John Osmond (ed.), *The National Question Again: Welsh Political Identity in the 1980s* (Llandysul, 1985), pp. 306–19, pp. 307–10.
19 Daniel Williams, 'Pan-Celticism and the Limits of Post-Colonialism: W. B. Yeats, Ernest Rhys and William Sharp in the 1890s', in Tony Brown and Russell Stephens (eds), *Nations and Relations: Writing Across the British Isles* (Cardiff, 2000), pp. 1–29, see especially pp. 5–11.
20 Alfred Thomas, *In the Land of Harp and Feather* (London, 1896).
21 R. Rice Davies, *The Cambrian Sketch-Book* (London, 1875).
22 James Kenwood, *For Cambria* (London, 1868), p. viii.
23 R. C. Halifax, *Among the Welsh Hills* (London, 1878).
24 Marie Trevelyan, *From Snowdonia to the Seas: Stirring Stories of North and South Wales* (London, 1895).
25 Alfred W. Rees, *Ianto the Fisherman and Other Stories of Country Life* (London, 1904).
26 Arthur Machen, *The Hill of Dreams* (London, 1907).
27 See D. P. Michael, *Arthur Machen* (Cardiff, 1971), p. 10.
28 Machen, *The Secret Glory* (London, 1922); for the date of writing see Michael, p. 34.
29 Ernest Rhys, *The Man at Odds* (London, 1904).
30 R. D. Blackmore, *The Maid of Sker* (London, 1872).
31 Matthew Arnold, *On the Study of Celtic Literatures and Other Essays* (London, 1910).
32 For a discussion of this story see Stephen Knight, 'Prowess and Courtesy: Chrétien de Troyes' *Le Chevalier au Lion*', ch. 3 of *Arthurian Literature and Society* (London, 1983), pp. 68–104.
33 Dai Smith, *Wales: A Question for History* (Bridgend, 1999), p. 93.
34 E. Everett Green, *Cambria's Chieftain* (London, 1903).
35 Owen Rhoscomyl, *The Jewel of Ynys Galon* (London, 1895).
36 Isaac Craigfryn Hughes, *The Maid of Cefn Ydfa* (Cardiff, 1881).
37 H. Elwyn Thomas, *The Forerunners* (Aberavon, 1910).
38 R. Dancey Green Price, *Rebecca, or A Life's Mistake: A Story of Country Life* (London, 1882).
39 ' "I came here a stranger": a view of Wales in the novels of Anne Beale (1815–1900)', *New Welsh Review*, 4 (1989), 27–32.
40 'A national seduction: Wales in nineteenth-century women's writing', *New Welsh Review*, 27 (1994–5), 31–8, see pp. 36–7; for the 'less snobbish' comment see *Pur fel y Dur*, p. 168.

[41] Rhoda Broughton, *Not Wisely But Too Well* (London, 1867), p. 6.

[42] Broughton, *Red as a Rose is She*, 2 vols (London, 1870), p. 8.

[43] Tamie Walters, introduction to repr. of *Belinda* (London, 1984 [1883]), pp. v–xv.

[44] Amy Dillwyn, *The Rebecca Rioter*, 2 vols (London, 1880); repr., with an introduction by Katie Gramich (Dinas Powys, 2001).

[45] Mallt and Gwenffreda Williams, *A Maid of Cymru* (London, 1901).

[46] Mallt and Gwenffreda Williams, *One of the Royal Celts* (London, 1889).

[47] Marion Löffler, 'A Romantic Nationalist', *Planet*, 121 (1997), 58–66, p. 60.

[48] Aaron, *Pur fel y Dur,* p. 209.

[49] See Sally [Roberts] Jones, *Allen Raine* (Cardiff, 1979), p. 14.

[50] Jones, *Allen Raine*, p. 2.

[51] Allen Raine, *Where Billows Roll: A Tale of the Western Coast* (London, 1909).

[52] Frederic Jameson, 'Third World Literature in the Era of Multinational Capitalism', *Social Text*, 15 (1986), 65–87.

[53] Jones, *Allen Raine*, p. 21.

[54] Aaron, *Pur fel y Dur,* p. 170.

[55] Jones, *Allen Raine*, p. 78; see also John Harris, '*Queen of the Rushes*: Allen Raine and her Public', *Planet*, 77 (1993), 64–72, p. 69.

[56] Gwyn Jones, *The First Forty Years: Some Notes on Anglo-Welsh Literature* (Cardiff, 1957); repr. in Sam Adams and Gwilym Rees Hughes (eds), *Triskel One: Essays on Welsh and Anglo-Welsh Literature* (Llandybïe, 1971), pp. 75–95, see p. 78.

[57] Jones, *Allen Raine*, pp. 85–6; Katie Gramich, introduction to repr. edn of *Queen of the Rushes: A Tale of the Welsh Revival* (Dinas Powys, 1998), pp. 7–9.

[58] The issue is discussed by Glenys Goetinck in her introduction to *Peredur: A Study of Welsh Tradition in the Grail Legends* (Cardiff, 1975), pp. 129–55; but there are many instances of this figure, including 'Laudine' in *Yvain*, discussed above and Guinevere (Gwenhwyfar) herself, whose marriage to Arthur confirms his kingship.

[59] Gramich, *Queen of the Rushes*, pp. 15–21.

[60] Allen Raine, *Torn Sails* (London, 1898).

[61] Jones, *Allen Raine*, p. 56.

[62] Raine, *Garthowen: A Story of a Welsh Homestead* (London, 1900).

[63] Gramich, *Queen of the Rushes*, p. 5.

[64] Raine, *A Welsh Witch: A Romance of Rough Places* (London, 1902).

[65] Raine, *Hearts of Wales: An Old Romance* (London, 1904).

[66] Raine, *Queen of the Rushes* (London, 1906).

[67] Aaron, *Pur fel y Dur*, p. 179.

[68] Williams calls him 'The first novelist I know of who had worked in a coalmine' in 'Working-class, Proletarian, Socialist: Problems in some Welsh novels', in H. Gustav Klaus (ed.), *The Socialist Novel in Britain* (Brighton, 1982), pp. 110–21, see p. 115.

[69] Joseph Keating, *Son of Judith* (London, 1900); Keating describes writing the novel in *My Struggle for Life* (London, 1916), p. 193.

[70] Keating, *Maurice* (London, 1905).

[71] Keating, *My Struggle for Life,* p. 222.

[72] Keating, *The Queen of Swords: The Story of a Woman and an Extraordinary Duel* (London, 1906).

[73] Keating, *Flower of the Dark* (London, 1917).

[74] D. Miles Lewis, *Chapel: The Story of a Welsh Family* (London, 1919).

[75] Irene Saunderson, *A Welsh Heroine: A Romance of Colliery Life* (London, 1911).

[76] The epithet is M. Wynn Thomas's in *Corresponding Cultures: The Two Literatures of Wales* (Cardiff, 1999), p. 19.

[77] See Jones, *The First Forty Years*, p. 78.

[78] John Harris, 'Caradoc Evans as Editor of "Ideas" ', *Planet*, 53 (1985), 52–62.

[79] Repr. in *Fury Never Leaves Us: A Miscellany*, ed. and with an introduction by John Harris (Bridgend, 1986), pp. 49–52.

[80] See Harris, introduction to *Capel Sion*, repr. edn (Bridgend, 2002), p. x.

[81] See Harris's introduction to *My People*, repr. edn (Bridgend, 1987), pp. 37–46, and T. L. Williams, *Caradoc Evans* (Cardiff, 1987), pp. 1–3, 20–1.

[82] Caradoc Evans, *My People* (London, 1915).

[83] Katie Gramich, 'The Madwoman in the Harness Loft: Women and Madness in the Literature of Wales', in Katie Gramich and Andrew Hiscock (eds), *Dangerous Diversity: The Changing Faces of Wales: Essays in Honour of Tudor Bevan* (Cardiff, 1998), pp. 20–33, see p. 21.

[84] See Harris, introduction to repr. edn of *My People*, p. 16.

[85] Evans, *Capel Sion* (London, 1916).

[86] Introduction to *Capel Sion*, repr. edn, p. xv.

[87] Evans, *My Neighbours* (London, 1919).

[88] Williams, *Caradoc Evans*, pp. 83–5.

[89] Evans, *Nothing to Pay* (London, 1930); repr. with afterword by John Harris (Manchester, 1989).

[90] Evans, *Wasps* (London, 1933).

[91] Evans, *The Earth Gives All and Takes All* (London, 1946), p. v.

[92] Glyn Jones, *The Dragon Has Two Tongues* (London, 1968); repr. edn, ed. Tony Brown (Cardiff, 2001), p. 73.

[93] T. W. H. Crosland, *The Perfidious Welshman* (London, 1910); *Taffy Was A Welshman* (London, 1912).

[94] Evans, *Fury Never Leaves Us*, pp. 164–218.

[95] Williams, *Caradoc Evans*, p. 89.

[96] Dearnley, *Distant Fields*, p. 1.

[97] Introduction to *Capel Sion*, p. xix.

[98] John Harris, 'Publishing *My People*: The Book as Expressive Object', *New Welsh Review*, 1 (1988), 23–9, see p. 28.

[99] The fullest account of the connections between Brown and Evans is by

Regina Weingartner, 'The Fight against Sentimentalism: Caradoc Evans and George Douglas Brown', *Planet*, 75 (1989), 86–92.

[100] John Harris, 'The Devil in Eden: Caradoc Evans and his Work', *New Welsh Review*, 1 (1992–3), 10–18, see p. 13.

[101] Quoted in John Harris's introduction to *Capel Sion*, p. viii.

[102] Quoted in John Harris's introduction to *My People,* p. 33.

[103] Barbara Prys-Williams, 'Fury Never Left Him', *New Welsh Review*, 8 (1995–6), 60–2, see p. 62.

[104] D. J. Williams, *Hen Dŷ Ffarm* (Aberystwyth, 1953).

[105] W. J. Rees, 'Inequalities: Caradoc Evans and D. J. Williams', *Planet*, 81 (1990), 69–80.

[106] Ibid., p. 77.

[107] Harris, '*Queen of the Rushes*: Allen Raine', p. 70.

[108] Hilda Vaughan, *The Battle to the Weak* (London, 1925).

[109] Vaughan, *The Invader* (London, 1928).

[110] Christopher W. Newman, *Hilda Vaughan* (Cardiff, 1981), p. 32.

[111] Vaughan, *The Soldier and the Gentlewoman* (London, 1932).

[112] Newman, *Hilda Vaughan*, p. 58.

[113] G. F. Adam, *Three Contemporary Anglo-Welsh Novelists: Jack Jones, Rhys Davies and Hilda Vaughan* (Bern, 1949), p. 76.

[114] Vaughan, *Here are Lovers* (London, 1926).

[115] Vaughan, *Harvest Home* (London, 1936).

[116] Vaughan, *A Thing of Nought* (London, 1934); repr. in Jane Aaron (ed.), *A View Across the Valley* (Dinas Powys, 1999).

[117] Vaughan, *The Fair Woman* (New York, 1942); as *Iron and Gold* (London, 1948).

[118] Vaughan, *Iron and Gold* (Dinas Powys, 2002).

[119] Sam Adams, *Geraint Goodwin* (Cardiff, 1975), p. 1.

[120] Geraint Goodwin, *Call Back Yesterday* (London, 1935).

[121] Adams, *Geraint Goodwin*, pp. 36–7.

[122] Goodwin, *The Heyday in the Blood* (London, 1936).

[123] Adams, *Geraint Goodwin*, p. 44.

[124] Ibid., pp. 7–8.

[125] Goodwin, *The White Farm and Other Stories* (London, 1937).

[126] Goodwin, *Come Michaelmas* (London, 1939); *Watch for the Morning* (London, 1938).

[127] Ceridwen Lloyd-Morgan, *Margiad Evans* (Bridgend, 1998), p. 7; see also Moira Dearnley, *Margiad Evans* (Cardiff, 1982).

[128] Evans, *Country Dance* (London, 1932).

[129] Lloyd-Morgan, *Margiad Evans*, p. 23.

[130] Clare Morgan, 'Exile and the Kingdom: Margiad Evans and the Mythic Landscape of Wales', *Welsh Writing in English*, 6 (2000), 89–115, p. 115.

[131] Evans, *The Old and the Young* (London, 1948); repr. with introduction by Ceridwen Lloyd-Morgan (Bridgend, 1998).

NOTES TO SECTION 2

[1] John Davies, *A History of Wales* (London, 1987), p. 469.
[2] See Eric Hobsbawm, *From 1750 to the Present Day: Industry and Empire*, vol. 3 of *The Pelican Economic History of Britain* (London, 1968), p. 298.
[3] Glyn Tegai Hughes, 'The Mythology of the Mining Valleys', in Sam Adams and Gwilym Rees Hughes (eds), *Triskel Two: Essays on Welsh and Anglo-Welsh Literature* (Llandysul, 1973), pp. 42–61; Hywel Teifi Edwards, 'The Welsh Collier as Hero 1850–1950', *Welsh Writing in English*, 2 (1996), 22–48.
[4] Gwyn A. Williams, *When Was Wales?* (London, 1985), p. 187.
[5] Davies, *A History of Wales*, p. 437.
[6] Chris Williams, *Capitalism, Community and Conflict: The South Wales Coalfield, 1898–1947* (Cardiff, 1998), p. 21.
[7] Davies, *A History of Wales*, p. 487.
[8] Ibid., p. 443.
[9] Ibid., p. 466. See also Kenneth O. Morgan, *Rebirth of a Nation: A History of Modern Wales* (Oxford, 1981), p. 241.
[10] Davies, *A History of Wales*, pp. 474 and 484.
[11] Davies, *A History of Wales*, p. 535.
[12] Chris Williams, *Capitalism, Community and Conflict*, pp. 69–70.
[13] *Chwalfa* (Aberystwyth, 1946), tr. Richard Ruck as *Out of Their Night* (Aberystwyth, 1954); *Traed mewn Cyffion* (Aberystwyth, 1936), tr. J. I. Jones as *Feet in Chains* (Denbigh, 1977).
[14] Joseph Furphy, *Such is Life* (Sydney, 1903).
[15] Early examples are the stories collected in *While the Billy Boils* (Sydney, 1896).
[16] Dai Smith, *Wales: A Question for History* (Bridgend, 1999).
[17] Davies, *A History of Wales*, p. 494.
[18] *The Miners' Next Step* (Tonypandy, 1912).
[19] Davies, *A History of Wales*, p. 491.
[20] D. K. Davies, 'The Influence of Syndicalism and Industrial Unionism on the South Wales Coalfield, 1898–1922: A Study in Ideology and Practice', Ph.D., University of Wales (Cardiff), 1994.
[21] See Stephen Knight, 'Anarcho-Syndicalism and Welsh Industrial Fiction', in *Anarchism in Twentieth Century British Literature*, H. Gustav Klaus and Stephen Knight (eds) (Cardiff, forthcoming, 2005).
[22] See Smith, *Wales*, pp. 139–40.
[23] Davies, *A History of Wales*, p. 471.
[24] Raymond Williams, *The Welsh Industrial Novel* (Cardiff, 1979), p. 7; repr. in Raymond Williams, *When Was Wales?*, ed. Daniel Williams (Cardiff, 2003), pp. 95–111.
[25] Glyn Jones, *The Dragon Has Two Tongues* (London, 1968; second edn, ed. Tony Brown, Cardiff, 2001), p. 41.
[26] Williams, *Capitalism, Community and Conflict*, p. 62.
[27] 'Under the Sway of Coal', *New Welsh Review*, 39 (1997), 29–31, see p. 29.

28 Rhys Davies, *The Withered Root* (London, 1927), pp. 241–2.
29 Hughes, 'The Mythology of the Mining Valleys', p. 49; Stephens, introduction to Meic Stephens (ed.), *Rhys Davies: Decoding the Hare* (Cardiff, 2001), p. 1.
30 Rhys Davies, *Print of a Hare's Foot* (London, 1969).
31 For a discussion of his work in this light see Stephen Knight, ' "Not a Place for Me": Rhys Davies's Fiction and the Coal Industry' in *Rhys Davies: Decoding the Hare*, pp. 54–70.
32 Dai Smith, 'Rhys Davies and his Turbulent Valley', in *Rhys Davies: Decoding the Hare*, pp. 29–39, see p. 31.
33 Rhys Davies, *My Wales* (London, 1937), pp. 102–3 and 46.
34 Davies, *My Wales*, pp. 97 and 98.
35 Smith, 'Rhys Davies and His Turbulent Valley', p. 31; see also his comments in *Aneurin Bevan and the World of South Wales* (Cardiff, 1993), p. 62.
36 See D. A. Callard, 'One Rainy Sunday Afternoon', in *Rhys Davies: Decoding the Hare*, pp. 138–46, see pp. 142–3.
37 Smith, 'Rhys Davies and His Turbulent Valley', pp. 35 and 36–9.
38 Davies, *The Withered Root*, p. 112.
39 Davies, *Print of a Hare's Foot*, p. 99.
40 Davies, *My Wales*, p. 14.
41 Jones, *The Dragon Has Two Tongues*, p. 107.
42 Rhys Davies, 'Writing about the Welsh', in John Gawsworth (ed.), *Ten Contemporaries: Notes Towards their Definitive Bibliography* (London, 1932), pp. 41–3, see p. 43.
43 Davies, *Rings on her Fingers* (London, 1930).
44 See J. Lawrence Mitchell, ' "I Wish I had a Trumpet": Rhys Davies and the Creative Impulse', in Belinda Humfrey (ed.), *Fire Green as Grass* (Llandysul, 1995), pp. 96–111, repr. in *Rhys Davies: Decoding the Hare*, pp. 147–61, see p. 151.
45 Daniel Williams, 'Withered Roots: Ideas of Race in the Writings of Rhys Davies and D. H. Lawrence' in *Rhys Davies: Decoding the Hare*, pp. 87–103
46 Stephens, introduction to *Rhys Davies: Decoding the Hare*, pp. 1–14, see p. 4.
47 Williams, 'Withered Roots', p. 100.
48 Davies, *The Red Hills* (London, 1932).
49 He finds the hills 'vivid in their Lawrentianism,' see Jeff Wallace, 'Lawrentianisms: Rhys Davies and D. H. Lawrence', in *Rhys Davies: Decoding the Hare*, pp. 175–90, p. 183.
50 M. Wynn Thomas, ' "Never seek to tell thy love": Rhys Davies's Fiction', *Welsh Writing in English*, 4 (1998), 1–21; repr. in *Rhys Davies: Decoding the Hare*, pp. 260–82, see p. 276.
51 Davies, *My Wales*, p. 138.
52 Davies, *Honey and Bread* (London, 1935).
53 Ibid., pp. 235–6.

[54] Michael Dixon, 'The Epic Rhondda: Romanticism and Realism in the Rhondda Trilogy', in *Rhys Davies: Decoding the Hare*, pp. 40–53, see p. 43.
[55] Ibid., p. 44.
[56] Davies, *A Time to Laugh* (London, 1937).
[57] Dixon, 'The Epic Rhondda', p. 47.
[58] Ibid., p. 46.
[59] Davies, *Jubilee Blues* (London, 1938).
[60] Davies, *Count Your Blessings* (London, 1932).
[61] Dixon, 'The Epic Rhondda', p. 49.
[62] Davies, *Tomorrow to Fresh Woods* (London, 1941).
[63] Mitchell, 'I Wish I had a Trumpet', p.156.
[64] Davies, *The Story of Wales* (London, 1943).
[65] Katie Gramich, 'The Masquerade of Gender in the Stories of Rhys Davies', in *Rhys Davies: Decoding the Hare*, pp. 205–15, p. 209.
[66] Jane Aaron, 'Daughters of Darkness: Rhys Davies's Revenge Tragedies', in *Rhys Davies: Decoding the Hare*, pp. 216–30, p. 229.
[67] Linden Peach, 'Eccentricity and Lawlessness in Rhys Davies's Short Fiction', in *Rhys Davies: Decoding the Hare*, pp. 162–74, see p. 171.
[68] Davies, *The Black Venus* (London, 1944).
[69] Kirsh Bohata, 'The Black Venus: Atavistic Sexualities', in *Rhys Davies: Decoding the Hare*, pp. 231–43.
[70] Jones, *The Dragon Has Two Tongues*, p. 11.
[71] Smith, *Wales*, p. 174.
[72] Jack Jones, *Unfinished Journey* (London, 1937).
[73] Keri Edwards, *Jack Jones* (Cardiff, 1974), p. 9.
[74] Jones, *Black Parade* (London, 1935).
[75] Smith, *Aneurin Bevan*, p. 115; Jones, *The Dragon Has Two Tongues*, p. 96; Williams, *The Welsh Industrial Novel*, p. 15.
[76] Edwards, *Jack Jones*, p. 14.
[77] Jones, *The Dragon Has Two Tongues*, p. 91; G. F. Adam, *Three Contemporary Anglo-Welsh Novelists: Jack Jones, Rhys Davies and Hilda Vaughan* (Bern, 1949), p. 27.
[78] Adam, *Three Contemporary Anglo-Welsh Novelists,* p. 37.
[79] Williams, *The Welsh Industrial Novel*, p. 17.
[80] Jones, *Rhondda Roundabout* (London, 1934).
[81] Smith, *Wales*, p. 174.
[82] Jones, *Bidden to the Feast* (London, 1938).
[83] Jones, *The Dragon Has Two Tongues*, p. 96.
[84] Morgan, *Rebirth of a Nation*, p. 261.
[85] Gwyn Jones, *Times Like These* (London, 1938).
[86] Raymond Williams, 'Region and Class in the Novel', in *Writing in Society* (London, 1983), pp. 229–38, p. 236.
[87] James A. Davies, ' "Two Strikes and You're Out": 1926 and 1984 in Welsh Industrial Fiction', in H. Gustav Klaus and Stephen Knight (eds), *British Industrial Fictions* (Cardiff, 2000), pp. 137–47.
[88] James A. Davies, 'Kinds of Relating: Gwyn Thomas (Jack Jones, Lewis

Jones, Glyn Jones) and the Welsh Industrial Experience', *Anglo-Welsh Review,* 86 (1987), 72–80, see p. 75

89 Dai Smith, 'A Novel History' in Tony Curtis (ed.), *Wales: The Imagined Nation: Studies in Cultural and National Identity* (Bridgend, 1986), pp. 129–58, see p. 141.

90 Adam, *Three Contemporary Anglo-Welsh Novelists,* p. 26.

91 'A White Birthday', repr. in Alun Richards (ed.), *The Second Penguin Book of Welsh Short Stories* (London, 1993); 'The Brute Creation', repr. in Alun Richards (ed.), *The Penguin Book of Welsh Short Stories* (London, 1976).

92 Dai Smith, *Lewis Jones* (Cardiff, 1982), p. 16.

93 Smith, *Wales,* p. 175.

94 Lewis Jones, foreword to *Cwmardy* (London, 1937), unpaginated.

95 Dai Smith, introduction to repr. edn of *Cwmardy* (London, 1979), unpaginated.

96 Williams, *When Was Wales?,* p. 271.

97 Smith, *Lewis Jones,* p. 78.

98 John Pikoulis, 'The Wounded Bard: The Welsh Novel in English: Lewis Jones, Glyn Jones, Emyr Humphreys', *New Welsh Review,* 26 (1994), 22–34.

99 Review of Lewis Jones, *We Live, Welsh Review,* 1 (1939), 235–6, see p. 236.

100 Andy Croft, *Red Letter Days: British Fiction in the Thirties* (London, 1990), p. 91.

101 Frank Kermode, *History and Value* (Oxford, 1988), pp. 89–90.

102 Hughes, 'The Mythology of the Mining Valleys', p. 51.

103 Davies, 'Kinds of Relating', p. 73.

104 As David Smith, 'Myth and Meaning in the Literature of the South Wales Coalfield', *The Anglo-Welsh Review,* 25 (1975), 21–42, pp. 26–7.

105 Carole Snee, 'Working-class Literature or Proletarian Writing', in Jon Clark *et al.* (eds), *Culture and Criticism in Britain in the 30s* (London, 1979), pp. 165–91.

106 Williams, 'Region and Class', p. 236.

107 B. L. Coombes, *These Poor Hands* (London, 1939).

108 Bill Jones and Chris Williams, *B. L. Coombes* (Cardiff, 1999).

109 See introduction by Bill Jones and Chris Williams to the repr. of B. L. Coombes, *These Poor Hands* (Cardiff, 2002), p. xiv.

110 Barbara Prys-Williams, 'A Miner "On Message" ', *New Welsh Review,* 48 (2000), 14–16 and ' "A Difficult Man, Your Coombes" ', *New Welsh Review,* 49 (2000), 55–60.

111 Introduction to *These Poor Hands,* pp. xiv–xv.

112 A segment of the surviving manuscript is reprinted in Bill Jones and Chris Williams (eds.), *With Dust Still in his Throat: A B. L. Coombes Anthology* (Cardiff, 1999).

113 Quoted by Jones and Williams, *B. L. Coombes,* p. 95.

114 Quoted in Ian Michael, *Gwyn Thomas* (Cardiff, 1977), p. 55.

115 Quoted in Dai Smith, introduction to Gwyn Thomas, *Sorrow for thy Sons* (London, 1986), p. 7.

116 Smith, introduction, p. 8.
117 Smith, introduction, p. 8.
118 Jack Jones, *Unfinished Journey*, p. 281.
119 Gwyn Thomas, *A Few Selected Exits* (London, 1968).
120 M. Wynn Thomas, *Internal Difference: Twentieth-Century Writing in Wales* (Cardiff, 1992), p. 43; Dai Smith, 'A Novel History', p. 147.
121 Thomas, *Where Did I Put My Pity?* (London, 1946).
122 Stephen Knight, 'The Voices of Glamorgan: Gwyn Thomas's Colonial Fiction', *Welsh Writing in English*, 7 (2001–2), 16–34.
123 'Myself my Desert' in *Where Did I Put my Pity?*, p. 193.
124 Smith, *Aneurin Bevan*, p. 143.
125 Smith, *Wales*, p. 185.
126 'The Dark Philosophers' in Jack Aistrop (ed.), *Triad One* (London, 1946).
127 Davies, 'Kinds of Relating', p. 81.
128 Thomas, *The Alone to the Alone* (London, 1947).
129 Victor Golightly, ' "We, who Speak for the Workers": The Correspondence of Gwyn Thomas and Howard Fast', *Welsh Writing in English*, 6 (2000), 67–88.
130 Golightly, ' "We, who Speak for the Workers" ', p. 71.
131 Thomas, *All Things Betray Thee* (London, 1949).
132 Smith, *Aneurin Bevan*, p. 121.
133 Davies, 'Kinds of Relating', p. 77.
134 Chris Meredith, 'Two from the Heart', *Planet*, 59 (1986), 98–9, see p. 99.
135 Jones, *The Dragon Has Two Tongues*, p. 108.
136 Smith, *Aneurin Bevan*, p. 273.
137 Williams, 'Region and Class', p. 237.
138 Raymond Williams, 'Working-class, Proletarian, Socialist: Problems in Some Welsh Novels', in H. Gustav Klaus (ed.), *The Socialist Novel in Britain: Towards the Recovery of a Tradition* (Brighton, 1982), pp. 110–21, see p. 118.
139 *All Things Betray Thee*, repr. edn (London, 1986), pp. ix–x.
140 Thomas, *The World Cannot Hear You* (London, 1951).
141 Thomas, *The Thinker and the Thrush* (Bridgend, 1988).
142 Thomas, *Now Lead Us Home* (London, 1952).
143 Thomas, *A Frost on my Frolic* (London, 1953).
144 Thomas, *The Stranger at my Side* (London, 1954).
145 Harri Pritchard Jones, *Poetry Wales*, 4 (1969), 45–50, see p. 47.
146 Jones, *The Dragon Has Two Tongues*, p. 107.
147 Quoted in Michael Parnell, *Laughter from the Dark* (London, 1988; repr. Bridgend, 1997), p. 220.
148 Ian Bell, 'How Green *was* My Valley?' *Planet*, 73 (1989), 3–9, p. 3.
149 Richard Llewellyn, *How Green Was My Valley?* (London, 1939).
150 *The Times Literary Supplement*, 7 October 1939, p. 575; Ben Ray Redman, 'An Age of Goodness I Knew', *The Saturday Review of Literature, XXI, no. 16, 10 February 1940, p. 5.
151 *New Statesman and Nation, XVIII, 450, 7 October 1939, p. 496.

[152] Smith, *Aneurin Bevan*, p. 94; 'A Novel History', p. 140; David Smith, 'Myth and Meaning', p. 33.

[153] Williams, *The Welsh Industrial Novel*, p. 17; Hughes, 'Mythology of the Mining Valleys', p. 60.

NOTES TO SECTION 3

[1] Leslie Norris, *Glyn Jones* (Cardiff, 1997), p. 4.

[2] Glyn Jones, *The Blue Bed and Other Stories* (London, 1937).

[3] *The Water Music and Other Stories* (London, 1944); Meic Stephens (ed.), *The New Companion to the Literature of Wales* (Cardiff, 1998), p. 378.

[4] Jones, *The Valley, the City, the Village* (London, 1956).

[5] M. Wynn Thomas, *Corresponding Cultures: the Two Literatures of Wales* (Cardiff, 1999), p. 107.

[6] Jones, *The Learning Lark* (London, 1960).

[7] Jones, *The Island of Apples* (London, 1965).

[8] Norris, *Glyn Jones*, p. 11.

[9] M. Wynn Thomas, *Internal Difference: Literature in Twentieth-Century Wales* (Cardiff, 1992), p. 29.

[10] Jones, *The Dragon has Two Tongues* (London, 1968); revised edn, ed. Tony Brown (Cardiff, 2001).

[11] Introduction to Walford Davies (ed.), *Dylan Thomas: Early Prose Writing* (London, 1971), pp. vii–xvi, p. ix.

[12] Dylan Thomas, *A Map of Love* (London, 1939).

[13] Davies, see note 11; Norris, introduction to Leslie Norris (ed.), *Dylan Thomas, Collected Stories* (London, 1983), pp. ix–xvii.

[14] Davies, introduction, p. xi.

[15] See Davies, introduction, p. x and Norris, introduction, p. ix.

[16] Dylan Thomas, *A Portrait of the Artist as a Young Dog* (London, 1940).

[17] Alun Lewis, *The Last Inspection* (London, 1942).

[18] John Pikoulis, *Alun Lewis* (Bridgend, 1984), p. 85.

[19] Alun Lewis, *In The Green Tree* (London, 1948 [actually published 1949]), p. 51.

[20] Tony Brown and M. Wynn Thomas, 'Colonial Wales and Functional Language', in T. Brown and R. Stephens (eds), *Nations and Relations: Writing Across the British Isles* (Cardiff, 2000), pp. 71–88, see p. 72.

[21] Michael Gareth Llewelyn, *Sand in the Glass* (London, 1943).

[22] Llewelyn, *Angharad's Isle* (London, 1944).

[23] Llewelyn, *The Aleppo Merchant* (London, 1945).

[24] Hilda Vaughan, *The Fair Woman* (New York, 1942).

[25] Llewelyn, *To Fame Unknown* (London, 1949).

[26] Menna Gallie, *Strike for a Kingdom* (London, 1959).

[27] D. J. Williams, *Hen Dŷ Ffarm* (Aberystwyth, 1953); for Gallie's uncle as the basis of the character, see Angela Fish, introduction to the reprint edition of *Strike for a Kingdom* (Dinas Powys, 2003), pp. ix–x.

[28]   Gallie, *The Small Mine* (London, 1962); Aaron, foreword to repr. edn of *The Small Mine* (Dinas Powys, 2000), pp. v–xiv, p. xiii.

[29]   Foreword to *The Small Mine*, p. ix.

[30]   Raymond Stephens, 'The Novelist and community: Menna Gallie', *Anglo-Welsh Review*, 14 (1964–5), 52–63, see p. 56.

[31]   Aaron, foreword to *The Small Mine*, p. xiii.

[32]   Gallie, *Man's Desiring* (London, 1960).

[33]   See Emyr Humphreys, in M. Wynn Thomas (ed.), *Conversations and Reflections* (Cardiff, 2002), p. 218.

[34]   See Tony Brown and M. Wynn Thomas, 'The Problems of Belonging', ch. 5 of M. Wynn Thomas (ed.), *Welsh Writing in English* (Cardiff, 2003), pp. 164–202, see pp. 191–2.

[35]   Brown and Thomas, 'Problems of Belonging', p. 192.

[36]   M. Wynn Thomas, *Emyr Humphreys* (Caernarfon, 1989), p. 10. Translations from the original Cymraeg have been approved by the author.

[37]   Emyr Humphreys, *A Toy Epic* (London, 1958); for Thomas's comments see his introduction to the reprint edition (Bridgend, 1989), pp. 8–10.

[38]   For discussion of the production of the final English version of *A Toy Epic*, see M. Wynn Thomas's introduction to the reprint edition, pp. 8–13.

[39]   See his comments about Greene and Malraux as the kinds of morally serious authors that the 'Protestant novel' should be equalling, in his essay originally titled 'The Protestant Novel', *The Listener*, 2 April 1953, 557–9, repr. as 'A Protestant View of the Modern Novel' in *Conversations and Reflections*, pp. 67–76. Ioan Williams comments on Greene's influence on Humphreys in *Emyr Humphreys* (Cardiff, 1980), p. 24.

[40]   The comments are recorded in Thomas, *Internal Difference,* p. 84.

[41]   See Emyr Humphreys, *The Taliesin Tradition* (London, 1983), p. 186.

[42]   Williams, *Emyr Humphreys*, p. 29.

[43]   Humphreys, *Hear and Forgive* (London, 1952).

[44]   See note 39.

[45]   Humphreys, *A Man's Estate* (London, 1955).

[46]   See Stanley Cooperman's review in *The Nation*, 183, 8 September 1956, 205–6, repr. in *Contemporary Literary Criticism*, 47, ed. Daniel G. Marowski and Robert Matuz (Detroit, 1988), p. 179; I. Williams, *Emyr Humphreys*, p. 24; and Linden Peach, 'The Woolf at Faulkner's Door: Modernism and the Body in Emyr Humphreys' 1950s Fiction', *Welsh Writing in English*, 6 (2000), 144–62.

[47]   See his comments in *Conversations and Reflections*, p. 217.

[48]   Brown and Thomas, 'Problems of Belonging', p. 195.

[49]   Humphreys, *Outside the House of Baal* (London, 1965).

[50]   One sequence of retrospective action was omitted from the first edition: Humphreys is reported as not remembering why, but as it involves a sexual encounter perhaps this was a form of editorial censorship. See pp. 318–27 of the text and note 110 (by M. Wynn Thomas) in the reprint edition (Bridgend, 1996), p. 408.

[51] Jeremy Hooker, 'A Seeing Belief: A Study of Emyr Humphreys' *Outside the House of Baal*', *Planet*, 39 (1977), 35–43, see p. 37.

[52] See the preface by Humphreys to the 1996 repr., p. 7.

[53] For the location see Humphreys's preface to the 1996 repr., p. 7; for the house name see Thomas, *Emyr Humphreys*, p. 13.

[54] Thomas, *Emyr Humphreys*, p. 46.

[55] M. Wynn Thomas, '*Outside the House of Baal*: The Evolution of a Major Novel', in Sam Adams (ed.), *Seeing Wales Whole: Essays on the Literature of Wales* (Cardiff, 1998), pp. 121–43, see p.127.

[56] *Conversations and Reflections*, p. 62.

[57] See Thomas, '*Outside the House of Baal*', pp. 124–6 and p. 143, n. 4.

[58] Thomas, *Emyr Humphreys*, p. 68.

[59] Preface, pp. 9, 12.

[60] Humphreys, *Jones* (London, 1984).

[61] Brown and Thomas, 'Problems of Belonging', pp. 192–3.

[62] Thomas, *Emyr Humphreys*, p. 24.

[63] Preface, p. 13.

[64] Thomas, '*Outside the House of Baal*', p. 134.

[65] Humphreys, *National Winner* (London, 1971).

[66] John Pikoulis, 'The Wounded Bard: The Welsh Novel in English: Lewis Jones, Glyn Jones, Emyr Humphreys', *New Welsh Review*, 26 (1994), 22–34.

[67] Humphreys, *Flesh and Blood* (London, 1974).

[68] Williams, *Emyr Humphreys,* p. 13.

[69] Jane Aaron and M. Wynn Thomas, ' "Pulling you through changes": Welsh Writing before, between and after two Referenda', ch. 9 in M. Wynn Thomas (ed.), *Welsh Writing in English*, pp. 278–309, see p. 284.

[70] Humphreys, *The Best of Friends* (London, 1978).

[71] Thomas, *Emyr Humphreys*, p. 25.

[72] Humphreys, *An Absolute Hero* (London, 1984).

[73] Humphreys, *Open Secrets* (London, 1988).

[74] See Thomas, '*Outside the House of Baal*', p. 142.

[75] Humphreys, *Bonds of Attachment* (London, 1991).

[76] Brown and Thomas, 'Problems of Belonging', p. 197.

[77] See introduction to Raymond Williams, *Who Speaks for Wales?: Nation, Culture, Identity*, ed. Daniel Williams (Cardiff, 2003), pp. xv–liii.

[78] *Border Country* (London, 1960). Williams describes his early attempts at novels in *Politics and Letters: Interviews with New Left Review* (London, 1979), pp. 277–8. The information about his father's death stimulating a new version of *Border Country* was conveyed by Merryn Williams, Williams's daughter, at a conference of the Association for Welsh Writing in English at Gregynog, March 2003.

[79] Introduction to *A View across the Valley: Short Stories by Women from Wales, c.1850–1950* (Dinas Powys, 1999), pp. ix–xx, pp. ix–xiv.

[80] See Raymond Williams, *The Welsh Industrial Novel*, The Inaugural Gwyn Jones Lecture (Cardiff, 1979); 'Working-Class, Proletarian, Socialist:

Problems in Some Welsh Novels', in H. Gustav Klaus (ed.), *The Socialist Novel in Britain: Towards the Recovery of a Tradition* (Brighton, 1982), pp. 110–21; and also the introduction to Gwyn Thomas's *All Things Betray Thee*, reprint edition (London, 1986), pp. iii–x. The first essay was reprinted in Raymond Williams, *Problems in Materialism and Culture* (London, 1980), pp. 213–89. All three essays are reprinted in Daniel Williams (ed.), *Who Speaks for Wales*, pp. 95–101, pp. 147–58 and pp. 159–64.

[81] Raymond Williams, *Second Generation* (London, 1964).

[82] Wiliams, *Politics and Letters*, p. 286.

[83] The statement was made by Williams's interviewers, and not contradicted by him, in *Politics and Letters*, p. 271.

[84] Introduction to *Who Speaks for Wales?*

[85] Williams, *The Country and the City* (London, 1973).

[86] These essays and reviews have been gathered in *Who Speaks for Wales?*

[87] Katie Gramich, ' "Both in and out of the Game": Welsh Writers and the British Dimension', ch. 8 in M. Wynn Thomas (ed.), *Welsh Writing in English*, pp. 255–77, see p. 272.

[88] Merryn Williams said this when launching Daniel Williams's *Who Speaks for Wales?* (see note 78); her comment contradicts the view reported by Fred Inglis (*Raymond Williams*, p. 190) that Terry Eagleton was the model for Peter Owen.

[89] Williams, *Television: Technology and Cultural Form* (London, 1974).

[90] Williams, *The Volunteers* (London, 1978).

[91] For a discussion of the novel as crime fiction see Stephen Knight, 'Raymond Williams's *The Volunteers* as Crime Fiction', *Welsh Writing in English*, 2 (1996), 126–37.

[92] Williams, *Loyalties* (London, 1985).

[93] Williams, *The Beginning* (London, 1989); *The Eggs of the Eagle* (London, 1991).

[94] Raymond Williams, 'People of the Black Mountains: Interview with John Barnie', *Planet*, 65 (1987), 3–13, pp. 7 and 3; the interview is reprinted in Williams (ed.), *Who Speaks for Wales?*, pp. 165–74.

[95] I am grateful to Dai Smith and Merryn Williams for their comments on the process by which Joy and Raymond Williams developed the 'Black Mountains' project.

[96] Williams, *The Volunteers*, p. 28.

[97] Tony Pinkney, *Raymond Williams* (Bridgend, 1991).

[98] A statement recorded in Inglis, *Raymond Williams*, p. 257.

[99] *The Guardian,* 3 June 1971, 15; repr. in *Who Speaks for Wales?*, pp. 3–4.

[100] See the interview with *Poetry Wales*, 'Marxism, Poetry, Wales', *Poetry Wales*, 13 (1977), 16–34; repr. in *Who Speaks for Wales?*, pp. 81–94, see p. 86.

[101] Stuart Evans, *Meritocrats* (London, 1974); *The Caves of Alienation* (London, 1977).

[102] Roland Mathias, 'Literature in English', in Meic Stephens (ed.), *The Arts in Wales* (Cardiff, 1976), pp. 207–38, see pp. 207–8; for Raymond Williams's

comment that 'Welsh writing became fashionable between the late thirties and the early fifties' see *Politics and Letters*, p. 279.

[103] For a discussion of this phenomenon see Stephen Knight, *Arthurian Literature and Society* (London, 1983), pp. 209–14.

[104] Richard Vaughan, *Moulded in Earth* (London, 1951).

[105] John Harris, 'Popular Images', ch. 6 in M. Wynn Thomas (ed.), *Welsh Writing in English*, pp. 203–21, see pp. 210, 212.

[106] Quoted by Tony Bianchi, *Richard Vaughan* (Cardiff, 1984), p. 39.

[107] Bianchi, *Richard Vaughan*, pp. 1, 5–6, and 5.

[108] Bianchi, *Richard Vaughan*, p. 39.

[109] Williams, 'The Welsh Industrial Novel', p. 109.

[110] Harris, 'Popular Images', p. 218.

[111] Chris Williams, 'Master of a Lost Past', *Planet*, 121 (1997), 12–18.

[112] Harris, 'Popular Images', p. 219.

[113] Mike Buckingham and Richard Frame, *Alexander Cordell* (Cardiff, 1999).

[114] Iris Gower, *The Copper Cloud* (London, 1976).

[115] Gower, *Return to Tip Row* (London, 1977).

[116] Gower, *The Copper Kingdom* (London, 1983); Harris, 'Popular Images', p. 220.

[117] 'Iris Gower', in Aruna Vasudevan (ed.), *Twentieth-Century Romance and Historical Writers*, 3rd edn (Detroit, 1994), pp. 274–5, see p. 275.

[118] Gower, *The Shoemaker's Daughter* (London, 1991).

[119] Gower, *Kingdom's Dream* (London, 2001).

[120] Cledwyn Hughes, *A Different Drummer* (London, 1947); *The Inn Closes for Christmas* (London, 1947).

[121] D. Gareth Owen, *The Place Where We Belong* (London, 1945); *Spring in the Air* (London, 1946); *Clouds Across the Moon* (London, 1947).

[122] Barbara D. Roberts, *Still Glides the Stream* (London, 1940); *Some Trees Stand* (London, 1945).

[123] Willian Glynne Jones, *Farewell Innocence* (London, 1950); *Ride the White Stallion* (London, 1951); *Legends from the Welsh Hills* (London, 1957).

[124] Nigel Heseltine, *Tales of the Squirearchy* (Carmarthen, 1946).

[125] Jane Aaron, introduction to *A View Across the Valley*, pp. ix–xx.

[126] Hana Sambrook, 'Bernice Rubens', in Neil Schlager and Josh Lauer (eds), *Contemporary Novelists*, 7th edn (Detroit, 2001), pp. 861–2, see p. 862.

[127] Bernice Rubens, *I Sent a Letter to My Love* (London, 1975); *Yesterday in the Back Lane* (London, 1995).

[128] Moira Dearnley, *That Watery Glass* (Llandybïe, 1973).

[129] Alun Richards (ed.), *The Penguin Book of Welsh Short Stories* (London, 1976); *The New Penguin Book of Welsh Short Stories* (London, 1993).

[130] Catherine Merriman, *State of Desire* (London, 1996).

[131] See 'Hog Roast', 'Mustard' and 'Learning to Speak Klingon' in *Of Sons and Stars* (Dinas Powys, 1997) and 'A Step away from Trouble' and 'Barbecue' in *Getting a Life* (Dinas Powys, 2001).

[132] Siân James, *A Small Country* (London, 1979); *Love and War* (London, 1994); *Storm at Arberth* (Bridgend, 1994).

133 James, *Not Singing Exactly* (Dinas Powys, 1996).
134 Lewis Davies and Arthur Smith (eds), *Mama's Baby (Papa's Maybe)* (Cardiff, 2000).
135 Tony Bianchi, 'Aztecs in Troedrhiwgair: recent fictions in Wales', in Ian A. Bell (ed.), *Peripheral Visions: Images of Nationhood in Contemporary British Fiction* (Cardiff, 1995), pp. 44–76.
136 Ron Berry, *Hunters and Hunted* (London, 1960).
137 Berry, *The Full Time Amateur* (London, 1966), p. 37.
138 Berry, *Flame and Slag* (London, 1968).
139 John Pikoulis, ' "Word-of-mouth cultures cease in cemeteries" ', *New Welsh Review*, 34 (1996), 9–15; Dai Smith discusses Berry in *Aneurin Bevan and the World of South Wales* (Cardiff, 1993), pp. 133–5; Ron Berry, *Collected Stories*, ed. and intro. Simon Baker (Llandysul, 2000).
140 Berry, *This Bygone* (Llandysul, 1996).
141 Berry, *So Long Hector Bebb* (London, 1970).
142 Pikoulis, 'Word-of-mouth cultures', p. 11.
143 For a discussion of these largely nostalgic industrial writers see Stephen Knight, ' "A New Enormous Music": Industrial Fiction in Wales', ch. 2 in M. Wynn Thomas (ed.), *Welsh Writing in English*, pp. 47–90, see pp. 81–3.
144 Alun Richards, *Dai Country* (London, 1973); *The Former Miss Merthyr Tydfil* (London, 1976).
145 Alun Richards, *Home to an Empty House* (Llandysul, 1973).
146 Katie Gramich, 'Both in and out of the Game', p. 266.
147 Dannie Abse, *Ash on a Young Man's Sleeve* (London, 1956).
148 Abse, *O. Jones, O. Jones* (London, 1970).
149 Christopher Meredith, *Shifts* (Bridgend, 1988).
150 Aaron and Thomas, ' "Pulling you through changes" ', p. 295.
151 Dafydd Johnston, 'Making History in Two Languages: *Y Pla* and *Griffri*, *Welsh Writing in English*, 3 (1997), 118–33.
152 Richard Poole, 'Afterword: Eggmen and Zeroes in Christopher Meredith's *Shifts*' to Christopher Meredith, *Shifts*, repr. edn (Bridgend, 1997), pp. 215–31; also published in *New Welsh Review*, 36 (1997), 60–6.
153 Christopher Meredith, *Sidereal Time* (Bridgend, 1998).
154 Thomas, introduction to *Welsh Writing in English*, p. 4.
155 Aaron and Thomas, ' "Pulling you through changes" ', p. 279.
156 Duncan Bush, *Glass Shot* (London, 1991).
157 Russell Celyn Jones, *Soldiers and Innocents* (London, 1990).
158 Jones, *An Interference of Light* (London, 1995).
159 Lewis Davies, *Work, Sex and Rugby* (Cardiff, 1993).
160 Davies, *Tree of Crows* (Cardiff, 1996).
161 Davies, *My Piece of Happiness* (Cardiff, 2000).
162 Richard John Evans, *Entertainment* (Bridgend, 2000).
163 Ato Quayson, ' "Looking Awry": Tropes of Disability in Post-Colonial Writing', in Rod Mengham (ed.), *An Introduction to Contemporary Fiction* (Cambridge, 1999), pp. 53–68.
164 Tom Davies, *Black Sunlight* (London, 1996).

165 Desmond Barry, *A Bloody Good Friday* (Macdonald, 2002).
166 Niall Griffiths, *Grits* (London, 2000).
167 Trezza Azzopardi, *The Hiding Place* (London, 2000).
168 John Williams, *Cardiff Dead* (London, 2000).
169 Stephen Knight, *Mr Schnitzel* (London, 2000).
170 Charlotte Williams, *Sugar and Slate* (Aberystwyth, 2002).
171 John Sam Jones, *Welsh Boys Too* (Cardiff, 2000); Erica Woof, *Mud Puppy* (London, 2002).
172 Rachel Trezise, *In and Out of the Goldfish Bowl* (Cardiff, 2000).
173 Williams, *When Was Wales?*, p. 305.
174 Emyr Humphreys, *The Taliesin Tradition*, pp. 229–30.
175 Wiliam Roberts, *Y Pla* (Bangor, 1987), tr. Elisabeth Roberts as *Pestilence* (Bridgend, 1991); Robin Llywelyn, *O'r Harbwr Gwag i'r Cefnfor Gwyn* (Caerdydd, 1994), tr. by author as *From Empty Harbour to White Ocean* (Cardiff, 1996).
176 Aaron and Thomas, ' "Pulling you through changes" ', p. 302.

INDEX